Asian/Oceanian Historical Dictionaries
Edited by Jon Woronoff

Asia
1. *Vietnam*, by William J. Duiker. 1989
2. *Bangladesh*, by Craig Baxter and Syedur Rahman, second edition. 1996
3. *Pakistan*, by Shahid Javed Burki. 1991
4. *Jordan*, by Peter Gubser. 1991
5. *Afghanistan*, by Ludwig W. Adamec. 1991
6. *Laos*, by Martin Stuart-Fox and Mary Kooyman. 1992
7. *Singapore*, by K. Mulliner and Lian The-Mulliner. 1991
8. *Israel*, by Bernard Reich. 1992
9. *Indonesia*, by Robert Cribb. 1992
10. *Hong Kong and Macau*, by Elfed Vaughan Roberts, Sum Ngai Ling, and Peter Bradshaw. 1992
11. *Korea*, by Andrew C. Nahm. 1993
12. *Taiwan*, by John F. Copper. 1993
13. *Malaysia*, by Amarjit Kaur. 1993
14. *Saudi Arabia*, by J. E. Peterson. 1993
15. *Myanmar*, by Jan Becka. 1995
16. *Iran*, by John H. Lorentz. 1995
17. *Yemen*, by Robert D. Burrowes. 1995
18. *Thailand*, by May Kyi Win and Harold Smith. 1995
19. *Mongolia*, by Alan J. K. Sanders. 1996
20. *India*, by Surjit Mansingh. 1996
21. *Gulf Arab States*, by Malcolm C. Peck. 1996
22. *Syria*, by David Commins. 1996
23. *Palestine*, by Nafez Y. Nazzal and Laila A. Nazzal. 1997
24. *Philippines,* by Artemio R. Guillermo and May Kyi Win. 1997
28. *People's Republic of China: 1949–1997*, by Lawrence R. Sullivan. 1997

Oceania
1. *Australia*, by James C. Docherty. 1992
2. *Polynesia*, by Robert D. Craig. 1993
3. *Guam and Micronesia*, by William Wuerch and Dirk Ballendorf. 1994
4. *Papua New Guinea*, by Ann Turner. 1994
5. *New Zealand*, by Keith Jackson and Alan McRobie. 1996

New Combined Series (July 1996)
25. *Brunei Darussalam*, by D. S. Ranjit Singh and Jatswan S. Sidhu. 1997
26. *Sri Lanka*, by S. W. R. de A. Samarasinghe and Vidyamali Samarasinghe. 1997
27. *Vietnam*, 2nd ed., by William J. Duiker. 1997
28. *People's Republic of China: 1949–1997*, by Lawrence R. Sullivan, with the assistance of Nancy Hearst. 1997
29. *Afghanistan*, 2nd ed., by Ludwig W. Adamec. 1997.
30. *Lebanon,* by As'ad AbuKhalil. 1997.

Historical Dictionary of Sri Lanka

S. W. R. de A. Samarasinghe and
Vidyamali Samarasinghe

Asian/Oceanian
Historical Dictionaries, No. 26

The Scarecrow Press, Inc.
Lanham, Md., & London
1998

SCARECROW PRESS, INC.

Published in the United States of America
by Scarecrow Press, Inc.
4720 Boston Way
Lanham, Maryland 20706

4 Pleydell Gardens, Folkestone
Kent CT20 2DN, England

British Library Cataloguing in Publication Information Available

Library of Congress Cataloging-in-Publication Data

Samarasinghe, S. W. R. de A.
        Historical dictionary of Sri Lanka / S. W. R. de A. Samarasinghe and
Vidyamali Samarasinghe.
                    p. cm. (Asian/Oceanian historical dictionaries : no. 10)
            ISBN 0-8108-3280-1 (cloth: alk. paper)
            1. Sri Lanka—History—Dictionaries. I. Samarasinghe, Vidyamali.
II. Title. III. Series.
DS489.5.S33   1998
954.93'003—dc21   96-29614

ISBN 0-8108-3280-1 (cloth : alk. paper)

♾™ The paper used in this publication meets the minimum requirements of
American National Standard for Information Sciences—Permanence of
Paper for Printed Library Materials, ANSI Z39.48–1984.
Manufactured in the United States of America.

To Padma Akka
with loving memories

CONTENTS

EDITOR'S FOREWORD

Few countries have experienced as much tragedy and violence in recent years as Sri Lanka. For some while, it seemed that the country would be torn apart or have to live with more or less permanent dividing lines, geographic, ethnic, and other. Even now it is far from certain that the wounds of the past can be healed and the people united. Yet, when Ceylon (as it was then called) became independent it was one of the most successful British colonies and one of the most promising new states. There have been other times before the emergency when it seemed that the right policies were being implemented and the economy was recovering. Even today, there are encouraging signs that Sri Lanka could become a much happier place.

This makes the *Historical Dictionary of Sri Lanka* a very worthwhile addition to our Asian series, especially at this juncture. It helps us look back at the past, not only the recent past but much earlier eras as well, to better understand what is happening at present. Even if we cannot quite make sense of the tragedy and violence, at least we can grasp some of the causes. We can also sense the possibilities residing in a rich soil, profusion of minerals and hardworking population which could restore some of the former luster, if not the ancient glory. This understanding is facilitated by hundreds of entries on significant places, institutions, and events as well as crucial aspects of the economy, society, and culture. Other entries inform us about important historical figures and present-day leaders. This is neatly tied up in a brief but insightful introduction and useful chronology. For those who wish to know more about specific subjects, there is a comprehensive bibliography.

This volume was written by the exceptional husband-and-wife team that knows Sri Lanka intimately, Stanley W. R. de A. and L. K. Vidyamali Samarasinghe. Both were born and educated in Sri Lanka and also taught there before moving to the United States. The former is an associate professor in the Department of International Health and Development at the School of Public Health and Tropical Medicine at Tulane University, New Orleans, Louisiana, and senior economist of the Development Studies Program at the Tulane Institute of International Development in Arlington, Virginia; and the latter is an associate professor at the International Development Program of the School of International Service at the American University in Washington, D.C. But this has not taken them away from Sri Lanka, for Stanley Samarasinghe is also a director of the International Centre for Ethnic Studies in Kandy, and they both have written and lectured extensively on the economic, social, and political problems of the country. This unusual position of insider-outsider makes it possible for them to observe and feel the situation and also describe it in terms that are readily accessible to a broader public.

Jon Woronoff
Series Editor

ACKNOWLEDGMENTS

We owe many debts to many people who helped us complete this project. First and foremost are the staff of the International Centre for Ethnic Studies in Kandy, Sri Lanka. Kanthi Gamage was most helpful at all times when we asked for information on numerous topics. She also helped us prepare the bibliography. Shyani Siriwardena also assisted in the preparation of the bibliography and the chronology of events. R. G. Seelawathie assisted us in the preparation of maps. Iranga Athukorale did some of the word processing work with her customary efficiency. Nalini Weragama, Chalani Lokugamage, and Samarakoon Bandara also helped whenever they had the opportunity to do so. Kingsley de Silva, G. H. Peiris, K. N. O. Dhramadasa and S. Thillainathan read some sections of the manuscript and offered useful comments.

Masako Motoyama of the Development Studies Program, Tulane University rendered valuable help to prepare the tables, graphs and the camera-ready copy.

Jon Woronoff, the series editor, not only guided us and helped us polish the raw manuscript with his immense editorial skills and knowledge of Asia, but also acted with great patience and forbearance to see the project through, numerous delays and setbacks notwithstanding.

To all the above we record our deep appreciation and thanks. However, we alone are responsible for any errors of omissions and commissions that may remain in this work.

S. W. R. de A. Samarasinghe
L. K. Vidyamali Samarasinghe

ix

ABBREVIATIONS AND ACRONYMS

A.D.	Of the Christian Era (Anno Domini)
AI	Amnesty International
AMDP	Accelerated Mahaweli Development Program
AW	Asia Watch
BA	Bachelor of Arts
B.C.	Before Christ
BIPZ	Biyagama Free Trade Zone
bl	billion
BMICH	Bandaranaike Memorial Intl. Conference Hall
BNP	*Bahujana Nidahas Pakshaya* (Multi-People Freedom Party)
BOC	Bank of Ceylon
BOI	Board of Investment of Sri Lanka
CB	Central Bank
CCC	Ceylon Chamber of Commerce
CCS	Ceylon Civil Service
CE	Common Era
CFS	Consumer Finance Survey
CIC	Ceylon Indian Congress
CNC	Ceylon National Congress
CP	Communist Party of Sri Lanka
CRB	Cooperative Rural Bank
CRM	Civil Rights Movement
CSE	Colombo Stock Exchange
CWC	Ceylon Workers Congress
CWE	Ceylon Wholesale Establishment
DDC	District Development Council
DFCC	Development Finance Corporation of Ceylon
DMK	*Dravida Munnetra Kasagam* (Dravidian Development Society)
DPA	District Political Authority
DUNF	Democratic United National Front
EDB	Export Development Board
EPF	Employees' Provident Fund
EPRLF	Eelam People's Revolutionary Liberation Front
EPV	Export Processing Village
ETF	Employees' Trust Fund
EUSL	Eastern University of Sri Lanka
FCCISL	Fed. of Chambers of Commerce & Industry of SL

FP	Federal Party
FPA	Family Planning Association
FTZ	Free Trade Zone
GCE(AL)	General Certificate of Education (Advanced Level)
GCEC	Greater Colombo Economic Commission
GDP	Gross Domestic Product
GNP	Gross National Product
GUES	General Union of Eelam Students
ha.	*hectare(s)*
HDFCSL	Housing Development and Finance Corporation of SL
HRTF	Human Rights Task Force
IGP	Inspector General of Police
ILO	International Labour Office
IMF	International Monetary Fund
IPKF	Indian Peace Keeping Force
IPPF	International Planned Parenthood Federation
IRDP	Integrated Rural Development Program
JGP	*Jathiya Galawagenime Peramuna*
JTF	Janasaviya Trust Fund
JVP	*Janatha Vimukthi Peramuna* (People's Liberation Front)
kg	*kilogram(s)*
km	*kilometer(s)*
LSSP	*Lanka Sama Samaja Party* (Lanka Equal Society Party)
LTTE	Liberation Tigers of Tamil Eelam
MDP	Mahaveli Development Program (People's United Front)
MEP	*Mahajana Eksath Peramuna*
MP	Member of Parliament
MPCS	Multi Purpose Cooperative Society
mw	megawatts
NAM	Non-Aligned Movement
NCMC	North Colombo Medical College
NIC	Newly Industrialized Country
NLSSP	*Nava Lanka Sama Samaja Party* (New Lanka Equal Society Party)
NSA	National State Assembly
OPEC	Organization of Petroleum Exporting Countries
PA	People's Alliance
PC	Provincial Council
PLOTE	People's Liberation Organization of Tamil Eelam
PR	Proportional Representation

PTA	Prevention of Terrorism Act
PVO	Private Voluntary Organization
RAW	Research and Analysis Wing
RRDB	Regional Rural Development Bank
SAARC	South Asian Association for Regional Cooperation
SAFG	South Asian Federation Games
SL	Sri Lanka
SLAS	Sri Lanka Administrative Service
SLFP	Sri Lanka Freedom Party
SLMP	*Sri Lanka Mahajana Pakshaya* (Sri Lanka People's Party)
SMB	*Sinhala Maha Sabha* (Great Sinhalese Assembly)
STF	Special Task Force
TC	Tamil Congress
TELA	Tamil Eelam Liberation Army
TELO	Tamil Eelam Liberation Organization
TNA	Tamil National Army
TS	Theosophical Society
TULF	Tamil United Liberation Front
UF	United Front
UN	United Nations
UNCTAD	United Nations Conference on Trade and Development
UNP	United National Party
US	United States
USA	United States of America
USAID	United States Agency for International Development
VOC	Verreenidge Oost-Indische Campagnie
WB	World Bank
WCIC	Women's Chamber of Commerce & Industry

CHRONOLOGY OF IMPORTANT EVENTS

B.C.

10,000	Stone Age Culture ("Balangoda" Man)
483	Arrival of Vijaya; migration of people from North India.
377	Establishment of the city of Anuradhapura.
210-240	The introduction of Buddhism to Sri Lanka by a missionary group led by Mahinda sent by the Indian Emperor Asoka in the reign of King Devanampiya Tissa. Theri Sangamitta arrived in Sri Lanka with a sapling of the Bo-tree. She also established the order of Buddhist nuns. *Thuparama*, the first stupa, is built by Devanampiya Tissa. *Mahavihara*, the historic center of orthodox Buddhism is established.
210-161	South Indian Chola conquerors rule from Anuradhapura.
161-137	King Dutugemunu unifies the island for the first time, expelling the Chola conquerors. Begins the tradition of building large stupas by constructing the *Ruvanwelisaya*.
103-89	South Indian (*Pancha-Dravida*) rulers in power in Anuradhapura.
89	Vattagamani defeats the Dravidian ruler and regains the throne. He established the Abhayagiri Viharaya, a Buddhist monastery that becomes a rival sect to the *Mahavihara*. The former were more receptive to the Mahayanist doctrine that the latter considered heretical to true Buddhism. This is the first schism in the *bhikkhu* order. Tri Pitaka, the sacred Buddhist text, was written at Aluvihara, Matale.
67	The founding of the Lambakanna dynasty by King Vasabha.
48	Anula, the first sovereign Queen of Sri Lanka, ascends the throne.

A.D.

59	The Vijayan dynasty comes to an end with the death of Yasalalaka Tissa.
67	Vasabha ascended the throne and founded the first Lambakanna dynasty; beginning of about 350 years of political stability and economic prosperity. Strong links were forged between the rulers and the *Sangha* during this period.
112	Gaja Bahu becomes king; Sri Lanka-Chola conflicts.
100-200	Sinhala used for literary purposes.

276-301   The reign of King Mahasena; 16 irrigation reservoirs, including Minneriya and Kavudula, constructed; Jetavana, the island's largest stupa built.

301-328   The reign of Sirimeghavanna (Kith Sirimevan). Established cordial relations with Samudra Gupta, the Maurya emperor of India. The Tooth Relic was brought to Sri Lanka.

339-365   King Buddhadasa, who is said to have compiled a treatise on medicine and established hospitals, ascends the throne.

400-500   Pali commentaries and canonical literature compiled by Buddhagosa, Buddhadatta, and Dhammapala; the best known of these is the *Visudhimagga* authored by Buddhagosa. *Dipavamsa*, the oldest of the surviving Pali chronicle, and, *Mahavamsa*, the most detailed, which describe the island's history up to the fourth century were also compiled around this time.

411   Fa-Hsien, the famous Chinese Buddhist traveler, visited Sri Lanka and stayed for two years.

429-455   Sad-Dravida rulers from South India establish their rule in Anuradhapura.

455   King Dhatusena (455-473) regains Anuradhapura for the Sinhalese and establishes the Moriya dynasty.

459   Dhatusena defeats the Kalabran ruler and becomes king, founding the Moriya dynasty.

477   Dhatusena is murdered by his eldest son, Kasyapa, who becomes king. Moggallana, the younger son, flees to India. Kasyapa built a palace on the Sigiriya rock, one of the best and most renowned secular structures of ancient Sri Lanka.

623   Silameghavanna ascends the throne. He purges the Abhayagiri Viharaya of "sinful" monks.

684-718   King Manvamma reestablishes the Lambakanna dynasty following a period of inter-dynastic disputes and war between the Lambakannas and Moriyas.

    Manavamma, son of Kasyapa II, arrives from India with a Pallava army and wrests the kingship; beginning of the Lambakanna dynasty.

769   Aggabodhi IV, as a result of frequent Tamil invasions, removes the seat of government from Anuradhapura to Polonnaruwa.

833-853	Sena I becomes king. Pandyans invade Sri Lanka and plunder Anuradhapura.
853-887	Sena II sends an expedition to the Pandyan Kingdom. The Sinhala army ransacks Madurai.
993	Chola army under Rajaraja I invades Sri Lanka and destroys Anuradhapura.
1017	Cholas attack Ruhuna and take Mahinda V prisoner.
1055	Vijayabahu becomes the ruler of Ruhuna.
1070	Cholas are expelled from the island by Vijaya Bahu.
1153-1186	The reign of Parakramabahu I. Trade, religious, and cultural links with Southeast Asia (Burma and Cambodia) established. *Gal vihara* sculptures constructed.
1187-1196	The reign of Nissanka Malla, the last of the Polonnaruwa kings to rule over the entire island. The last Sri Lankan expeditionary force to India was sent.
1200-1300	Chulavamsa, compiled by Dhammkitti to survey the history of Sri Lanka up to reign of Parakramabahu I (1153-86).
1215	Magha of Kalinga, South India, takes over Polonnaruwa.
1232-36	Vijayabahu III moved the capital to Dambadeniya and established the Dambadeniya dynasty.
1238	King Bhuvanekabahu sends a mission to the Egyptian court using Arab traders living in Sri Lanka.
1287-93	The reign of Parakramabahu III, the last to rule from Polonnaruwa.
1200-1300	An independent Tamil kingdom established in the Jaffna peninsula.
1341-51	Bhuvanekabahu IV rules from Gampola. His brother Parakramabahu V rules in Dedigama.
1344	The rise of Nissanka Alagakkonara of Raigama. Ibn Batuta, the Arab traveler arrives in Sri Lanka. Lankatilaka and Gadaladeniya temples completed.
1353	An invasion force from Jaffna invades the south.
1369	Alagakkonara III establishes the Fort at Kotte.
1371-1408	Rules from Kotte in the latter part of his reign.
1405	Cheng-ho from China under Ming emperors leads a naval expedition to Sri Lanka to demand the tooth relic. Mission fails.
1410	The Sinhalese King Vira Alakesvara captured by Cheng Ho and taken to China.

1411-66	Parakramabahu VI consecrated king after vanquishing all his opponents. He moves from Raigama to Kotte in 1415.
	Salalihini Sandesaya collection of poems written by Sri Rahula Maha Sthavira.
1450	Unification of Ceylon under Parakramabahu VI with the capture of the Jaffna Kingdom by Prince Sapumal.
1477-89	Reign of King Vira Parakramabahu; internal rebellion against the Kotte king.
1479-1519	Jaffna kingdom regains its independence under King Pararajasekeram.
1505	The arrival of a Portuguese fleet under the command of Don Lourenco d'Almeida in the reign of Parakramabahu VIII.
1512	20,000 Sinhalese besieged the Fort at Colombo for seven months.
1521	The partition of the Kingdom of Kotte into Kotte, Sitavaka, and Raigama, following the *Vijayaba Kollaya*, the assassination of Vijayabahu.
1527	Mayadunne, king of Sitavaka, wages war against Bhuvanekabahu of Kotte, and retreats when the Portuguese reinforcements arrive.
1543	Dharmapala, grandson of Bhuvanekabahu, crowned in effigy by King John III in Lisbon.
1545	Joint Sitavaka-Kotte attack on the Udarata (hill country) ruler Jayavira.
1546	Unsuccessful Kotte-Portuguese invasion of Kandy.
1550	Bhuvanekabahu shot dead by a Portuguese soldier. Dharmapala is installed king of Kotte by the Portuguese.
1557	The ruler of Kotte, Dharmapala, converted to Roman Catholicism by the Portuguese.
1560	Portuguese dispatch an expedition to Jaffna to punish its ruler for acting against converts to Roman Catholicism.
1565	Portuguese get Dharmapala to abandon Kotte and move to Colombo Fort, which was under the control of the former.
1571-82	Portuguese construct a fort in Galle.
1574	Rajasingha I of Sitavaka launches an invasion of Kandy. Portuguese launch destructive forays into Sitavaka territory in the southwest coastal region.
1579-81	The siege of Colombo Fort by Rajasingha I.

1580	Dharmapala bequeaths the whole island to the crown of Portugal.
1581	Rajasingha I succeeds to the throne of Sitavaka on Mayadunne's death.
1582	Rajasingha I annexes the Kingdom of Kandy (*Udarata*).
1587-88	The great siege of Colombo by Rajasingha I of Sitavaka. The Portuguese ravage the coastal towns.
1591	Portuguese expeditionary force sent to Jaffna.
1594	Vimaladharma Surya builds the *Dalada Maligawa* and the king's palace in Kandy. Failed Portuguese expedition to Kandy to install Dona Catherina as queen.
1594-1619	A series of revolts against Portuguese rule of Kotte.
1595-96	The arrival of Dutch ships in Asian waters.
1597	Death of Dharmapala.
1603	Death of Vimaladharma Surya.
1618	Revolt by a Christian Group in Jaffna against the ruler.
1619	Portuguese send an expeditionary force to Jaffna. The Jaffna ruler is captured with the help of the Christian minority and brought to Colombo.
1623	Portuguese seize the port city of Trincomalee from the Kandyan kingdom.
1627	Dutch mission to the Kandyan court of Rajasingha II.
1628	Portuguese capture the Kandyan port city of Batticaloa.
1638	A Portuguese army under the command of Diego De Melho and Domian Battado invades Kandy, and ransacks the city but is surrounded and destroyed by Rajasingha II at Gannoruwa. The Dutch capture Trincomalee and Batticaloa from the Portuguese and return them to the Kandyan king.
1640	The Dutch capture Negombo and Galle from the Portuguese.
1645	Truce between the Portuguese and the Dutch, which lasted till 1650.
1656	Colombo falls to the Dutch from the Portuguese following a 12-month siege.
1658	Jaffna surrenders to the Dutch after a siege of three and a half months. Mannar taken by the Dutch.
1660	Robert Knox and several of the crew of the English frigate, *Anne* taken prisoners at Kottiyar and removed to Kandy.

1665	Trincomalee captured by the Dutch.
1668	Batticaloa captured by the Dutch.
1670	The Dutch declare that the export of certain Sri Lankan products such as elephants, and pearls and the import of certain goods such as cotton goods will be the monopoly of the Dutch company VOC.
1670-75	The Kandyans attack Dutch-held area.
1675	The Dutch and the Kandyan King Rajasingha II declare a truce.
1679	Robert Knox escapes from Kandy and reaches Arippu.
1687	Vimaladharma Surya II succeeds to the Kandyan throne vacated by the death of Rajasingha II.
1707	Sri Vira Parakrama Narendra Simha (1707-39), who built the Temple of the Tooth, becomes the king of Kandy.
1716-20	The Kandyan kingdom closes its frontier to the Dutch.
1722	The Dutch introduce coffee cultivation to Sri Lanka.
1731	The first printing press in Sri Lanka established by the Dutch.
1732-34	The Kandyan kingdom closes its frontiers to the Dutch.
1739	Sri Vijaya Rajasingha becomes the King of Kandy and inaugurates the Nayakkar dynasty of Telugu origin in Madura.
1747	Kirti Sri Rajasingha succeeds to the Kandyan throne.
1753	A mission of *bhikkhus* arrive in Kandy from Thailand to revive the *sasana* in Sri Lanka, and the *upasampada* for *bhikkhus* is restored.
	Siam sect of the monkhood established.
1757	Uprising of cinnamon peelers in the Dutch areas against the Dutch administration.
1762	A British envoy from Madras visits the Kandyan court.
	Dutch at war with the Kandyan kingdom.
1764	The Dutch send an expeditionary force that destroys Kandy.
1766	Peace treaty with the Dutch Governor Falck. The Kandyan king concedes sovereignty of Matara, Galle, Colombo, Jaffna, Kalpitiya, Mannar, Trincomalee, and Batticaloa to the Dutch.
1773	The Kandyan king refuses to join to demarcate new boundaries. The Dutch unilaterally do it.
1775	The procession of the Temple of the Tooth is added to the Kandy *Perahara*.
1780	The Dutch build the Star Fort in Matara.

1796	Colombo, Trincomalee, Jaffna, and Kalpitiya surrender to the British, and Dutch power in Sri Lanka ends. The British govern their areas in Sri Lanka from Madras.
	A police service is established.
1797	Rebellion against the British led by Sinno Appu.
1798	Death of Rajadhi Rajasingha; Sri Vikrama Rajasingha is raised to the Kandyan throne by Prime Minister Pilimatalauve.
	Frederick North made governor; Ceylon Civil Service established.
1799	Supreme court established.
	Torture prohibited.
1800	A British embassy led by Hay Macdowell sent to Kandy.
1801	Supreme Court of Sri Lanka established.
1802	*The Government Gazette* commenced publication.
	The Treaty of Amiens signed ceding Sri Lanka to the British by the Dutch.
	Sri Lanka made a crown colony.
1803	Two detachments of the British Army take possession of Kandy.
	British hostilities against the King of Kandy commenced.
	Muttuswami proclaimed king by the British.
	Kandyans attack the British Garrison in Kandy.
	Muttuswami is delivered at the desire of the Kandyans and put to death.
1805	The Kandyans invade British territory and are repulsed.
	London Missionary Society established in Sri Lanka.
1806	Muslim laws sanctioned by the British administration.
	Construction of the Kandy Lake completed.
	Roman Catholics in the territory under the British relieved of the restrictions on worship imposed upon them by the Dutch.
	British Naval Yard established in Trincomalee.
1811	Pilimatalauve beheaded for a conspiracy against the Kandyan king.
1812	Colombo Public Library established.
	Trial by jury established.
	A Royal Botanical Garden established in Gampaha.
	Baptist Mission established.
1814	Ehelepola, chief *adigar* of the king, rebels and takes refuge in Colombo; his wife and four children are put to death in Kandy.

	Molligoda succeeds Ehelepola. First-ever population census under the British.
1815	The Kandyan Convention convened and treaty between the British and the Kandyan Chiefs signed. British annexed Kandyan provinces, ending nearly 2,357 years of Sinhala independence. British declare war on the Kandyan provinces.
1816	American mission established in Sri Lanka. The ex-king of Kandy and his family sent to Vellore, Madras.
1817	Sunday declared a public holiday. The Kandyan Rebellion against British rule breaks out in Uva and Vellassa.
1818	Martial law declared in the Kandyan provinces and the rebellion suppressed. Church Missionary Society established.
1821	Peradeniya Botanical Gardens established. Colombo-Kandy road opened for traffic. The first edition of *Ceylon Blue Book*.
1822	Bridge of Boats over the Kelaniya river near Colombo completed.
1823	Unsuccessful insurrection at Matale. The first large-scale coffee plantation established in Singhapitiya, Gampola.
1824	Second population census of Sri Lanka.
1826	The infliction upon women of capital punishment by drowning is abolished in the Kandyan provinces. Uduvil Girls' Boarding School established in Jaffna by American Missionaries.
1827	Coffee exported for the first time.
1828	First batch of immigrant laborers from India arrive in Sri Lanka.
1829	The Colebrooke-Cameron Commission of Enquiry to probe into and report on all matters relating to the administration of the Government of Sri Lanka appointed.
1831	The Colebrooke Report on the administration presented to the government. Colombo-Kandy road completed.
1832	The Kandy Mail Coach, the first of its kind in Asia, started. *Rajakariya* (compulsory service to the state) abolished on the recommendation of Colebrooke.

The Colombo Journal, the first newspaper in Sri Lanka, published by Governor Robert W. Horton.

Cameron's report on law reform presented to the British administration.

Ceylon Savings Bank established.

1833 Sri Lanka divided into five provinces.

Judicial reforms based on the Cameron Report implemented.

An executive council and a legislative council established.

1834 *The Ceylon Observer*, the first independent newspaper of Sri Lanka, commenced publication.

1836 The Colombo Academy (later Royal College) established.

1838 The Galle Mail Coach started.

1839 Ceylon Chamber of Commerce established.

1841 Central School Commission established.

Ceylon Bank opened for business.

1844 Total abolition of slavery in Sri Lanka.

1845 A new province, the North-Western province, created.

1846 *The Ceylon Times* newspaper commenced publication.

1847 The custody of the sacred Tooth Relic handed over to the *bhikkhus* and headmen of the Kandyan provinces.

1848 Abortive rebellion in the Kandyan provinces.

Martial law imposed and later abolished in the areas affected by the rebellion.

1858 First telegraph line between Colombo and Galle.

Undersea cable laid between Sri Lanka and India for telegraphic communication.

1860 The first Sinhala newspaper *Lanka Lokaya* published.

1861 The Volunteer Force of the Sri Lanka army established.

1864 Capture of the bandit Sardiel.

The first Tamil newspaper *Udaya Tarakai* published.

The *bhikkhu* sect Sri Lanka Ramanna Nikaya established.

1865 Colombo Municipal Council established.

The Ceylon League formed.

1866 Municipal councils established in Kandy and Galle.

1867 Railway service between Colombo and Kandy commenced.

1870 Tea exported from Sri Lanka for the first time.

1871 First general census.

1872 Rupees and cents currency inaugurated in Sri Lanka.

1873 "Panadura Debate," the religious controversy between Buddhists and Christian missionaries took place.

North-Central province created.

Vidyodaya Pirivena, the Buddhist seat of learning founded.

1875	*Vidyalankara Pirivena*, the Buddhist seat of learning, founded.
	The Prince of Wales visits Sri Lanka.
1877	The National Museum opened in Colombo.
1879	Appointment of Harry Dias, the first Sinhalese to be a judge of the supreme court.
	A system of state-aided schools established.
1880	The founding of the Buddhist Theosophical Society by Col. Henry Steel Olcott.
1881	Census of population.
1882	Ceylon Native Agricultural Association formed.
1883	First public auction of teas in Colombo.
1884	Col. Henry Steel Olcott left on a mission to London to discuss the problems of the Buddhists with the British colonial administrators.
	Attorney general's department established.
	Buddhists Defense Committee founded.
1885	The official Buddhist flag ceremonially hoisted for the first time.
	Post Office Savings Bank inaugurated.
	Sinhala and Hindu New Year day declared a public holiday.
1886	Pettah English Buddhist School (Ananda College) established.
1887	Commencement of the new landing jetty in the Colombo harbor.
	Inauguration of the Ceylon Branch of the British Medical Association.
1889	The Sabaragamuwa province formed; Sri Lanka divided into nine provinces.
	Archaeology department established.
1891	Population census.
1894	Colombo Technical College established.
	Colombo Tea Traders Association founded.
1895	Colombo gets electricity.
1897	Waste Lands Ordinance.
1898	Young Men's Buddhist Association founded.
1899	First motor car imported to Sri Lanka.
1900	Department of Irrigation established.
1901	Census of population.
1904	Ceylon Agricultural Society founded.
1905	First Sinhala novel *Meena* written by A. Simon Silva published.

1907	Dutch-Burgher Union founded.
1908	Low-Country Products Association founded.
1911	Census of population.
1912	Reform of the Legislative Council.
	First cooperative society established.
1914	Indo-Lanka rail link established.
1915	Martial law rescinded.
	The publication of Sinhala newspapers suspended under Martial law.
	Martial law declared.
	Riots between Sinhalese and Muslims erupted in Kandy.
1921	University College, Colombo established.
	Census of population.
	All Ceylon Tamil Mahajana Sabha founded.
	Reform of the Legislative Council.
1922	The Prince of Wales visits Sri Lanka.
1924	Colombo Radio Broadcasting Station opened.
	Death of Sir Ponnambalam Arunachalam.
1925	Tea Research Institute, Talawakele, opened.
1927	Mahatma Gandhi arrives in Sri Lanka.
	Donoughmore Commission on Constitutional Reform begins sittings.
1928	Report of the Donoughmore Commission published.
	Labor Party of Ceylon founded.
1929	College of Indigenous Medicine founded.
	The Legislative Council accepts Donoughmore proposals for governmental reform.
1930	Death of Sir Ponnambalam Ramanathan.
1931	Elections to the first State Council through universal franchise.
	Mrs. A. F. Molamure, Sri Lanka's first woman legislator, elected to the State Council.
1932	The Colombo Art Gallery opened.
1933	Women permitted to enter the legal profession.
	Death of Anagarika Dharmapala.
1935	Sri Lanka's first woman barrister, Mrs. E. Deraniyagala took her oaths.
	Sinhala dictionary first published.
	Lanka Sama Samaja Party (LSSP) established.
	Land Development Ordinance enacted.
1936	Elections to the Second State Council.
1938	Ratmalana airport opened.

	Radio Ceylon starts a Sinhala service.
1939	Bank of Ceylon established.
	Indian Association of Ceylon (later CWC) established.
1940	The Board of Ministers of the State Council resign.
1941	Rice and sugar rationed by the government.
	Minipe Ela irrigation scheme inaugurated.
1942	University of Ceylon established, replacing University college.
	Japanese bomb Trincomalee and Colombo.
1943	Communist Party of Ceylon founded.
1944	All Ceylon Tamil Congress founded.
	Soulbury Commission appointed to inquire and report on constitutional affairs.
	Death of Sir D. B. Jayatilaka.
	The Supreme Commander of the Allied Forces in Southeast Asia transfers his headquarters from New Delhi to Kandy.
1945	Soulbury Commission Report published.
	Free Education introduced from kindergarten to university with Sinhalese or Tamil as the medium of instruction.
1946	Census of population.
	United National Party formed.
	New constitution based on the Soulbury proposals promulgated.
1947	Independence bill passed in parliament. Inaugural meeting of the first parliament.
	Agreement signed between Colombo and London granting Sri Lanka full independence.
	First parliamentary elections.
	First Sinhala Film *Kadavunu Poronduwa* (Broken Promise) screened.
1948	
February 4	Sri Lanka gains Independence, ending 152 years of British rule.
July 31	Duncan White of Sri Lanka wins the Olympics Silver Medal in the 400 hurdles, Sri Lanka's first-ever Olympic medal.
November 15	Ceylon Citizenship Act No. 18, 1948 enacted.
December 18	The Federal Party of Ceylon (*Ilankai Tamil Arasu Kadchi*) formed.
1949	
August 28	Laxapana hydropower project inaugurated.

October 10	An Act of Parliament to establish the Sri Lanka Army passed.
December 16	Central Bank of Ceylon established.

1950

January 18	Jawaharlal Nehru, the prime minister of India visits Sri Lanka.
January 23	Air Lanka inaugurates international flights.
February 13	The National Flag formally adopted.
July 1	The Colombo Plan founded.
July 21	Ceylon Chamber of Commerce founded.
August 28	Sri Lanka becomes a member of the International Monetary Fund (IMF) and the World Bank.

1951

September 2	Sri Lanka Freedom Party (SLFP) founded.
November 22	The National Anthem formally adopted.

1952

February 14	Indo-Lanka Trade Pact signed.
March 22	Death of Prime Minister D. S. Senanayake.
March 26	Dudley Senanayake appointed prime minister.
April 8	First parliament dissolved.
May 24	Second parliamentary elections.
November 7	Rice-Rubber commodity trade pact between Sri Lanka and China signed.

1953

February 3	Settlement of colonists in Gal Oya Scheme commences.
March 20	Population census.
August 12	General strike (*hartal*) organized by the left parties and trade unions; curfew imposed.
August 20	Curfew lifted.
October 12	Prime Minister Dudley Senanayake resigns; Sir John Kotelawala succeeds Senanayake.

1954

January 18	Kotelawala-Nehru agreement on Indian Tamils in Sri Lanka.
February 26	Bribery Act passed in parliament.
April 11	Elizabeth II, the Queen of England, arrives in Colombo for an official visit.
April 28	Asian Prime Ministers Conference inaugurated in Colombo.
July 17	The last British governor-general, Viscount Soulbury leaves Sri Lanka to be succeeded by Sir Oliver Goonetilleke, the first Sri Lankan governor-general.

1955

January 6   Sinhala and Tamil made the medium of instruction in secondary schools starting 1957.

April 4   The Industrial Corporations Act enacted.

June 20   Ceylon Institute of Scientific and Industrial Research established.

December 14   Sri Lanka admitted as a member of the United Nations Organization.

1956

January 13   Dudley Senanayake resigns from both the Parliament and the UNP.

February 3   Buddhist Commission Report released.

February 18   Second parliament dissolved.

February 22   *Mahajana Eksath Peramuna* led by the SLFP formed.

April 5,7 & 10 General elections won by the *Mahajana Eksath Peramuna*; S. W. R. D. Bandaranaike becomes prime minister.

May 17   Death penalty suspended.

June 5   Federal Party stages a *Satyagraha* (nonviolent protest) against the Sinhala only bill.

June 15   The Sinhala only bill passed in the House of Representatives.

August 16   The Department of Official Languages established.

October 1   The Department of Cultural Affairs established.

1957

January 3   Chinese Prime Minister Chou-En-lai makes an official visit.

January 14   Decision to teach in Sinhala, Tamil, and English media in the University of Ceylon from 1960 announced.

January 19   Tamil campaign against the *Sri* motor vehicle number plate commences.

March 17   Indian Prime Minister Jawaharlal Nehru makes an official visit.

May 17   Regional Councils bill gazetted.

May 23   *Buddha Jayanthi* celebrated.

May 28   Japanese Prime Minister Nobousuki Kishi makes an official visit, the first-ever such visit by a Japanese prime minister.

July 25   Bandaranaike-Chelvanayakam pact.

October 15   The Trincomalee air and naval base handed over to Sri Lanka by the British.

November 1   British air force base in Katunayake handed over to Sri Lanka.

December 19	Sri Lanka and the Soviet Union establish diplomatic relations.
	Paddy Lands bill passed in the House of Representatives.
December 22	Major floods in the North Central and Eastern provinces.

1958

January 1	Bus transport service nationalized.
	Prime Minister Bandaranaike abandons the Bandaranaike-Chelvanayakam Pact.
	Sarvodaya movement founded.
April 1	Campaign of obliterating Tamil name boards commenced.
May 27	Communal riots break out; curfew imposed.
July 7	Curfew lifted.
July 18	Victoria Park, Colombo, renamed Vihara Maha Devi Park.
August 1	Sri Lanka State Plantations Corporation established.
	Colombo Port nationalized.
August 14	Tamil Language (Special Provisions) Act.
November 28	Employees Provident Fund established.

1959

January 1	*Vidyodaya* and *Vidyalankara* universities commenced operations.
April 30	Law College admits candidates who sit for the entrance examination in Sinhala or Tamil.
May 18	Philip Gunawardena resigns from the cabinet.
June 13	*Jathika Sevaka Sangamaya* the UNP-oriented trade union established.
September 25	Prime Minister S. W. R. D. Bandaranaike assassinated.
September 26	W. Dahanayake assumed office as the fifth prime minister of Sri Lanka.

1960

January 6	Third parliament dissolved.
March 19	Fourth parliamentary elections; the UNP obtains 50 seats as against 46 won by the SLFP.
March 21	Dudley Senanayake becomes prime minister of a UNP government.
April 22	The Dudley Senanayake government is defeated in parliament.
April 26	Fourth parliament is dissolved.
July 20	General elections held for the fifth parliament. Sri Lanka Freedom Party secures 75 seats and Mrs. Sirimavo Bandaranaike becomes world's first woman prime minister.

August 2	Prime Minister Sirimavo Bandaranaike appointed to the Senate.

1961

January 14	State-assisted schools taken over by the government.
April 14	Federal Party launches a civil disobedience campaign.
April 18	Islandwide curfew; Federal Party banned.
May 29	Ceylon Petroleum Corporation established; retail petroleum distribution nationalized.
July 1	People's Bank established.
July 27	Bank of Ceylon nationalized.

1962

January 1	Insurance Corporation of Ceylon established.
January 27	Abortive coup d'etat against the government.
March 2	William Gopallawa succeeds Oliver Gunatilake as the governor-general of Sri Lanka.
September 6	The first batch of American Peace Corps volunteers arrives in Sri Lanka.

1963

January 1	Sinhala made the official language of Sri Lanka.
April 30	Emergency regulations lifted after 743 days.
May 1	*Grama Sevaka* system replaces the Headman system.
	Sri Lanka Administrative Service replaces the Ceylon Civil Service.
June 25	Ayurvedic Medical Council inaugurated.
July 5	Population census.
August 12	United Left Front founded.
August 30	Press Commission appointed.

1964

August 1	Private practice by government doctors prohibited.
October 15	Press takeover bill presented to parliament.
October 30	Sirimavo-Shastri Agreement signed.
November 12	Bureau of Sri Lanka Standards established.
December 3	Fourteen members of the ruling party join the opposition.
December 17	Government defeated by 74 votes to 73 in parliament; fifth parliament dissolved.

1965

March 22	Sixth general elections — The United National Party (UNP) gains 66 seats, led by Dudley Senanayake for a coalition government comprising the UNP, the Federal Party, the Sri Lanka Freedom Socialist Party, the Tamil Congress, the *Mahajana Eksath Peramuna*, the

	Janatha Vimukthi Peramuna and the *Lanka Prajathanthravadhi Pakshaya.*
August 26	River Valleys Development Board established.
December 19	Lester James Peiris's *Gamperaliya* wins the Golden Peacock award at the New Delhi International Film Festival.

1966

January 1	*Poya* day — Buddhist holy day — substituted for Sunday as a holiday.
January 8	Tamil Language (Special) Provisions Act; street demonstrations against the Act.
May 2	Industrial Development Board established.
July 7	Army Commander Richard Udugama taken into custody as a suspect in a coup plot.
November 1	Female students admitted to the two Buddhist universities, Vidyodaya and Vidyalankara.

1967

January 5	Sri Lanka Broadcasting Corporation established.
March 20	Oruwela Steel Corporation starts production.
March 23	Kelani Tyre Corporation starts production.
September 18	Prime Minister of India Mrs. Indira Gandhi makes an official visit.
October 14	Sigiri frescoes damaged by vandals.
November 22	Rupee devalued.

1968

March 8	Katchchatiuve islands officially declared as a part of Sri Lanka.
April 22	National Science Council of Sri Lanka established.
June 8	Opposition demonstrates against the District Councils bill.
June 26	District Councils bill presented to parliament.
September 30	Mahaveli diversion scheme at Polgolla inaugurated.

1969

January 23	National Youth Service Council established.
July 6	Work on Stage I of the Mahaveli Diversion Scheme inaugurated.
October 1	Atomic Energy Authority established.
November 1	Ceylon Electricity Board established.

1970

March 25	Sixth parliament dissolved.
May 3	Mahaveli Development Board established.
May 27	Seventh parliamentary elections held.

May 30	Mrs. Sirimavo Bandaranaike assumes office as prime minister.
July 19	Inaugural meeting of the Constituent Assembly.
October 25	Demonetization of the Rs 50/= and Rs 100/= currency notes.
December 4	Pope Paul VI makes an official visit to Sri Lanka.

1971

March 16	State of emergency declared.
March 29	Paddy Marketing Board established.
April 4	*Janatha Vimukthi Peramuna* (JVP) insurrection against the government begins.
April 7	Government bans the JVP.
June 12	The trial of the accused in the April 1971 insurrection begins.
July 2	State Graphite Corporation established.
August 24	Sunday restored as the regular weekend holiday.
September 22	State Pharmaceutical Corporation established.
September 29	National Savings Bank established.
October 2	The Senate (Upper House of Parliament) abolished.
October 9	Census of population.
November 1	State Gem Corporation established.
November 15	The Court of Appeal replaces the Privy Council of England as the highest court of appeal.
December 1	*Janatha* (People) Committees established.
December 12	Rohana Wijeweera, the JVP leader, sentenced to 20 years in prison.

1972

January 24	State Film Corporation established.
February 12	All state universities integrated into one University of Sri Lanka.
April 5	Criminal Justice (Special) Commissions Act passed.
May 22	The First Republican Constitution promulgated and Sri Lanka declared a republic; the name of the country officially changed from Ceylon to Sri Lanka.

1973

March 23	Language of the Courts (Special Provision) bill passed in parliament.
April 13	Death of former Prime Minister Dudley Senanayake.
May 27	Bandaranaike Memorial International Conference Hall (BMICH) opened.
July 20	Lake House Group of Newspapers taken over by the government.
October 19	*Satyagraha* campaign started by the opposition UNP.

December 1	Official bread rationing in cities.
December 11	M. J. M. Lafir wins the World Amateur Snooker Championship.

1974

January 1	Administration of Justice Law becomes operable.
January 2	Five-day week for public sector workers.
April 20	*Davasa* Group of Newspapers sealed.
June 28	A formal agreement on Kachchatievu signed by Prime Ministers Indira Gandhi and Sirimavo Bandaranaike.
August 14	Women jurors selected for a jury for the first time.
October 6	The Jaffna University campus established.

1975

September 14	Land Reform Law to takeover foreign-owned public company estates passed.

1976

February 19	Communist Party of Ceylon leaves the United Front government.
May 6	Satellite Earth Station at Padukka inaugurated.
August 30	Fifth Non-Aligned Summit inaugurated in Colombo; Sri Lanka's Mrs. Sirimavo Bandaranaike elected chairperson.
October 15	Government College of Ayurveda elevated to university status.
December 8	Private "channeled" practice by government medical consultants stopped.

1977

January 3	*Janawasa* Commission established.
February 15	Emergency declared by the government.
March 12	Rupee revalued by 20 per cent.
March 31	*Davasa* Group of Newspapers resumed publication.
May 18	Parliament dissolved.
July 23	Eighth parliamentary elections; UNP wins 139 seats and returns to power.
October 21	Criminal Justice Commission Act repealed.
November 2	Rohana Wijeweera, the JVP leader, released from prison on a presidential pardon.
November 11	Sansoni Commission appointed to inquire and report on the communal violence of 1977.

1978

February 4	J. R. Jayewardene sworn in as the first executive president of Sri Lanka.
February 6	R. Premadasa appointed prime minister.

March 9	Greater Colombo Economic Commission commenced operations.
March 29	Special Presidential Commission appointed to inquire and report on the abuse of power.
May 19	A law enacted proscribing the Liberation Tigers of Tamil Eelam (LTTE) and other similar organizations.
August 27	Ruhuna University College established.
September 7	The Second Republican Constitution promulgated. Air Lanka's Avro 748 destroyed by a terrorist bomb attack.
October 15	*Udagama* (Village Awakening) Movement inaugurated.
November 23	Cyclone weather causes severe damage in the Batticaloa, Ampara and Polonnaruwa districts, rendering 150,000 homeless, and leaving about 500 persons dead.

1979

January 10	Air Lanka incorporated.
April 10	Private bus transport services commence.
May 19	Local government elections.
June 4	Government takeover of the private Independent Television Network.
July 12	Prevention of Terrorism Act passed in parliament.
August 14	Death of N. M. Perera, leader of the LSSP.
September 4	TULF ends its boycott of parliament.
October 3	Essential Public Services Bill passed in Parliament.
October 18	National Textile Corporation dissolved.
December 27	State of emergency declared in Jaffna.

1980

January 18	Free school textbook distribution scheme started.
February 14	Cabinet reshuffle.
March 4	Work on the national TV complex commenced.
June 19	Open University of Sri Lanka commenced operations.
July 18	State sector employees strike for higher pay.
October 11	Kotelawala Defense Academy established.
October 16	Former Prime Minister Mrs. Sirimavo Bandaranaike deprived of her civic rights and expelled from parliament.
November 26	Mrs. Ranganayaky Pathmanathan takes oaths as the first Tamil woman MP since independence.

1981

January 29	Singapore prime minister arrives for an official visit.
March 17	Population census.
June 2	Curfew in Jaffna.
June 4	Emergency imposed.

	Elections for District Development Councils.
June 9	Emergency lifted.
July 21	Sri Lanka attains Test Playing Status in cricket.
July 27	First private Agency Post Office established.
August 17	State of emergency declared.
August 28	Death of Dr. S. A. Wickramasinghe, the leader of the Communist Party of Sri Lanka.
September 17	Institute of Fundamental Studies inaugurated.
September 25	Private North Colombo Medical College inaugurated.
October 4	*Divayina,* the Sinhala daily, commenced publication.
October 15	*Gramodaya Mandala* (Village Awakening Councils) inaugurated.
October 21	Queen Elizabeth II and Prince Philip arrive in Sri Lanka in connection with the celebrations to commemorate the 50 years of Universal Franchise in Sri Lanka.
November 29	Sri Lanka Cricket Foundation established.

1982

February 17	Inaugural Cricket Test Match between Sri Lanka and England in Colombo.
March 7	*Swarnabhoomi* Land Grant Program inaugurated.
April 29	Parliament moved to the new complex at Sri Jayawardhanapura Kotte.
June 1	Natural Resources, Energy and Science Authority replaces the National Science Council.
July 2	New company law.
July 30	Emergency declared and a curfew imposed in Galle; Sinhala-Muslim communal clashes in Galle.
August 4	Curfew in Galle lifted.
October 20	Presidential election.
October 28	Curfew imposed in the Jaffna district.
December 22	Referendum to extend the eighth parliament for six years.

1983

March 4	One Million Houses Program inaugurated.
May 19	The UNP wins 14 of the 17 parliamentary by-elections.
May 24	The fifth amendment to the constitution.
June 10	Ministry of Women's Affairs established.
July 23	13 soldiers including an officer killed and two others seriously injured in an attack by the LTTE at Tinnevely.
July 25	Anti-Tamil rioting breaks out in several parts of Colombo and curfew imposed in the city.
July 26	Anti-Tamil rioting spreads to outside Colombo. All-island curfew imposed.

July 30	*Janatha Vimukthi Peramuna, Nava Sama Samaja Party,* and the Communist Party proscribed.
July 30	The Communist Party organ *Attha* sealed.
August 4	The sixth amendment to the constitution making espousal, promotion, financing, encouraging, or advocacy of the establishment of a separate state in Sri Lanka illegal, passed in parliament.
August 11	The new District of Kilinochchi constituted.
October 1	Coast Conservation Act becomes law.
November 8	Anura Bandaranaike becomes the leader of the opposition.
December 21	Talks begin in Colombo to end the ethnic conflict.

1984

January 3	Gopalaswami Parthsarathi, the special emissary of the Indian Prime Minister Mrs. Indira Gandhi, arrives in Colombo for talks on the ethnic conflict.
January 10	All-Party Amity Conference begins.
March 24	Ministry of National Security established.
April 17	The ban on the *Attha* newspaper lifted.
August 18	Sri Jayawardhanapura Hospital opened.
October 22	Terrorist bombs explode in Colombo.
November 22	A countrywide curfew declared for two days.
December 24	Cyril Mathew ceases to hold cabinet office.
December 26	Government abandons the proposals of the All-Party Conference on ethnic peace.

1985

April 11	British Prime Minister Margaret Thatcher commissions the Victoria Project.
July 5	Ethnic peace talks in Thimpu.
July 10	The government lifts the eight-month-long night curfew in the Northern Province.
August 9	The second round of ethnic peace talks in Thimpu.
August 23	The Kotmale Reservoir Project commissioned.
September 2	Two former TULF MPs, Messrs. V. Dharmalingam and A. Alalasundaram, murdered.
December 5	President J. R. Jayewardene leaves for Bangladesh to attend the SAARC summit.

1986

January 1	President J. R. Jayewardene restores the civic rights of Mrs. Sirimavo Bandaranaike, former prime minister and Mr. Felix Dias Bandaranaike, former Cabinet minister (posthumously).
March 23	Waters of the Randenigala Reservoir impounded.

May 3	A bomb explosion in an Air Lanka plane bound for Male at the Katunayake International Airport kills 17 passengers and injures about 24.
June 25	All Party Conference to resolve the ethnic crisis begins at the BMICH.
October 8	Eastern University, Sri Lanka (EUSL), the country's eighth university inaugurated.
November 15	President Jayewardene leaves for Bangalore to attend the second SAARC Summit.

1987

April 17	Terrorists massacre 128 civilians and injure more than 60 near Kitulottuwa along the Habarana-Trincomalee Road.
April 21	A bomb explosion kills 113 persons and injures more than 300 in Pettah, Colombo.
June 3	Indian flotilla sent to Jaffna with supplies, turned back at Sri Lanka territorial waters by the navy.
July 27	A 72 hour islandwide curfew imposed.
July 29	Prime Minister of India, Rajiv Gandhi, arrives in Sri Lanka and signs the Indo-Sri Lanka Peace Accord with President J. R. Jayewardene.
	Induction of the Indian Peace Keeping Force (IPKF).
August 18	An unidentified assailant throws two grenades into the committee room where the government parliamentary group chaired by President J. R. Jayewardene, was in session. Several government parliamentarians are injured and one is killed.
November 1	President J. R. Jayewardene leaves for Kathmandu to attend the third SAARC summit.
November 9	A bomb explosion at Maradana, Colombo, kills 31 people and injures 106.
November 12	The Provincial Councils bill passed unanimously and the 13th amendment to the Constitution by a two-third majority in parliament.

1988

February 16	Assassination of Vijaya Kumaranatunga, popular film actor and leader of the *Sri Lanka Mahajana Pakshaya*.
April 28	The first ever Provincial Council election takes place for the North Central, Sabaragamuwa, North Western and Uva Provincial Councils.

September 7   President J. R. Jayewardene issues a proclamation merging the Northern and Eastern provinces into a single administrative unit.

September 26   King Birendra of Nepal visits Sri Lanka in his capacity as chairman of the South Asian Association for Regional Cooperation (SAARC).

JVP gunmen assassinate Lionel Jayatilleke, minister of Rehabilitation & Reconstruction.

October 21   J. R. Jayewardene commissions the Randenigala Multi-Purpose Reservoir project.

December 19   R. Premadasa of the UNP wins the presidential election.

1989

January 2   R. Premadasa takes oath as the second executive president.

January 11   R. Premadasa signs a proclamation to revoke the state of emergency in force in the country.

February 15   The ninth parliamentary election held for the first time under a proportional representation scheme.

February 18   R. Premadasa appoints a 22-member Cabinet and 49 ministers of state.

July 13   Tamil United Liberation Front (TULF) leader A. Amirthalingam and former TULF MP Yogeswaran assassinated by LTTE gunmen.

President R. Premadasa addresses the first ceremonial sitting of the ninth parliament.

September 13   An All-Party Conference held in Colombo to find a solution to the prevailing unrest in the country.

September 18   Sri Lanka and India sign an agreement in Colombo providing for the withdrawal of the IPKF from the North and East by December 31 and the suspension of offensive military operations against the LTTE from the 20th onward.

October   International Committee of Red Cross arrives in Sri Lanka. Indian Peace Keeping Force (IPKF) begins its withdrawal from Ampara. The Tamil National Army and the Sri Lankan Army move into the areas vacated by the IPKF.

November 13   Government announces the death *of Janatha Vimukthi Peramuna* leader Rohana Wijeweera.

November 14   Government announces the death of the general secretary of the *Janatha Vimukthi Peramuna*—Upatissa Gamanayake.

1990

January	The LTTE takes over areas vacated by the IPKF in the North and East.
February	President R. Premadasa holds talks with the LTTE.
March	President R. Premadasa imposes direct control on Northeast Provincial Councils.
May 12	Justice Minister Hameed and the LTTE leader Prabhakaran hold talks.
December	Brigadier Wijeratne, the highest ranking soldier to be killed in the war to date, dies in Trincomalee.

1991

March 2	Minister of Plantations and Deputy Minister of Defense Ranjan Wijeratna killed in a car bomb explosion.
March 24	The last of the Indian Peace Keeping Forces leaves the island.
May 11	The UNP wins local government elections.
June	Fighting breaks out between government troops and the LTTE in what is dubbed as Eelam War II.
December 21	Sixth summit of the South Asian Association for Regional Cooperation held in Colombo.
Dec. 22-30	South Asian Federation Games held in Colombo.

1992

May	No-confidence motion against government defeated.
	Failed impeachment motion against the president.
August 8	Deaths of General Denzil Kobbekaduwa, General Wijaya Wimalaratne, Rear-Admiral Mohan Jayamaha, and seven others when an explosive devise destroyed the jeep in which they were traveling in Kayts.
November	Navy Commander Clancey Fernando killed by an LTTE suicide bomber in Colombo.

1993

April 24	Former national security minister and leader of the DUNF Lalith Athulathmudali, assassinated.
May 1	Assassination of President R. Premadasa by a suicide bomber.
	D. B. Wijetunga sworn in as the new president.
May 5	Ranil Wickramasinghe sworn in as the new prime minister.
May 17	Provincial Council elections.

1994

February 5	Two peace delegations, one led by the Anglican Bishop of Colombo Rev. Kenneth Fernando and the other led by the Sarvodaya Leader A. T. Ariyaratne, visit Jaffna.

March 2	Southern Provincial Council elections; the PA wins.
May 19	Gamini Dissanayake returns to parliament as UNP MP.
June 24	Ninth parliament dissolved.
August 16	General elections for the tenth parliament; the PA wins a plurality, beating the UNP.
August 19	Mrs. Chandrika Kumaratunga sworn in as the 14th prime minister, and the People's Alliance government installed in office.
August 25	First session of the tenth parliament.
October 13	First round of peace talks between the government and the LTTE in Jaffna.
October 24	Gamini Dissanayake, the leader of the opposition and UNP candidate at the presidential elections and several top leaders of the party assassinated by a suicide bomber.
October 27	The UNP nominates Mrs. Srima Dissanayake, the widow of its slain candidate Gamini Dissanayake as the substitute candidate for the presidential election.
November 9	The PA candidate Mrs. Chandrika Kumaratunga wins the presidential elections polling 62 per cent of the votes cast.
November 12	Mrs. Chandrika Kumaratunga assumes office as the fourth president.

1995

January 3	Government-LTTE talks — second round.
January 7	Cessation of hostilities in the war between the government and the LTTE.
January 14	Government-LTTE talks — third round.
January 20	The visit of Pope John Paul II to Sri Lanka.
April 10	Government-LTTE talks — fourth round.
April 19	The LTTE attacks government naval installation and resumption of hostilities.
July 9	Government security forces in the north commence Operation Leap Forward.
August 3	Government officially announces its Peace Package.
September 21	Media censorship on military and security news.
October 17	Government security forces in the north commence Operation *Riviresa*.
October 20	The LTTE terrorist attack on Colombo oil installation facilities.
November 2	Motion of no confidence against minister M. H. M. Ashraff defeated in parliament.

December	The LTTE moves its theater of operations from Jaffna to Kilinochchi
December 5	Operation *Riviresa* military campaign concluded with the taking of Jaffna from the LTTE.
December 20	Media censorship on military and security news lifted.

1996

January 3	North Central and Sabaragamuwa Provincial Councils are dissolved.
January 4	The LTTE explode the telecommunication exchange in Kalmunai. Tigers kill a TELO member in Eravur.
January 9	Draft legal document of devolution proposals introduced.
January 17	Military operation *Rivikirana* is launched against the LTTE.
January 21	Sri Lanka lose the Benson and Hedges World Series in Australia amidst controversy over spinner Muralitharan's bowling action.
January 22	A Russian-built transport Mi-17 Sri Lanka Air Force helicopter carrying 39 security forces personnel including seven officers shot down east of Point Pedro by the LTTE.
January 29	14 soldiers die in an LTTE attack in Pulmudai near Trincomalee.
January 31	A suicide bomb explosion by the LTTE at the Central Bank building in Colombo kills more than 100 civilians and seriously wounds 1,300 others.
February 5	The Australian cricket team decides not to play in Sri Lanka in the sixth World Cup match.
February 9	President Chandrika Kumaratunga opens Parliamentary sessions for 1996.
February 12	A lorry loaded with 144 kgs of explosives was discovered by the police at a Buddhist temple in Kotahena.
February 15	The LTTE vessel "Horizon" containing arms destroyed by the Sri Lankan navy 21 miles off Mullaitivu.
February 16	All schools closed indefinitely for security reasons.
February 21	President Chandrika Kumaratunga and the leader of the opposition Ranil Wickramasinghe discuss the government devolution package.
February 24	The LTTE attack the Pesalai security forces detachment.
March 5	The Maha Sangha gather at the BMICH to show their opposition to the devolution package.
March 7	UNP tables no confidence motion against Minister Lakshman Kadirgamar over the Thawakkal issue.
March 17	Sri Lanka wins the Wills World Cricket Cup in Lahore.

March 25	Tigers blast 300 line telephone exchange in Akkaraipattu.
March 30	Navy boat Dvora is blasted by the Sea Tigers.
April 1	18 STF men die in an LTTE attack.
	UNP and PA supporters clash at Anamaduwa.
	Government Medical Officers Association strikes over a post-intern merit list.
April 9	Government bans *Sirasa* Sinhala news telecast as a punishment for announcing an emergency declaration as a curfew order.
April 12	The LTTE makes an abortive pre-dawn attack on the Colombo harbor
April 18	600,000 estate workers commence a five-day work stoppage.
April 19	Two naval gunboats *Suraya* and *Ranasuru* in the Trinco naval dockyard sunk by the LTTE.
	Military operation *Riviresa* II launched by the government security forces to liberate Vadamarachchi and Thennamarachchi.
	Press censorship is imposed.
April 27	3,000 doctors report sick over the failure of the government to appoint 460 doctors who had just completed internship.
May 1	Lt. Gen Rohan Daluwatte is appointed new army commander.
May 15	Operation *Riviresa* III launched.
May 16	Army captures Vadamarachchi in Operation *Riviresa* III.
May 17	Army captures Valvetithurai, the birth place of the LTTE leader Prabhakaran and Point Pedro.
May 24	Time in Sri Lanka is advanced by one hour to save day light.
May 29	A three-day work stoppage by Ceylon Electricity Board workers commenced.
June 6	A power cut of 10 hours per day started.
June 11	The LTTE killed 14 Sinhalese villagers in a small hamlet in the Puttalam district.
July 4	A suicide bomber kills Brig. Ananda Hamangoda and injures Minister Nimal Siripala de Silva in Jaffna.
July 18	Nearly 1,400 soldiers killed in an LTTE attack on the Mullaitivu military camp.
July 14	Two bombs explode in Colombo commuter train killing more than 60.
July 16	Military operation *Sathjaya* commences in Jaffna.

July 17	Government forces capture the northern town of Paranthan, the gateway to Kilinochchi.
August 1	India bans the LTTE. Government considers banning the LTTE as a political party.
	The Liberal Party Leader Dr. Chanaka Ameratunga dies in a motor car accident.
August 8	The pocketed herd of elephants at Handapangala is driven to Yala.
August 16	Professor Ediriweera Sarachchandra dies at 82.
August 22	Former minister of state and UNP stalwart Anandatissa De Alwis dies at the age of 76.
September 7	Sri Lanka beats Australia by 50 runs in the four-nation Singer World Series cricket final in Colombo.
September 12	The LTTE attacks a bus at Arantalawa near Ampara killing 11 passengers.
September 29	Government troops capture Kilinochchi.
September 30	Veteran Left Leader Vivian Goonewardena dies at the age of 80.
October 7	The tenth Brigade army camp at Pooneryn is vacated.
October 8	The six-month long media censorship is lifted.
October 15	Kilinochchi is occupied by forces of operation *Sathjaya.*
October 26	The clock is put back by half-an-hour
October 30	Shirani Bandaranayake a 37 year old professor of law at the Colombo University named as the country's first woman Supreme Court judge.
November 1	The first executive President J. R. Jayewardene dies after a brief illness at the age of 90.
	Former army commander Cecil Waidyaratne is remanded on corruption charges.
November 6	Deputy Minister of Finance and Justice and Constitutional Affairs Minister, Prof. G. L. Peiris presents the PA's third budget in parliament.
November 18	The soldiers suspected of the gang-rape and murder of Jaffna school girl, Krishanthi Kumaraswamy and the killing of three others appear in the Colombo high court.
December 17	STF deputy chief SSP Sahabandu dies after a suicide bomber rams into his vehicle in Ampara.

INTRODUCTION

Sri Lanka is a pear-shaped island in the Indian Ocean, 65,610 square kilometers in extent lying off the southern tip of the Indian sub-continent, between latitudes 5 55' to 9 50' N and longitudes 79 42' to 81 53' E. The Palk Strait and the Gulf of Mannar separate Sri Lanka from India. The Bay of Bengal lies to its north and east, and the Arabian sea to its west.

The name Sri Lanka, meaning the "resplendent island," has been used by the Sri Lankans themselves for a very long time. However, until 1972 it was known to the rest of the world as "Ceylon," derived from the Portuguese term "Ceilao." To ancient seafarers it was also known as *Ratnadvipa*, the island of gems, or *Serendib*. The Greeks, who could not pronounce the name *Thambapanni*, another Sinhalese name by which the island was known, named it Taprobane, the name used by the second-century cartographer Ptolemy in his map of the island.

In mid-1996 Sri Lanka's population was 18.2 million. Thus, with 276 persons per square kilometer, it has one of the highest population densities for any country in the world. Sri Lanka has a multiethnic society. The two principal ethnic groups, the Sinhalese and the Tamils, speak two different languages. The society is also multireligious with adherents of four of the world's great religions, Buddhism, Christianity, Hinduism, and Islam, being found in the country. This reflects the history of an island nation that is located in close proximity to a vast and relatively densely populated landmass, the Indian subcontinent. It also reflects the location of the island on a strategic sea route that was used by sailors and traders in the Indian ocean region from antiquity. This location factor has been decisive in shaping the island's 2,500-year-old recorded history and even today exerts a powerful influence on the destiny of the nation.

Geography

A large part of the geology of the island is composed of highly metamorphosed ancient crystalline rocks. Only about one-tenth of its geological structure is formed by narrow belts of Jurassic, Miocene, Pleistocene, and recent rocks of sedimentary origin. The island's surface morphology consists of three major regions, i.e., central highlands, the plains, and the coastal region. The central highlands consist of a series of peaks, escarpments, and valleys. The highest point is Pidurutalagala (8,282 ft.). From the central highlands the land falls in steps to the plains, which are narrow in the southern and southwestern sectors and broader in the north. The elevation of the plains range from sea level to 300 ft. The coastal region consists of sand dunes, sand bars, and spits, lagoons, and marshes. The Mahaveli, the longest river in Sri Lanka (206 miles), originates in the western sector of the central highlands and literally cuts across the highlands

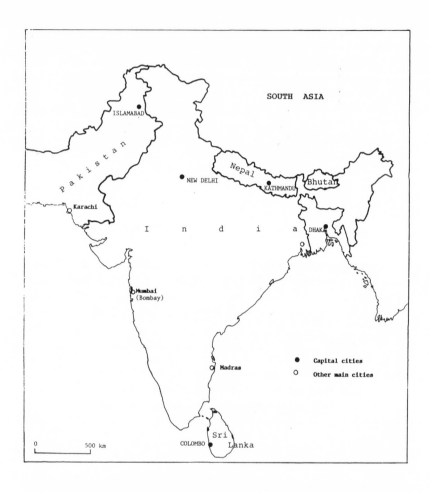

and falls into the sea at Trincomalee in the east coast of the island. All other rivers flow radially from the central highlands to the sea.

The climate of Sri Lanka is determined by its tropical location, its insularity, the location of its highlands in the central region, and its proximity to the landmass of the Indian subcontinent. Mean monthly temperatures in the lowlands of Sri Lanka fall between 78° and 85° F with relatively little seasonal or diurnal variations. Due to higher altitude, temperatures in

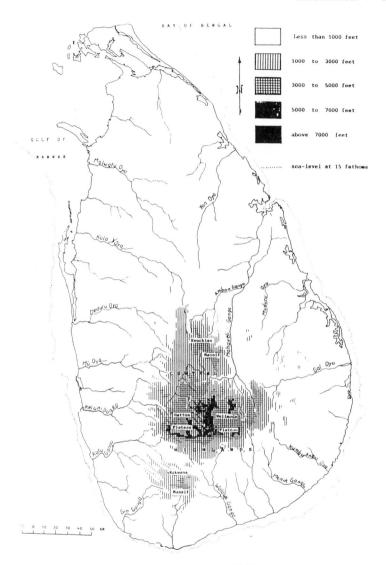

BAT OF BENGAL

GULF OF

MANNAR

	Less than 1000 feet
	1000 to 3000 feet
	3000 to 5000 feet
	5000 to 7000 feet
	above 7000 feet

.... sea-level at 15 fathoms

Malwatu Oya

Yan Oya

Kala Yara

Amban Ganga

Maduru Oya

Deduru Oya

CENTRAL

Knuckles

Ramai

Mahaveli Ganga

Mi Oya

Gal Oya

Kelani Ganga

Hatton Plateau

Wellawaya Plateau

HIGHLANDS

Kulu Ganga

Kumbukkan Oya

Rakwana

Menik Ganga

Massif

Walawe Ganga

Gin Ganga

0 10 20 30 40 50 KM

Morphological Layout of Sri Lanka

Nuwara Eliya located in the central highlands, range from a mean of 55° F in December to 70° F in May. It is mainly the rainfall that brings a spatial and a seasonal variation in climate. The southwestern quadrant of the island, known as the wet zone, receives rainfall from both the southwest and northeast monsoons and also in the form of convectional rain. Consequently, rainfall is relatively heavy, well distributed seasonally, and reliable. Mean

Sri Lanka: Administrative Boundaries and Main Towns

annual rainfall is more than 75 inches and in the windward sector of the central highlands it rises to more than 150 inches. The dry zone, which covers the north and the east of the island including the eastern sector of the central highlands, receives most of its precipitation from the northeast monsoons and has a period of drought during the southwest monsoon season. The mean annual rainfall is less than 75 inches, seasonal in character and less reliable.

Approximately 82 percent of the wet zone consists of red-yellow podzolic soils. These soils are suitable for growing tree crops, and respond well to fertilizers. Reddish brown earths are the main soil group of the dry zone lowland areas. Strips of alluvial soil are found among the lower courses of the rivers. If well drained, this soil variety could be used for intensive cultivation of field crops.

The lowland wet zone of Sri Lanka has tropical evergreen forests, and some parts of the highland wet zone have subtropical evergreens. At high altitudes forest trees are stunted. In the dry zone the forests consist of semi-evergreen flora. However, most of the forest cover has disappeared due to settlements and expansion of agriculture. In the driest part of the island the vegetation consists of stunted, thorny shrubs. The savannalike grasslands found in the eastern dry zone are believed to be a result of periodic burning.

The minerals of commercial value found in Sri Lanka are gemstones, graphite, ilmenite, limestone, quartz, mica, industrial clays, and salt. There are no known deposits of petroleum or coal. There are scattered deposits of iron ore. Gemstones and graphite remain the most valuable mineral products of Sri Lanka. High-value gemstones such as sapphire, ruby, chrysoberyl, spinel, and beryl, and semiprecious stones such as moonstones, garnet, zircon, tourmaline, and feldspar are among the gemstones commercially extracted in Sri Lanka. Graphite (Crystalline carbon) deposits of high quality are found in north-central, western, and southwestern segments of the island.

The People

Sinhalese account for 13.4 million (74 percent) of the total population of 18.1 million, Sri Lanka Tamils 2.2 (12 percent), Indian Tamils 1.1 (6 percent), Muslims 1.3 (7 percent), and Burghers (Eurasians) and others account for the balance, 176,000 (1 percent). The Sinhalese speak Sinhala. They trace their origins to settlers who came to the island from Bengal in northeast India starting around the fifth century B.C. Historically they probably are the descendants of waves of migrants from several parts of India, including Orissa in the west coast of the subcontinent mixed with the native tribal population called the *Veddas*.

The Tamils speak Tamil, a Dravidian language spoken in Tamil Nadu in South India. The Tamils arrived in the island in antiquity and settled mostly in the northern part of the island, especially in the Jaffna peninsula. The Muslims speak mostly Tamil, but some are Sinhala speakers. They trace their origins to Arab traders who came to the island especially after the 12th century. However, it is more probable that the Muslims also have highly mixed origins. Some of the community can trace back their origins to

Islamic settlers from the southern coastal regions of India. The Burghers, who number about 65,000, are primarily the descendants of the Dutch. They generally consider themselves to be racially distinct from the rest of the population because of their European origin. Their native language typically is English. However, the Burgher population declined sharply after the mid-1950s due to large-scale migration to Australia, Canada and other western countries. Those who remain are more integrated than in the past with the larger ethnic communities.

There are also a few small minority communities, each numbering from as little as a few thousand to about 20,000. The Malays, who first came to Sri Lanka under Dutch rule, constitute one such minority. The Parsees, Borahs, and Sindhis are small minorities of Indian origin who live largely in Colombo and are engaged primarily in business. Today there are not more than a few thousand at most who belong to the original indigenous tribe of the country, the *Veddas*.

More than 90 percent of the Sinhalese are Buddhist and the balance are Christians, mostly Roman Catholics. About 80 percent of the Tamils are Hindus and the rest Christians. The Muslims consider themselves to be a distinct ethnic group because of their adherence to Islam.

Approximately 75 percent of the population of the country is rural and the balance, 25 percent urban. However, these estimates must be treated with caution. Urban areas are officially defined as those that have municipal councils or urban councils as local authorities. There are large populations in close proximity to the larger cities and towns (especially Colombo) who live in urbanized environments, but outside municipal and urban council jurisdiction. However, Sri Lanka has experienced a slower rate of urbanization than many other developing countries. This is partly due to the combined effect of several factors, including the relatively slow pace of industrialization, the stress of government policy on rural development and small farmer agriculture, availability of cheap public transport from rural areas to urban centers, and the comparatively satisfactory quality of facilities, especially in health and education, in rural areas.

About two-thirds of the country's population live in the wet zone where the density is about 600 per square kilometer. The eastern, northern and southeastern plains that comprise the dry zone with the exception of the Jaffna peninsula are relatively thinly populated. This variation in density is directly related to employment opportunities and the quality of natural resources available, especially cultivable land in the two zones. The wet zone has abundant water and is suitable for the plantation crops as well as for rice and other subsidiary food and cash crops. The dry zone is suitable for agriculture, but perennial cultivation usually requires irrigated water, which is relatively scarce and expensive to provide. Moreover, Sri Lanka's manufacturing industries and commercial activities are also largely concentrated in and around Colombo.

One of the striking features of Sri Lanka's demography is the transition that is currently taking place in its population growth. Sri Lanka began to experience a slow decline in its mortality rate from the early 1920s, mainly due to improvement in living standards and better access to food and health care for the ordinary people. Largely due to an effective reduction in the incidence of Malaria, this decline accelerated dramatically in the second half of the 1940s when the crude death rate fell from more than 21 per 1,000 in 1945 to 10 per 1,000 in the mid-1950s. The decline continued into the next several decades. The current crude death rate is 6 per 1,000, and the infant mortality rate is 18 per 1,000 live births—one of the lowest for a developing country with a per capita income of less than US$ 700. In the 1950s and the early 1960s the crude birthrate remained practically unchanged around 35 per 1,000 producing a sharp rise in the natural rate of growth of population from about 1.5 percent in the mid-1940s to over 2.5 percent in the mid-1950s to mid-1960s. The population in the country doubled from 6.7 million in 1945 to 13.0 million in 1973. This sharp rise also radically altered the population age structure. In 1950 only 25 percent of the population were under the age of 15 and only 40 percent under 25. In 1981 these numbers were 35 percent and 56 percent respectively.

From the early 1970s the crude birthrate also began to decline slowly. The current rate is 20 per 1,000. The female fertility rate has dropped from 4.3 in 1970 to 2.1 in 1991. This trend is attributable to a number of factors, the most significant being improved female education leading to more formal employment for females, an increase in the age of marriage and a rising contraceptive prevalence rate. The low infant mortality rate and urbanization are also important factors that have contributed to a smaller family size.

The final point that must be noted about Sri Lanka's population is its geographical distribution in terms of ethnicity. Approximately 90 percent of the Sinhalese live in the "south," defined to mean the two-thirds of the country excluding the northern and eastern provinces. About 90 percent of the Indian Tamils and two-thirds of the Muslims also live in the south. The latter are scattered in pockets in many areas, but the former are concentrated in the central highland tea-growing districts of Kandy, Badulla, and especially Nuwara Eliya where they are an absolute majority of the population. About three-quarters of the Sri Lankan Tamils and about 10 percent of the Indian Tamils live in the northern and eastern provinces. About 70 percent of the population in that region is Tamil. The major political implication of this distribution is that it permits the Sri Lankan

Tamils to make the claim, generally rejected by the Sinhalese, that the northeast region is an exclusive Tamil homeland.

Early History

The Sri Lankan civilization has a history stretching back to more than 2,500 years. *The Mahavamsa,* the great chronicle of the Sinhalese that serves as a principal source for the construction of the island's early history, has an "origin myth" about the first settlers on the island. According to that story, a band of 700 young men led by Vijaya, a strong-headed young prince from Bengal who was banished by the king, his father, as punishment for misconduct, reached the shores of the island in 483 B.C. Vijaya established himself as the first ruler of the land. He first took a local tribal woman for his consort, but later married a princess from South India. Thus a kingship was established that continued after Vijaya.

Anuradhapura was established as the capital city of the new kingdom in 377 B.C. The ancient Sinhalese civilization was heavily influenced by India. However, it was not a copy of any Indian model. The Sinhalese civilization developed its own unique characteristics and individuality. The fact that the country was separated from the mainland by a strip of sea, albeit narrow, was helpful. Most importantly, it was primarily Buddhism that gave the Sinhalese civilization its own unique personality. Buddhism was officially introduced to the country in 250 B.C. by the great Indian Emperor Asoka, who sent his own son as a missionary to Sri Lanka. Indeed, as Buddhism gradually diminished in importance in India under the onslaught of Hinduism, the Sinhalese viewed it as their sacred mission to protect Buddhism and considered Sri Lanka to be the repository of the Buddhist doctrine in its pristine form.

The economic prosperity of this civilization, which was based in *Rajarata* as the northern plain came to be known, was based on rice cultivation that in turn depended on an increasingly complex irrigation system. Successive kings built increasingly large reservoirs, locally known as "tanks," to tap rivers to collect water for cultivation in the drier months. The reservoirs were connected by a system of canals. It was one of the most sophisticated hydraulic systems in the ancient world. Using the dual pillars of Buddhism and the rice economy, the ancient Sinhalese developed a sophisticated lifestyle for that era. For example, in the fourth century, the physician king Buddhadasa built hospitals to treat the sick. Scholars, especially *Bhikkhu* (monk) scholars, wrote works of history, religion, and literature.

The irrigation system proved to be the strength as well as the weakness of the ancient Sinhalese civilization. The interconnected system was highly vulnerable to enemy attack—a fact that invaders from South India were soon to realize and exploit.

From ancient times Sri Lanka has had what one might call a love-hate relationship with India. For powerful South Indian rulers Anuradhapura was a tempting target and many sent expeditionary forces, sometimes merely to loot and pillage. Some South Indian invaders such as King Elara in the second century B.C. were more ambitious and stayed on as rulers. South India was the obvious refuge to organize and gather an army for members of the Sinhalese ruling family or others who wanted to challenge a Sri Lankan ruler. Such challengers often cultivated the patronage of a south Indian king, with whose help an army was raised. They returned to the island with the mercenary force to do battle and capture the throne. There were also a number of instances where a Sri Lankan king would send an army to invade an Indian kingdom. However, the more frequent occurrences were in the opposite direction. One reason that led to the abandonment of Anuradhapura as the capital city in 993 in favor of Polonnaruwa, which is located to the southeast of the former, was to discourage such invasions. An army invading Polonnaruwa from the north had to cross an important river barrier, Sri Lanka's principal river, the Mahaveli.

There probably were economic reasons as well for moving the capital. One was the superior physical base of the Thamankaduwa plains on which Polonnaruwa is located for irrigated agriculture. The emergence of seaports along the eastern seaboard as centers of trade with southeast Asia would have been another factor. Polonnaruwa continued in the great tradition of the Sinhalese civilization established by Anuradhapura. The Polonnaruwa kings continued irrigation development. It was during the reign of King Parakramabahu I in the second half of the 12th century that Polonnaruwa reached the zenith of its grandeur and power. However, Polonnaruwa also eventually succumbed to invaders from South India. After the 13th century, Polonnaruwa was abandoned, and the capital city of Sinhalese kings gradually moved south, first to Dambadeniya, and later to Yapahuwa, Gampola, Kotte, and Sitavaka, and finally to Kandy.

Sometime in the 13th or early 14th century a Tamil kingdom was established in Jaffna. Over a certain spell of time it was practically independent of the southern rulers. However, at other times it acknowledged the suzerainty of the latter.

There is no one explanation for the eventual collapse of the ancient Sinhalese civilization in the *Rajarata*. South Indian invasions were an important factor. Scholars also speculate that malaria might also have played an important role in it.

Portuguese Rule

The arrival of the Portuguese in the island in 1505 coincided with a relatively weak and declining period in Sri Lanka's premodern civilization. The Portuguese, on the other hand, represented a Europe that was rising in military and economic might with an increasingly global reach. Thus the two sides were somewhat mismatched, a fact that was reflected in the relationship that developed between the Sri Lankans and the Portuguese.

The 16th century was a period of crisis in Sri Lankan history. There were numerous internecine disputes that at times led to succession wars. The Portuguese cleverly exploited these rivalries to consolidate their influence and power over the maritime provinces by virtually controlling the court of Kotte. From about 1600 to 1658 they actually ruled the maritime provinces, and also controlled the kingdom of Jaffna in the north. However, they failed to subjugate the kingdom of Kandy. They sent expeditionary forces to Kandy three times, but on all three occasions they were soundly defeated in battle. The Portuguese were finally expelled from the island in 1656 by the Dutch, who made an alliance with the king of Kandy for this purpose.

The Portuguese had two principal interests in Sri Lanka. One was to capture the island's export trade, especially in spice for which the country was renowned. The other was to spread Catholicism among the native population. Political power and control of territory were incidental to these two goals. For the first their only serious rivals were Arab traders, who had virtually dominated the market when the Portuguese arrived in the country. The rivalry between the two groups continued. The Portuguese won the competition, at least in the Kotte kingdom and the south and southwestern part of the country. However, the Arab traders managed to get the patronage of the Kandyan kings to carry on their trade from the eastern seaboard of the island.

The campaign of the Portuguese to proselytize the local population met with stiff resistance from Buddhist monks, the *Sangha*. On occasion the Portuguese used cruel and destructive tactics, including killing of those who resisted and pillage of temples, to achieve their aspirations to establish Catholicism.

The Portuguese left behind in Sri Lanka their influence on religion and culture that remains to this day. Roman Catholicism took root, especially in the maritime provinces. Today it is the most important and powerful Christian denomination in Sri Lanka with about 700,000 adherents. Some of the Catholic churches built by the Portuguese are of considerable architectural value. The Portuguese also made a contribution to Sinhala and Tamil languages by adding a host of new words. Portuguese music and dance forms became an integral element of the popular culture.

Dutch Rule

The Dutch arrived in Sri Lanka in the second quarter of the 17th century. Their main goal was to capture the spice trade from the Portuguese. Toward that end they formed an alliance with the Kandyan kingdom. Between 1639 and 1658 they succeeded in defeating the Portuguese in a series of battles and in taking over the key fortresses at Trincomalee, Negombo, Colombo, Mannar, and Jaffna, in that order. The Dutch established a strong administration in the maritime areas under their control and embarked on a long campaign to gain full mastery of the island by subjugating the Kandyan king. The goal of the Dutch was to get the king to acknowledge their right to rule the areas that they controlled and to win recognition of their right to a monopoly of the island's external trade. The Kandyan kings never formally conceded any of these. It was an uneasy relationship that was based on the principle "live and let live".

The Dutch East India Company (VOC) that administered the Dutch territory developed a flourishing trade in cinnamon. The Dutch administration also encouraged the cultivation of food crops, especially rice. Most important, Sri Lanka got locked into the international trading system as never before. Perhaps the long-term impact of the Dutch on Sri Lanka was less tangible than that of the Portuguese. Nevertheless, it was not entirely negligible. They developed a network of canals in the Colombo area for transport purposes. In education, for example, they took over the schools left behind by the Portuguese and handed them over to missionaries of the Dutch Reformed Church. The linkage between education and proselytization continued under the Dutch as before under the Portuguese. The Dutch expanded and improved the school system. They took over the local system of administration and adapted it to meet their own needs. However, it did not lead to any radical changes in the system. In the legal system, however, the Dutch made a lasting impact by introducing the Roman-Dutch Law in areas such as property rights. In architecture they left behind a more enduring legacy than the Portuguese did, primarily because they ruled the littoral for a longer period than the latter. For example, some of the Dutch churches are considered to be fine works of architecture of that period.

The Dutch lost their Sri Lankan territory essentially as a result of events in Europe and in the Indian subcontinent. For quite sometime the British did not want to get involved in Sri Lanka for fear of offending the Dutch. However, that constraint disappeared when Dutch power in Asia began to decline. In 1782 the British attacked and captured for a brief spell the fort of Trincomalee on the northeast coast. From that time up to about 1796 there was periodic friction between the Dutch (and the French) on the one side and the British on the other for control of places like Trincomalee and Nagapatnam in the north.

The British established contact with the Kandy king, who resented the fact that he was the ruler of a landlocked state and had to depend on the Dutch to have access to a port for trade. The first British contact with the Kandyan kingdom in 1762 was done cautiously. However, when the prospect of a French takeover of Dutch territory in Asia loomed large toward the 1790s, the British stepped in and took over from the Dutch. On that occasion it was a peaceful transfer of power that was agreed to by a treaty signed in Europe.

British Rule

The first British administration in Sri Lanka from 1796 to 1802 was under the British East India Company that operated from Madras. In 1802 the London Colonial Office made Sri Lanka a crown colony. The British made an unsuccessful bid to capture Kandy in 1803. They succeeded in their second attempt in 1815 with the help of some of the key ministers of the last king of Kandy Sri Vickrama Rajasingha. The king and his family were captured by the British troops and deported to Vellore (Madras).

The British entered into a treaty with the Kandyan chieftains that gave the latter certain assurances regarding the administration of the Kandyan provinces. In particular the British promised to protect Buddhism by providing state patronage as Sri Lankan kings had done for over 2,000 years. However, soon disillusionment set in among the Kandyan leadership. The result was the 1818 Kandyan rebellion led by a section of the Kandyan aristocracy. The rebellion had a Kandyan nationalist flavor to it. It was also the last effort of the Sri Lankan (Kandyan) aristocracy to regain power. The British, using their superior military might, had no difficulty in ruthlessly suppressing it.

Of the three western powers that occupied Sri Lanka over a period of 450 years, it was the British who made the most radical changes in the life of the country and charted it into new waters. The British unified the country under a single administration, something that had not happened for 400 years before that. Like the Portuguese and the Dutch before them, the British also adapted the native administrative system to suit their own requirements. However, they also introduced a more centralized and modern administrative structure.

For a while the British used some elements of the feudal system that they found in the country. For example, people were required to work in public works for a certain number of days every year. However, in the Colebrooke-Cameron reforms of 1833, they officially abolished all feudal obligations. This was a turning point in the social and economic history of Sri Lanka. The British, in doing so, had laid the foundation for the development of a modern capitalist economy.

The original motive of the British for taking over Sri Lanka from the Dutch was largely strategic. The British simply wanted to preempt a takeover by the French that would have threatened their position in India. However, the British soon realized that the new colony had considerable economic potential. Thus the colonial government took the initiative to experiment with coffee growing. The pilot project proved to be a success. The first regular coffee plantation was opened in 1827. Soon prospective British planters came to Sri Lanka in ever-increasing numbers to open new plantations. The government assisted them in every possible manner, especially by providing them with land. For this purpose the British enacted an ordnance in 1840 that decreed that all land for which no title could be shown will be vested in the Crown. Sri Lankan villagers generally enjoyed land rights by tradition, and they were hard put to make legal claims under the new law. Thus a large extent of the country's land resources were automatically vested in the state. It is this land that was sold very cheaply to British planters.

Coffee proved to be a lucrative crop. It was grown in the central highland area. The capital and technology were British. The labor was Indian. The Sinhalese who inhabited that part of the country were not willing to work as laborers on the plantations. Thus the workers for the coffee plantations came almost entirely from South India as indentured labor. By 1880 Sri Lanka had over 140,000 ha. under coffee. Annual coffee exports had reached the 112 million lb. mark around this time.

In the 1870s the Sri Lankan coffee plantations were devastated by the leaf blight, *hemileia vastratrix.* The planters then switched over to tea as an alternative crop that proved to be even more successful than coffee. By the turn of the century tea had not only completely replaced coffee but had exceeded the area covered by coffee to reach 165,000 ha. In the 1890s rubber was also introduced as a commercial plantation crop. There was a rapidly growing market for rubber in the West, especially to meet the demands of new industries such as automobiles. By 1914 area under rubber had grown from less than 1,000 ha in 1900 to over 60,000 ha.

Tea and rubber, together with coconut, established a classic commodity export dual economy in Sri Lanka. The country exported virtually the entire product of the first two crops and also coconut products and other minor cash crops such as cinnamon. It imported food and other consumer goods, intermediate goods such as fuel and cement and capital goods. A modern service sector, including banking, insurance, and transport grew, around the export-import sector to cater to its needs. The government used the tax revenue generated by the economy to improve the physical infrastructure such as roads and communications. It also invested in education and health care that were essential to run the system smoothly. The traditional economy and the vast rural population that lived in the hinterland derived some benefits from this activity. For example, up to about 1850 "native coffee" exceeded in volume the coffee produced on the plantations. However, the traditional economy centered on rice cultivation—the other part of the dual system—continued at a subsistence level.

The rebellion of 1848 against the colonial administration partly reflected economic dissatisfaction felt by some sections of the community, especially in the context of a recession that hit the economy around that time. But more importantly, it was due to the traditional resentment of foreigners on the part of the Kandyan people. The rebellion was confined to Kandy and some adjacent areas in the more central parts of the country. The British administration had no difficulty in crushing it with its armed might. Except for this episode, the period after 1830 in the 19th century was politically uneventful. The legislative council, which was largely an advisory body to the British governor underwent a slow evolution with more unofficial members being appointed to represent the various ethnic communities. In the first quarter of the 20th century, provision was made to elect some of them by limited franchise.

After the end of World War I a movement for self-government began to gather momentum. Inspired by the contemporary movement in India for independence, Sri Lankan political leaders established the Ceylon National Congress in 1919 to work toward that goal. It was led by a set of leaders who were deeply committed to working with the British authorities and winning their demands through peaceful negotiation. Thus, the Sri Lankan independence movement hardly, if ever, took a militant stance. Their efforts paid early dividends when in 1931 the British accepted the recommendations of the Donoughmore Commission and granted "internal self-government" under a legislative body—the State Council—that was directly elected by the people. Thus, Sri Lanka became the first nonwhite British colony to enjoy universal franchise, one of the principal privileges of a democratic polity.

This was also the time when the Buddhist revivalist movement, whose origins can be traced back to the last quarter of the 19th century, assumed a particularly militant profile. The leaders, most notably Anagarika Dharmapala, advocated rejection of things foreign and extolled the virtues of indigenous—Sinhala Buddhist—culture and values.

The Great Depression of the 1930s affected the Sri Lankan economy very adversely. The export sector that served as the engine of growth spluttered. The country suffered a massive reduction in export earnings and severe unemployment in the plantation and commercial sectors. This focused the attention of the national political leadership on the vulnerability of the export economy to external shocks and the need for a more self-reliant economy. The result was the beginning of a resolute effort to produce more goods, especially rice and other basic consumer goods, at home for the domestic market. It took about three more decades and well after independence for this inward orientation to gather momentum. However, the seed for change was sown in the 1930s. It was the economic facet of the nationalist movement that was pressing the British for independence.

The Second World War diverted the attention of the British authorities to the war effort. The local British administration got thoroughly engaged in defense activity after Japan joined the Axis powers in the war. Japan's military successes in Malaya and Burma alarmed the local administration that took the threat posed by Japan to Sri Lanka seriously. The Sri Lankan nationalist leadership gave its strong support to the British and cooperated with the local British officials in the defense of the country. They had hope of being rewarded with generous constitutional reform, and perhaps independence, in return for the loyalty that they showed in this hour of need. When Britain's new postwar Labour government under Prime Minister Clement Atlee decided to give independence to India and Burma, granting independence to Sri Lanka became a mere formality. The country won its independence from 150 years of British rule on February 4, 1948.

Independence

The postindependence history of Sri Lanka easily lends itself to convenient periodization that breaks up the past 45 years into four analytically convenient subperiods. The first from 1948 to 1956 was associated with the liberal democratic regime of the United National Party (UNP) that ruled the country in the first eight years of independence. This was followed by 20 years of Sinhalese nationalist and socialist administrations under Sri Lanka Freedom Party (SLFP) regimes led by S. W. R. D. Bandaranaike (1956-1959) and his wife Sirimavo Bandaranaike (1960-1965 and 1970-1977). The 1965-1970 UNP regime under Dudley Senanayake was, at best, an interlude between the administrations of the Bandaranaikes. The third period, from 1977-1994 (August), is associated with a UNP administration that was substantially different from the previous UNP regimes. The fourth period begins in August 1994 with the defeat of the UNP after having been in office for 17 years. It is, as yet, premature to judge the historical significance of the new People's Alliance government. It may or may not turn out to be a fresh chapter in the country's history.

1948-1956: Era of Liberal Democracy

The UNP administration under Don Stephen Senanayake that took over from the British also inherited, inter alia, a reasonably prosperous economy, a relatively large foreign reserve, and a sophisticated bureaucracy. In foreign policy the government was strongly pro-western. It signed a defense agreement with the British government that permitted the latter to retain a naval base in Trincomalee and an air force base in Katunayake.

On issues concerning interethnic relations, the Senanayake administration followed somewhat mixed policies. On the one hand, it took in the Tamil Congress, the then premier Tamil political party, as a junior partner in government. It was also committed to having Sinhala and Tamil as official languages. However, it also enacted the Ceylon Citizenship Act of 1948 that effectively made about three-fourths of the Indian Tamil plantation workers stateless "immigrants" and also made them lose their franchise.

The UNP administration, especially Prime Minister Senanayake, was very enthusiastic in promoting domestic agriculture through land colonization. Under colonization, state land in the dry zone was distributed in small parcels of five to eight acres to landless peasants moved from other parts of the country where there was a shortage of land. The government also spent large sums of money to develop irrigation facilities and the physical infrastructure such as roads, schools, hospitals, and townships in the colonization schemes. Some of these settlements later proved to be a principal bone of contention between the Sinhalese and Tamils. The former viewed it as a legitimate use of the country's land resources. The latter viewed the settlements as a deliberate attempt on the part of the Sinhalese-dominated government to settle Sinhalese in the northern and especially eastern province, which they (Tamils) claimed as their traditional homeland.

The economic consequences of the settlement schemes, on balance, proved to be beneficial. The resettlement of people from the more densely populated southwest quarter of the country reduced population pressure in that part of the country and also helped to slow down the pace of urbanization. More importantly, the increased production of rice in the new settlements helped to cut back rice imports and make the country almost self-sufficient in the staple food.

In general, the policies of the UNP were conservative and reflected the preferences of the western-educated elite who took over the country from the British. This created an obvious opening for someone to exploit the more radical nationalist strand of politics that was yearning for leadership. S. W. R. D. Bandaranaike, one of the senior cabinet ministers of the UNP administration, understood the significance of this political vacuum and stepped in to fill it. He broke away from the UNP and formed the SLFP in

1951. It advocated the policy of Sinhalese as the only official language and presented a program that appealed to the Sinhalese-Buddhist nationalist elements.

Stephen Senanayake died in March 1952 and was succeeded by his son Dudley to the premiership. Two months later Dudley Senanayake led the UNP to a decisive electoral victory in parliamentary elections. However, a few months later he ran into bitter opposition led by the left parties and the trade unions that they controlled when he tried to cut the consumer rice subsidy to balance the budget. Senanayake resigned from the premiership and was succeeded by Sir John Kotelawala. Kotelawala's stewardship was relatively uneventful. However, the UNP governed with confidence. Little did it realize that the mood of the country, especially in the south, was changing rapidly under a wave of Sinhalese-Buddhist nationalism. Kotelawala dissolved parliament one year ahead of schedule and called for general elections to obtain a fresh mandate. In the elections held in April 1956, the UNP suffered a resounding defeat at the hands of the *Mahajana Eksath Peramuna* (MEP), a coalition of parties headed by the SLFP under Bandaranaike.

1956-1965: Nationalism and Socialism

The 1956 election was a major turning point in the country's post-independence history. The Bandaranaike government policies gave expression to the demands of the Sinhalese-Buddhists to restore to them their due position in the life of the country that they believed was lost during 450 years of Western occupation. Thus, Sinhala was made the only official language in 1956. A ministry of cultural affairs was created to work for the advancement of Sinhalese culture and Buddhist religion.

The government also tried to boost the image of the vernacular (Sinhala) teachers, Ayurvedic doctors, and others associated with the local, especially Sinhalese culture. This was also the time when there was a renaissance in Sinhala literacy and cultural activities. For example the Sinhala creative writer Martin Wickremasinghe published some of his best works during this period, and E. R. Sarachchandra produced his groundbreaking stage play *Maname* around the same time.

In economic policy the government was committed to a socialist program. Thus private bus companies were nationalized in 1958 and a state monopoly was created in that sector. The ports were also taken over in 1958. The cooperative movement was strengthened as a counterweight to the private sector in retail and wholesale trading. In rice cultivation the rights of tenants were strengthened at the expense of those of the land-owners.

In foreign policy, Bandaranaike moved away from the pro-western foreign policy of the UNP and became an enthusiastic supporter of the concept of nonalignment. He also persuaded the British to withdraw their naval and air force bases from Sri Lanka.

Bandaranaike's language policy encountered the opposition of the Tamils. In response he reached agreement with S. J. V. Chelvanayakam, the leader of the Tamil Federal Party, to settle the grievances of the Tamils. Under the so-called Bandaranaike-Chelvanayakam Pact of 1957, legal provision was to be made for the use of the Tamil language in state business. More importantly, a system of regional government was proposed to devolve power to the Tamil areas. In retrospect, had this agreement been implemented, the country might have been spared the ethnic violence that it has suffered over the last 15 years. Unfortunately, there was vehement opposition to the agreement from both within the MEP administration as well as from without. Bandaranaike was forced to abrogate the pact in 1958. However, he did enact legislation to make provision for the use of the Tamil language in state transactions.

Bandaranaike was assassinated in 1959. He was succeeded by his widow, Sirimavo Bandaranaike, who entered active politics only after her husband's death. Her party won the July 1960 elections with a comfortable margin. Her first administration from 1960 to 1965 was notable for several radical programs that were undertaken. The western oil companies were nationalized in 1962. The American oil companies refused to accept the quantum of compensation offered, and consequently the United States government suspended aid to Sri Lanka. The Bandaranaike administration also created state monopolies in banking and insurance. It had a vigorous program of import substitution industrialization with protection given to the new industries by having high tariffs, import quotas, or outright bans on imports. Many of the larger and more capital-intensive industries were undertaken by the state itself through para-statal corporations. The government also took over almost all the schools that hitherto were in the hands of private religious organizations that ran them with the help of a state subsidy.

In foreign policy Prime Minister Bandaranaike became a prominent leader of the Non-Aligned Movement. She developed a close rapport with the leading figures of the movement, such as Marshal Tito of Yugoslavia and Julius Nyerere of Tanzania. Her most notable foreign policy achievement during this period was the signing of an agreement with Indian Prime Minister Lal Bahadur Shastri to settle the question of stateless Indian Tamil plantation workers in Sri Lanka. Under the Sirimavo-Shastri agreement India promised to take back 350,000 people and their natural increase, and Sri Lanka promised to give citizenship to 200,000 and their natural increase.

The fate of the balance 100,000 was to be decided at a later stage. The agreement was not implemented in full or in accordance with the original 15 year time frame. However, it greatly assisted in the resolution of the issue that eventually ended with India taking almost 500,000 people and Sri Lanka granting citizenship to the balance.

The radical policies of the Bandaranaike government resulted in the first-ever military coup attempt in Sri Lanka in 1962 led by a group of high-ranking military officers who were unhappy with the socialist ways of the government. The coup, however, failed and the leaders were arrested and prosecuted in court. The government eventually was defeated two years later in parliament on its proposal to takeover Sri Lanka's foremost newspaper publishing house, the Lake House. The Bandaranaike administration viewed the privately owned newspaper group as an anti-SLFP government and pro-UNP entity. Thus, in 1964 it brought legislation to parliament to nationalize the group. The government was defeated, resulting in fresh general elections that returned the UNP to power.

1965-1970: Liberal Interlude

The 1965-1970 UNP administration under Dudley Senanayake was an interlude between two Bandaranaike administrations. Senanayake was a liberal who believed in the classical parliamentary model. In retrospect, these were the last five years in Sri Lanka's postindependence history that the country enjoyed a sense of freedom that a true liberal democracy would offer. Senanayake tried to address the Tamil issue by inviting the Federal Party to join the government. In return for the latter's support in parliament, Senanayake offered to establish a form of devolved government in the provinces, and also strengthen the implementation of the legislation that provided for the use of Tamil in state business. These proposals, like similar ones before, also had to be abandoned due to strong opposition from Sinhalese interest groups from both inside and outside the government.

In the economic front, Senanayake took some tentative steps toward liberalization. For example, he loosened foreign exchange control and eased import restrictions. However, he lacked the confidence and vision to make any fundamental changes. His significant achievement was in agriculture. The government launched a "cultivation movement" that encouraged higher productivity, especially in rice and subsidiary food crops. This policy showed considerable success. In particular, rice production reached record levels. This success in domestic agriculture was not sufficient to meet the rising expectations of the population, especially the young. The labor force had begun to grow rapidly after 1960 as a result of the population boom that the country experienced following the sharp decline in the death rate after the Second World War. The growth rate of the economy was simply insufficient to provide employment to all the new workers who were joining the labor force seeking employment. In the May 1970 general elections, the majority of these young voters were successfully wooed by the SLFP-led United Front (UF) left-of-center coalition. Thus, the UNP led by Senanayake suffered a humiliating defeat at the hands of the UF, which won a two-thirds majority in parliament.

1970-1977: Socialism in Crisis

The program of the second Sirimavo Bandaranaike administration took off from where it had stopped in 1965. Two major events, one internal and the other external, early in the life of the government shaped much of its policies in the seven years that the regime lasted. The internal event was the rebellion of the *Janatha Vimukthi Peramuna* (JVP—People's Liberation Front), an almost exclusively Sinhalese Marxist-Nationalist group. It supported the UF in the general elections. However, the JVP leadership was not satisfied with the slow pace of the government in implementing a socialist program of work. Therefore, it organized an armed insurrection in April 1971. The government crushed the rebellion deploying its superior military forces. Several thousand people, mostly supporters of the JVP, lost their lives in the insurrection. This unfortunate episode profoundly influenced government policy.

The external event was the first oil crisis of 1972 that quadrupled oil prices. Sri Lanka's already weak balance of payments faced a crisis of unmanageable proportions. The government responded to the two events outlined above by resorting to measures that strengthened the role of the state in the economy and even in fields such as university education. The foreign exchange shortage created by the oil crisis compelled the government to impose rationing of several basic consumer goods such as sugar and flour that were imported. Price control was extended to cover a wide range of goods. State monopolies were created in several areas of export and import trade. The policy of import substitution was pursued with greater vigor.

The JVP insurrection was a key factor that persuaded the government to undertake a major program of land reform in 1972 and 1975 that led to the nationalization of tea and rubber plantations. With this move the government brought under its bulk of control the production of the two principal agricultural export commodities. Given the already extensive state involvement in manufacturing industry, trade, banking, and insurance, the nationalization of the plantations gave the state almost complete control over key areas of the "modern" sector of the economy.

The social sector policies of the Bandaranaike administration were also in line with its socialist-statist orientation. On the positive side, it made every effort, subject to fiscal constraints, to maintain social sector expenditure on health, education, and social welfare. There was some scaling back of the consumer rice subsidy, but it significantly affected only the taxpayers who were a small fraction of the population enjoying relatively high incomes. The JVP used some of the university campuses as key bases to organize its insurrection. The government reacted by abandoning the liberal policy that it promised on universities at the 1970 elections in favor of legislation that imposed centralized state control over the university system. As subsequent events proved, this alienated a large segment of the intellectual community who had supported the UF in 1970.

In the political sphere the major change that took place during the 1970-1977 period was the introduction of the First Republican Constitution in 1972. Parliament was convened as a constituent assembly to draft the new constitution. The new constitution did away with the upper house (Senate) and created a unicameral parliament. Sri Lanka was changed from a dominion to a republic. A president with nominal powers replaced the Queen of England as head of state. The new constitution retained the previous parliamentary form of government. However, it deviated from the 1948 constitution in some other key areas. For example, it gave more powers to the cabinet of ministers in the control of the bureaucracy. It also excluded the safeguards found in the 1948 constitution that were designed to protect minorities against discriminatory legislation. The latter resulted in the Tamil MPs of the opposition boycotting the proceedings of the constituent assembly.

Prime Minister Sirimavo Bandaranaike's greatest triumphs were in foreign policy. In 1974 Mrs. Bandaranaike successfully negotiated a second agreement with Indian Prime Minister Indira Gandhi to settle the issue of the residual Indian Tamil population—about 150,000—whose citizenship status was left unresolved in the 1964 Sirimavo-Shastri agreement. The more prominent event was the holding of the fifth non-aligned summit in Colombo in August 1976. In keeping with the tradition of the movement, Prime Minister Bandaranaike, as the head of government of the host country, assumed the chairmanship of the movement at the summit.

In general, the 1970-1977 Bandaranaike administration faced a series of political difficulties that made governing difficult. The JVP insurrection was the first. The serious disagreements on important policy matters between the SLFP and its principal partner in the ruling coalition, the *Lanka Sama Samaja Party* (LSSP), was another. These eventually led to the latter being expelled from the coalition in 1975. In 1976 the government made an abortive attempt to extend the life of parliament by securing an amendment to the constitution. This move, however, was opposed by several cabinet ministers of the SLFP as well as the Communist Party, the sole remaining coalition partner of the SLFP.

1977-1994: Triumph of the Market & Challenge of Tamil Separatism

At the general election held in May 1977, the UNP was returned to power with a landslide victory. The party won 140 seats out of 168 seats in parliament. The second UNP era in Sri Lankan postindependence history was very different from the first. The UNP under J. R. Jayewardene, who took over the leadership in 1973 on Dudley Senanayake's death, had a new outlook. It no longer carried the image of the party of the privileged class. Many of the new UNP MPs came from ordinary backgrounds and had strong grassroots bases. Jayewardene had built up a powerful party machine with an organizational network that no other major political party could match. Most importantly, he was determined to make some radical changes in economic policy.

In its first budget in November 1977, the Jayewardene administration announced a series of measures to liberalize the economy. Import controls and price controls were mostly eliminated, tariffs were reduced and the tariff structure was simplified, the rupee exchange rate was devalued, exchange control was relaxed, income tax rates were reduced, and a number of other measures were taken to encourage private enterprise. Popularly known as the "open economy" policy, the goal was to increase economic growth via a market and export-oriented economic strategy. The new economic policy had the strong support of the donor community led by the World Bank and the International Monetary Fund (IMF). Between 1978 and 1994 Sri Lanka received more than US$ 7.5 billion in assistance.

The Jayewardene administration identified what it called "lead projects" to spearhead the economic strategy. In the export sector it established free trade zones (FTZ) under a "one-stop" authority called the Greater Colombo Economic Commission (1978), renamed the Board of Investment of Sri Lanka (BOISL) in 1992. The first FTZ was established in Katunayake adjacent to the Colombo international airport. A second was established in Biyagama, a suburb to the north of Colombo in 1987. A third FTZ was opened in the south of the country in 1990, and a fourth in Kandy in the central province in 1993. As at the end of 1994 the FTZs provided 122,000 jobs. In that year they exported goods worth Rs 87.0 billion. In agriculture and power the government decided to telescope the implementation of the Mahaveli River Development Project from 30 years to ten. Renamed the Accelerated Mahaveli Development Program (AMDP) (1978-1987), it involved the construction of six major dams and hydropower generating plants with an aggregate capacity of 800 MW per year and providing irrigation to 150,000 ha. of new land in the dry zone, mainly for rice cultivation. AMDP planned to settle 100,000 families in new farmsteads, and create many thousands of new jobs in secondary activity in industry and services.

AMDP has cost the government Rs 58 billion up to the end of 1994. About 80 percent of the funds came from donor contributions either as grants or loans on easy terms. Up to the end of 1994 it had settled 90,570 families and provided irrigation to 134,000 ha. of new land. In 1993, 47 percent of the national power supply came from Mahaveli. In 1993 a detailed cost-benefit analysis of the AMDP was completed. It revealed that, contrary to popular assertions, the program has in fact generated a rate of return considerably higher than that estimated in the original master plan. The government could not strictly adhere to its original plan for AMDP, in part due to factors beyond its control. The construction was not completed in ten years. Some work is still in progress. Some of the downstream work cannot be completed because the current ethnic war affects those areas. The Kotmale dam of the AMDP sprung a leak due to a structural weakness that resulted in several hundred million rupees in additional expenditure to effect repairs. However, defenders of the project point out that a strict monetary calculation does not capture the full benefits of the project. For example, it is argued that if not for the Mahaveli hydropower the country would have faced a severe power shortage. The social benefits of the new farmer settlements too may be considerable but difficult to quantify.

In the rural sector, the lead project has been a series of Integrated Rural Development Programs (IRDPs) in 14 different districts. These were also funded with donor contributions. IRDPs were designed to have local-level development programs that directly address grassroots needs. In theory IRDP projects were to be executed with maximum grassroots participation. However, due to a complex of reasons this objective was never fully realized. The results of IRDPs have been decidedly mixed. In general, IRDPs were less successful than the FTZ or the AMDP in achieving their goals.

In the social sector the lead project was housing. The Jayewardene government started its ambitious housing program with the 100,000 houses program in 1978-1982. It was followed by a 500,000 program in 1981-1985 and a 1 million program in 1986-1990. The current program is for 1.5 million houses between 1990-1996. These numbers must be qualified in several respects. Both new housing units as well as upgraded old units are included in this number. Moreover, it is unlikely that the targets were completed in any given five-year period. Thus, the last three programs ran concurrently in terms of the targets to be achieved. However, the important point is that the government was very successful in improving the housing stock at all levels. At the beginning, the government invested a substantial amount of its own funds for house construction. After 1983, government subsidies for this sector were substantially reduced. The new strategy was to provide mortgage loans to individuals, and in the case of middle-class housing, to corporate house builders as well. In the case of low income groups the government provided assistance to individual builders with small loans and cheap materials, and encouraged "self-help" construction.

The open economy strategy produced mixed economic results. On the positive side, economic growth picked up in the first five years to average more than 5 percent per annum. The rate of unemployment was cut from 25 percent to 12 percent. On the negative side, inflation increased from single digits in the mid 1970s to more than 10 percent per annum in the early 1980s. Import liberalization helped create many jobs by easing the supply of raw material, spare parts, and capital equipment. Recession in previously protected industries such as handloom textiles created considerable social problems for those who lost employment. Income distribution also worsened because the new policies favored income from profits, rent, and high-level managerial and professional employment. However, the drastic reduction in unemployment, especially in the informal sector, probably helped to reduce the incidence of poverty.

At the macroeconomic level the strategy had one major weakness, its unsustainability. The rate of investment rose from about 15 percent to 20 percent in the mid 1970s to more than 30 percent in the late 1970s and the early 1980s. This increase was financed almost entirely with foreign assistance. A substantial amount of this investment was in the public sector in projects such as AMDP with long gestation periods. Some other programs such as housing development had substantial social benefits, but their short-term direct economic benefits were limited. The government was forced to trim expenditure by 10 percent in most programs in 1982. The period of political instability that followed the 1983 ethnic disturbances damaged investor confidence, both local and foreign, and caused a decline in the level of economic activity. The growth rate also dropped to an average of about 4 percent per annum for the rest of the decade.

The economy showed signs of recovery after 1990. Tourism and foreign investment picked up. The government undertook a vigorous program of privatization to restructure the economy. However, the long-term sustainability of the economic program will largely depend on restoring confidence in the economy by settling the ethnic war.

Overall, the Jayewardene administration (1977-1989) can claim credit for its economic achievements. The same cannot be said regarding its politics. At the beginning of his administration he made a genuine attempt to address the ethnic question. He modified the scheme of admissions to universities to meet some of the Tamil concerns. He also established a system of district development councils (DDC) to devolve power to the districts. The Tamil leadership cooperated with Jayewardene to work the DDC system. However, it eventually failed because Colombo simply did not give the new councils enough power to make them meaningful to the Tamils. Whereas the traditional Tamil leadership that negotiated with the government lost its credibility, the rebel groups increased their credibility by engaging the government in a direct armed confrontation. The intensity of the conflict intensified severalfold after the July 1983 ethnic riots. In August 1985 the government agreed to attend Indian-sponsored peace talks between the government and the rebel groups in Thimpu, but the talks ended in failure. In June 1986 the government initiated "All Party" talks to reach a settlement, but that met with the same fate that befell the Thimpu talks. In 1987 the government decided to escalate its war effort in the hope of defeating the Liberation Tigers of Tamil Eelam (LTTE), which now controlled the Jaffna peninsula. The Indian government warned Jayewardene that it would not tolerate a military defeat of the LTTE, and the government had to stop its campaign. Instead, under intense Indian pressure, Jayewardene signed an Indo-Lanka Peace Accord with Prime Minister Rajiv Gandhi in July 1987.

The Peace Accord and connected exchange of letters between President Jayewardene and Prime Minister Gandhi addressed two somewhat separate sets of issues. One related to the foreign policy concerns of India. For example, Sri Lanka agreed not to permit any foreign military activities that would be prejudicial to the interests of India.

The second aspect dealt with the ethnic conflict. The Peace Accord brought temporary peace to the island. The principal provision was the establishment of a system of provincial councils to devolve power. The northern and eastern provinces were temporarily amalgamated, and a single provincial council was established in terms of the accord. It lasted only about three years from 1987 to 1990. In any event, peace broke down when the LTTE refused to be disarmed and abide by the terms of the accord. Within three months of signing the accord, fighting broke out between the LTTE and the Indian Peace Keeping Forces (IPKF). As the war intensified, the IPKF numbers increased to more than 60,000 by mid 1988. In the south, the JVP unleashed an antigovernment terror campaign using the presence of the IPKF as a factor to mobilize support among the Sinhalese for its cause. By mid 1988, the entire country was in the grip of terror and violence. The second presidential election held in December 1988 proved to be one of the most violent such events Sri Lanka had ever seen. The JVP that called for a boycott of the election launched a campaign of terror to intimidate party workers and voters. What is remarkable is that the threat of violence and intimidation notwithstanding, more than 60 percent of the voters came to the polls. It was by no means the cleanest of elections held in the country. Local and international groups that observed the elections reported a large number of incidents of violence, intimidation, and other violations of regulations governing the poll. It is difficult to judge whether such events had a decisive outcome on the result. Be that as it may, the election was narrowly won by the UNP candidate R. Premadasa, defeating his nearest challenger, SLFP's Sirimavo Bandaranaike.

In 1978 Jayewardene replaced the first republican constitution with a new second republican constitution that converted Sri Lanka from a parliamentary government to an executive presidency. This change was justified by him on the grounds that a strong executive authority free of parliamentary control was essential to take quick and decisive decisions to develop the country. In practice, the presidential system proved to be very authoritarian. Jayewardene's first major political act after winning the first presidential election in October 1982 was to substitute the parliamentary elections that were due in 1983 with a referendum to extend the life of the 1977 parliament by another six years. The UNP that campaigned for the extension "won" the referendum. However, its victory was questioned on grounds of campaign and poll malpractice.

There were several other acts of commission and omission during the Jayewardene administration that further undermined liberal democracy in Sri Lanka. On one occasion supreme court judges were intimidated by a gang of thugs who had the tacit approval of the UNP leadership. A police officer who was found guilty by courts for violating human rights was rewarded by the government with an immediate promotion to a higher rank. In general adherence to the rule of law and due process weakened during the 1980s. This was further compounded by the neglect of accountability and transparency in government that in turn led to widespread corruption in public life. Of course one can arguably qualify this by pointing to the threat of terrorism that the Sri Lankan government had to contend with during this period, and the gross violation of human rights by Sinhalese and Tamil rebel groups who also resorted to arbitrary killing and torture of their opponents and civilians on a large scale. However, the international human rights groups and the donor community focused mostly on violations of human rights by the state military and police.

President Premadasa led the UNP to a convincing parliamentary election victory in March 1989. Getting the Indian Peace Keeping Force (IPKF) out of the country was one of his chief campaign promises during both elections. For this purpose he had an ally in the LTTE with whom he had peace talks for more than one year until June 1991. The Indians eventually agreed to leave and all IPKF troops were pulled out by March 1990. However, his peace talks with the LTTE failed and fighting broke out between government troops and the LTTE in June 1991 in what has been dubbed the second Eelam war.

Premadasa led a populist but authoritarian administration. A primary strength of his administration was the president's own indefatigable capacity for work, and his strong leadership focused on development. Premadasa understood that in a fundamental sense, Sri Lanka's development dilemma was one of satisfying the basic needs of about one-third of its population that lived below the poverty line, while at the same time making a concerted effort to modernize the economy to take the country to the 21st century. He tried to find a concept of poverty alleviation. The other was framed in the concept of "NIC" (Newly Industrialized Country) by the year 2000.

Premadasa's populism stemmed from his conviction that as a man from an ordinary (nonelite) background, it was his duty to work for the poor and dispossessed. He had a vision of Sri Lanka that would eliminate poverty and provide jobs and a decent living standard for everyone. Premadasa accepted the superiority of the market as a method for organizing production. However, he also saw the social ruthlessness of the market that could make it politically unacceptable to many, especially the poor. He was one leader who searched for a formula to harmonize market economic efficiency with the greater social good. His answer was to persuade capitalists and workers that they had a common goal to achieve by working together. To realize his vision he launched a poverty alleviation program, the ultimate goal of which was to make every family self-reliant. He started a 200-garment factory scheme to take factory industry to the village. He also continued his Village Awakening and house construction schemes that were begun during the Jayewardene administration. Not every scheme and program that Premadasa undertook passed the test of strict economic rationality. But none can doubt his commitment to hard work, and his desire to give a better deal to the poor.

In some ways Premadasa was an insecure man who felt that the Sri Lankan establishment never fully accepted him as a leader. To compensate, he had no compunctions about using the enormous powers that the presidency bestowed on him. Many were the instances when power was abused if not by the president himself, at least in his name. The authoritarian element of his rule led to an eventual breakup of his first cabinet. In 1992 two of his most senior ministers, Lalith Athulathmudali and Gamini Dissanayake, led a group of UNP rebels in parliament to propose a motion to impeach the president. The attempt failed and the rebels were expelled from the party. They also lost their seats in parliament. Premadasa's vision for Sri Lanka was abruptly cut short when he was assassinated by an LTTE suicide bomber in May 1993 in Colombo.

Prime Minister D. B. Wijetunga succeeded Premadasa to the presidency. The new president's more open and less-authoritarian style of government was welcomed by the people at large. However, in general, there was continuity of UNP policy under the new administration. The market-oriented economic policies were pursued with the same vigor as before. However, the government failed to seriously address the ethnic war. Indeed the new president alienated some segments of the minority population by suggesting that the northern issue was nothing more than one of "terrorism". Neither did the Wijetunga administration make a serious bid to address the issues of corruption at the higher level of government, arbitrary use of power by the military and the police, and other such concerns that engaged the public mind after 17 years of UNP rule. Thus, notwithstanding a steady economic recovery after 1989 and some outstanding achievements in the economic sphere, the UNP lost, thcugh narrowly, the tenth parliamentary elections of Sri Lanka held on August 16, 1994.

1994: The New Dispensation

The new People's Alliance (PA) administration is led by Mrs. Chandrika Bandaranaike Kumaratunga, the charismatic second daughter of two former prime ministers, S. W. R. D. Bandaranaike and his wife, Sirimavo. For Mrs. Kumaratunga it was a meteoric rise from chief minister of a provincial government in 1993 to the prime ministership and later to the presidency within less than 18 months. The new government took a few steps, such as cutting the price of bread, resuming peace talks with the LTTE, and initiating investigations into charges of corruption against members of the former UNP administration that were clearly aimed at the electorate preparing to vote in the third presidential election scheduled for November 9, 1994. The PA nominated Mrs. Kumaratunga and the UNP nominated its leader of the opposition Gamini Dissanayake. The latter was assassinated by an LTTE suicide bomber in October before the election, and was replaced by his widow Mrs. Srima Dissanayake.

In the presidential election the PA, and especially Mrs. Chandrika Kumaratunga, consolidated power when the latter scored one of the most impressive victories ever in Sri Lankan politics at the national level. Mrs. Kumaratunga polled an unprecedented 62.8 percent (4 million votes) of the total valid poll as against her UNP opponent Mrs. Srima Dissanayake's 38 percent (2.75 million votes). The disarray in the UNP campaign caused by Gamini Dissanayake's assassination was a major setback for the UNP and its bid for the presidency. However, the large margin of Mrs. Kumaratunga's victory suggests that even if Dissanayake had lived, the PA would probably have won convincingly.

From a political point of view, what is important to note is not only the size of the PA victory but also its nature. Mrs. Kumaratunga won handsomely in every district of the country and won a clear majority in every constituency bar one. (In the northern districts under the LTTE control the poll was limited to a small area.) She got overwhelming support from the Sinhalese-Buddhist majority, and nearly 100 percent support from the ethnic minorities, especially those living in the north and east affected by the war. The PA interpreted this as a full endorsement of its policies and leadership by the electorate.

The Kumaratunga administration completed more than 16 months in office by the end of 1995. Perhaps the single most important achievement of the new administration has been on the diplomatic front. The fresh and clean image of the new president and her government, her strong commitment to find a political solution to the ethnic conflict, and the steps that the PA administration took in the first few months in office to improve the human rights situation contributed toward building a more positive international image of Sri Lanka. This has been particularly helpful to the new president in her efforts to mobilize support abroad for her campaign against the LTTE.

From the very beginning the government found that there were severe political and economic constraints against delivering on the extravagant promises made to the electorate. On the political side the four big promises were to establish democratic practices in full, including media freedom, stamp out bribery and corruption, abolish the executive presidency, and end the ethnic civil war and restore peace in the north. Of the four the starkest failure has been in regard to the third of these promises. President Kumaratunga herself set July 15, 1995 as the deadline for this act. Now the president and the government say that the executive presidency will be abolished only when the constitution is amended comprehensively on some future indeterminate date. Critics of the government view that as a cynical excuse on the part of Mrs. Kumaratunga to enjoy the powers of the presidency, especially in a situation where the PA government is not sure of a majority in parliament.

Critics also do not believe that the PA in power is as committed to democratic values and practices as it said it would be when on the campaign trail. It is generally conceded that there is a climate of freedom and no serious fear of intimidation by the government of its opponents and critics, something that was missing during the Premadasa administration. However, the PA has failed to live up to initial expectations created by its own rhetoric. For example, the editor of a Sunday newspaper generally critical of the president and the government was assaulted by a gang that many believe was sent by somebody connected with the administration. The government has also indefinitely postponed its own proposal to denationalize the Lake House group of newspapers. It imposed press censorship on military and security news in September 1995 for about three months during the military campaign to retake Jaffna from the LTTE. Censorship on military news was reimposed in April 1996. Even more disappointing has been the postponement of local government elections. They were originally due in mid 1995 but were put off thrice to the end of 1996.

The PA administration has strengthened the anticorruption laws and appointed a string of presidential commissions to probe the misdeeds of members of the former UNP regime. However, the government has already had its own quota of accusations of misuse of power and corruption.

The peace talks with the LTTE that commenced in October 1994 ended abruptly in April 1995. There has been mutual recrimination regarding who was responsible for the breakdown. However, most independent observers believe that it was the LTTE and not the government that must take the blame. Since then, the government has adopted a two-pronged strategy. On the one hand, it is taking military action to crush what it calls "LTTE terrorists." To date the most notable success was the takeover of Jaffna in late 1995 that drove the LTTE to the jungles of Kilinochchi in the mainland south of the Jaffna peninsula. This was a major psychological and logistical blow to the LTTE that ran a quasi-independent mini-state in Jaffna for more than five years. The second element of the government strategy is to seek a political settlement through more devolved power. It announced what is known as a "Peace Package" in August 1995, and has since been earnestly canvassing support for it. Since the withdrawal of the LTTE from the peace talks the government has been working with other Tamil groups. However, as of mid 1996, there is no clear and quick end in sight for the ethnic war. The Peace Package has encountered strong opposition from some influential sections of the Sinhalese community. The UNP also opposed some of its key proposals, such as the abolition of the unitary state and the merger of the northern and eastern provinces. The LTTE has established itself in the jungles of the Vanni area and moves freely in the eastern province.

The greatest disappointments of the Kumaratunga administration have been in the economic field. The PA election manifesto included fiscally extravagant promises ranging from cheap bread to a dole for the unemployed. Almost none of these have been yet fulfilled. An ill-advised attempt to cut the price of bread had to be ended after one year. The cost of living has steadily risen unabated. The anticipated savings ("peace dividend") from ending the war have not been realized for obvious reasons. Foreign and local investors are still not confident of the future despite presidential assurances of an investor-friendly economic climate. The business community is still wary of the left-wing elements in the government. The share price index of the Colombo stock market has dropped by half since mid 1994. Jobs in the formal sector are scarce and the number of jobless is rising. The official target to raise Rs 13.5 billion for privatization of state enterprises in 1995 fell short by as much as 85 percent. The tourist industry that began to expand in the early 1990s continued its progress with tourist arrivals exceeding 400,000 for 1994, a figure that was last matched in 1982. However, the climate of uncertainty that was created by acts of terrorism in Colombo in late 1995 and early 1996, especially the partial destruction of the Kolonnawa petroleum facility, the bombing of the Central Bank building in the heart of Colombo city, and by the resumption of the war itself, have reversed the trend in the fourth quarter of 1995.

Sri Lanka is marching toward the 21st century along an uncertain path that is not wholly within its powers to chart. The country, especially its relatively small economy in global terms, is increasingly getting integrated into the world economy. It will have to absorb and adjust to the external shocks that such linkage normally brings in its wake. However, it will also benefit enormously from the world economy as a market for its products and as a source of capital and technology, provided the domestic political and economic conditions are stable. There is no doubt that there are many positive features such as the commitment to democracy, strength of state and civil society institutions, a literate population, a high degree of socio-economic equity for a low-income country, not to mention the natural beauty and tropical climate of the island that helps agriculture that give Sri Lanka a significant edge over many other developing countries. However, mainly owing to political instability and poor political judgment the country has never been able to exploit these advantages to the maximum to achieve broad-based sustainable development over a long period of time. The prospects for that happening in the next decade will largely depend on the settlement of the ethnic conflict, and developing a political culture that resonates more with democratic values.

DICTIONARY

A

AGRICULTURE. The Sri Lankan economy is predominantly dependent on agriculture. About 2.3 million ha of land is under cultivation. About 2.4 million workers accounting for 40 percent of the labor force are directly engaged in agriculture. Agriculture directly accounts for about 25 percent of the gross domestic product and indirectly much more. Rice is the main crop in domestic agriculture that caters to the local market. Coconut, vegetables, potatoes, onions are among the more important subsidiary crops in this sector. About 60 percent of the agricultural labor force and as much of the total cultivated area (2.3 million ha.) are in the domestic sector. The balance of 40 percent is in plantation (commercial) agriculture. Food producers are mostly small farmers, either owner cultivators or tenants who retain a part of the crop for their own consumption and sell the rest. However, in the last two decades small farming has been more commercialized with some producing for the export market. The major export crops are tea (q.v.), rubber (q.v.), and coconut (q.v.) which account for about one-third of gross export earnings. Tea and rubber are predominantly plantation crops cultivated in relatively large units under commercial conditions. Coconut is a more mixed crop with both large plantations as well as numerous smaller units.

AIR LANKA. Sri Lanka's wholly state-owned international airline that succeeded Air Ceylon, also a state company in 1979. It serves 11 destinations in south, southeast, and east Asia, eight in the middle east, and six in Europe. Until 1991 it was making large losses that were subsidized by the treasury. Since then it has trimmed expenses and has made a modest profit. However, it has been heavily criticized by a presidential commission, the World Bank (q.v.), and others for mismanagement. The airline's major contribution to the economy is the tourist traffic it brings, especially from Europe. The government is expected to restructure and privatize the company in 1996.

AMIRTHALINGAM, APPAPILLAI (1927-1989). Educated at a village school in Pannakam and Victoria College, Chullipuram, University of Ceylon (Colombo), and Ceylon Law College. Lawyer and politician, Amirthalingam's involvement in the politics of Jaffna began as early as 1950 as a sympathizer of the S. J. V. Chelvanayakam's (q.v.) Federal Party. He joined the party in 1952 and organized its youth front. In 1956 he was elected MP for Vaddukodai, and retained his seat till his defeat in the general election in 1970. On two occasions he was placed under detention during periods of ethnic tension. In 1977 he was returned to parliament as MP for Kankesanturai and became the leader of the opposition. Amirthalingam played a key role in establishing the Tamil United Front and later its successor the Tamil United Liberation Front (TULF) (q.v.) that was an amalgam of several Tamil parties led by the Federal Party. Amirthalingam also played a major role in negotiations with the Jayewardene administration to establish District Development Councils. He forfeited his seat in parliament in 1983 when he together with the other TULF MPs refused to take an oath of allegiance to the Sri Lankan constitution. After July 1983 he spent much of his time in self-imposed exile in Madras. He was assassinated by the Liberation Tigers of Tamil Eelam (LTTE) (q.v.) gunmen in Colombo in 1989.

AMNESTY INTERNATIONAL (AI). AI has been generally highly critical of Sri Lanka's human rights (q.v.) record since about 1980. It has periodically sent delegations to investigate the human rights situation and alleged abuses. Some recommendations of AI to improve the human rights situation have been accepted and implemented by the government. AI has been found fault with by government spokespersons and others in Sri Lanka for focusing on human rights abuses by government troops while often ignoring those committed by the Tamil rebel groups, most notably the Liberation Tigers of Tamil Eelam (LTTE) (q.v.) and by *Janatha Vimukthi Peramuna* (JVP) (q.v.). In more recent AI reports human rights violations by rebel groups have also been cited.

ARMED FORCES. Sri Lanka's armed forces consisting of the army, air force, and the navy were officially established in October 1949 following independence. The army is the largest of the three with about 120,000 troops at the end of 1995. The navy and the air force each had about 10,000. In addition there is a paramilitary force known as the Special Task Force (STF) numbering about 4,000 men that is a branch of the police (q.v.). However, the STF is also deployed on combat duty in the current ethnic war. Until the outbreak of the 1971 *Janatha Vimukthi Peramuna* (JVP) rebellion (q.v.) Sri Lanka's armed forces were small in number—around 10,000 men—and were considered to be nothing more than a largely ceremonial force. The 1971 rebellion was the first major combat test that the Sri Lankan armed forces faced. However, it was the ethnic war after 1980 that led to a major effort tostrengthen the armed forces. The troop strength has grown over twelve-fold in the last decade and all three branches have acquired increasingly sophisticated equipment to fight the war against the Liberation Tigers of Tamil Eelam (LTTE) (q.v.) led Tamil rebels. Whereas a decade ago not more than 2 percent of the gross national product (GNP) was absorbed by the armed forces, in recent years it has climbed to over 7 percent. As for the war against the Tamil rebels, the success of the armed forces has been mixed. Their greatest success to date has been the takeover of Jaffna in late 1995 from the LTTE that ruled the area for over five years. On two separate occasions, once in 1962 and later in 1967, some members of the armed forces were legally charged for trying to stage a coup d'etat against the government.

ASIA WATCH (AW). An international human rights group that watches and reports on the human rights abuses in Asia. Since 1980, on several occasions Sri Lanka received adverse comments from AW for its alleged human rights (q.v.) abuses.

ASIAN DEVELOPMENT BANK (ADB). Sri Lanka has been a member of the ADB since its inception in December 1966. At the end of 1993 the country had held 0.61 percent of ADB's subscribed capital and 0.87 of its voting power. It is the second largest multilateral donor to the country behind the World Bank (q.v.), having lent $1,495 million (3.3 percent of total ADB lending) over the period 1966-1993.

ATHULATHMUDALI, LALITH (1936-1993). Athulathmudali, a lawyer and politician, was the eldest son of D. D. Athulathmudali, a member of the State Council (q.v.) from 1931 to 1935. Lalith Athulathmudali was educated at Oxford and Harvard universities. In Oxford he was elected the president of the Oxford Union. He taught law at the University of Singapore before returning to Sri Lanka in 1964 to practice law and enter politics. He became an active member of the United National Party (UNP) (q.v.) and was returned to parliament in the 1977 parliamentary elections (q.v.). He was made the minister of Trade and Shipping in the first Jayewardene administration.

　　Athulathmudali was a strong advocate of economic liberalization. He reformed the administration of the Colombo port and turned it into one of the most efficient in the region. He was one of the principal architects of the 1978 second republican constitution (q.v.). In 1984 he took over the portfolio of National Security and was in charge of the military operations against the Tamil rebels until 1989. He strengthened the armed forces with both more men and better equipment. The successful Vadamarachchi operation (q.v.) was conducted by the military in 1987 under his leadership. He was one of the principal campaigners for R. Premadasa (q.v.) when he contested for the presidency in 1988. In the Premadasa cabinet he became the minister of Agriculture and later minister of Education and Higher Education. Disenchanted with Premadasa's authoritarian style of government, Athulathmudali together with Gamini Dissanayake (q.v.) led a rebel group of UNP ministers and MPs to sponsor an impeachment motion against President Premadasa in 1992. The motion failed and Athulathmudali was expelled from the party. Consequently he lost his seat in parliament. Athulathmudali helped form a new political party, Democratic United National Party (DUNF) (q.v.) and became its first leader. He was in the midst of leading the party's campaign in the May 1993 provincial council elections when he was assassinated by a lone gunman while addressing a party propaganda meeting in April in Colombo. The identity and motive of the gunmen are still not fully resolved.

B

BALANCE OF PAYMENTS. Sri Lanka's balance of (international) payments has been running a chronic deficit since the late 1950s, with payments generally exceeding receipts in the current account, particularly in the trade balance. The traditional export crops have not done too well especially because the price of tea (q.v.), the principal commodity export, had been generally weak in the international markets, and Sri Lanka's rubber (q.v.) production has stagnated after the mid 1960s. In the last two decades manufacturing exports, especially in garments, have expanded to help the balance of payments. However, mainly due to developmental needs, imports (q.v.) have always kept ahead of exports (q.v.). The remittances from Sri Lankans working abroad, especially in the Middle East (q.v.) after the mid 1970s has made a significant contribution to the credit side of the balance of payments in the last 15 years. After economic liberalization (q.v.) in 1977, substantial foreign aid (q.v.) has helped to sustain the expanding level of imports. Foreign private investment (q.v.) also increased after that year but suffered a setback after the 1983 July ethnic violence and its aftermath. Foreign investment picked up in the early 1990s but became sluggish toward the middle of the decade, largely owing to the uncertain investment climate.

BANDARANAIKE, ANURA P. S. D. (1949-) The son of two prime ministers, S. W. R. D. Bandaranaike (q.v.) and Sirimavo Bandaranaike (q.v.), he received his B.A. from London University. On his return from London he took to politics by assuming the leadership of the youth wing of the Sri Lanka Freedom Party (SLFP) (q.v.) in 1975. In the 1977 parliamentary elections (q.v.) he was returned to parliament from the Nuwara Eliya electorate. In 1984 he became the leader of the opposition, the youngest ever to hold that position, when the leader of the Tamil United Liberation Front (TULF) (q.v.) who held that position departed from parliament (q.v.). He is one of the most skillful debaters in parliament. Anura Bandaranaike, who was the acknowledged leader of the right wing faction of the SLFP, had a protracted battle with his more left-leaning sister, Chandrika Bandaranaike Kumaratunga (q.v.), to succeed their mother to the leadership of the party. The latter, who was favored by the mother, won and Anura Bandaranaike left the party and joined the United National Party (UNP) (q.v.) in 1992. He briefly served in the last UNP cabinet. From August 1994 he has been a leading member of the opposition in parliament.

BANDARANAIKE, FELIX R. DIAS (1931-1985). A lawyer cum politician and nephew of S. W. R. D. Bandaranaike (q.v.), he played a major role in the two Sirimavo Bandaranaike administrations. In 1960 at the age of 29 he entered parliament (q.v.) as a Sri Lanka Freedom Party (SLFP) (q.v.) MP and was given the key portfolio of Finance and also made the deputy minister for defense and external affairs. In the 1970-1977 administration he held the portfolio of Justice. In 1977 he suffered a stunning defeat in the general elections. In 1980 he lost his civic rights for six years following a presidential commission of enquiry that found him guilty of abuse of power when in office.

BANDARANAIKE, SIRIMAVO R. D. (1916-) Born to a Kandyan aristocratic family, Sirimavo Ratwatte married S. W. R. D. Bandaranaike (q.v.) in 1940. She led a sheltered life until her marriage. As the wife of a prominent politician and prime minister, she participated in public activity on a limited scale but confined herself largely to social work. The assassination of Prime Minister S. W. R. D. Bandaranaike in 1959 paved the way for her to enter politics. She was invited by the Sri Lanka Freedom Party (SLFP) (q.v.) to step into the leadership vacuum that was created by the death of her husband. She led the SLFP to victory in the July 1960 parliamentary elections. She herself did not contest a seat on that occasion but chose to sit in the Senate (q.v.) and lead the government as the first woman prime minister of the world. The Sirimavo-Shastri Pact (q.v.) that helped resolve the problem of the stateless Indian Tamales (q.v.), the nationalization of the foreign-owned oil companies, and the establishment of several state industries and the state takeover of privately managed schools were some of the more notable achievements during her first stint in office. In the 1965 parliamentary elections she won her seat but her party was defeated. She became the leader of the opposition.

In 1970 she led the United Front (q.v.) coalition to a landslide victory in the polls. In her second administration she nationalized the plantations, established state monopolies in several sectors of trade, and generally increased state involvement in the economy. She also took over the privately owned Lake House Press. In 1972 her administration introduced Sri Lanka's first republican constitution (q.v.) that ended the country's dominion status (q.v.). The first *Janatha Vimukthi Peramuna* (JVP) rebellion (q.v.) took place in 1971, and Mrs. Bandaranaike successfully crushed it, obtaining the assistance of several friendly countries and deploying the military. She was a prominent leader in the nonaligned movement. Sri Lanka hosted the fifth nonaligned summit in 1976 and she assumed the chair of the movement. However, Mrs. Bandaranaike's government became unpopular, especially on account of the economic difficulties that the people had to face during her administration. She extended the life of the parliament by two years to 1977. However, when elections were held in May of that year, the Sri Lanka Freedom Party (SLFP) suffered a humiliating defeat at the hands of the United National Party (UNP) (q.v.). Mrs. Bandaranaike won her seat in parliament. However, she lost it when her civic rights were suspended for six years in 1980. She continued as the leader of the SLFP, although she could not contest elections for six years. In 1988 she contested the presidential elections but lost to R. Premadasa (q.v.). In 1989 she was returned to parliament and became the leader of the opposition.

In November 1994 she assumed the office of prime minister for the third time in the new PA administration. This time, however, she is practically powerless in government. Her daughter Chandrika Kumaratunga (q.v.) exercises a total executive power as the president. Mrs. Bandaranaike has no specific ministry assigned to her. Her tasks have become mostly ceremonial.

BANDARANAIKE, S. W. R. D. (1899-1959) The fourth prime minister of Sri Lanka, Bandaranaike came from one of the most elite families in the country. He took his B.A. from Oxford where he was active in the Oxford Union, having held the post of secretary. On his return from Oxford, he joined the Ceylon National Congress (q.v.) and became its joint secretary and later its president. In 1931 he entered the newly formed State Council (q.v.) and retained his seat in the 1936 election. In the 1936 council he became the minister of local government. In 1936 he formed his own political organization the *Sinhala Maha Sabha* (q.v.). In 1946 when the United National Party (UNP) (q.v.) was formed by D. S. Senanayake (q.v.), Bandaranaike brought his *Sinhala Maha Sabha* into it. In the 1947 parliament he was the leader of the house and de facto deputy prime minister. Bandaranaike was more sympathetic than his fellow UNPers to the aspirations of the Sinhalese Buddhist (q.v.) nationalist forces. Thus in 1951 he resigned from the UNP to form his own party, the Sri Lanka Freedom Party (SLFP) (q.v.), which articulated policies that were more sympathetic to such forces. The UNP easily defeated his new party in the 1952 parliamentary elections (q.v.) and Bandaranaike became the leader of the opposition. However, in the 1956 general elections he won a landslide victory. Bandaranaike legislated for Sinhala (q.v.) to be the only official language. He nationalized the ports and private bus companies. However, his tenure as prime minister was brought to a tragic end by his assassination at the hands of a *bhikkhu* gunman.

BANDARANAIKE FAMILY. The most prominent political family of Sri Lanka. S. W. R. D. Bandaranaike (q.v.) was the founder of the Sri Lanka Freedom Party (SLFP) (q.v.), one of Sri Lanka's principal political parties, and was prime minister from 1956 to 1959. His widow, Sirimavo Bandaranaike (q.v.), became the world's first woman prime minister in 1960. She is the prime minister in the current (1994-) PA (q.v.) administration of her daughter President Chandrika Kumaratunga (q.v.). She also serves as the leader of the SLFP. Her only son, Anura Bandaranaike (q.v.), who was the acknowledged leader of the right-wing faction of the SLFP, left the party in 1991 following a struggle for party leadership with his more left-oriented sister Chandrika and joined the United National Party (UNP) (q.v.).

BANDARANAIKE-CHELVANAYAKAM (B.C.) PACT. An agreement negotiated in 1957 between Prime Minister S. W. R. D. Bandaranaike (q.v.) and S. J. V. Chelvanayakam (q.v.), the leader of the Federal Party (q.v.) that represented the Tamils. Under the B.C. Pact the use of the Tamil language in government would have been ensured and power would have been devolved to the northern and eastern provinces where the majority of the Sri Lankan Tamils (q.v.) live. However, succumbing to intense opposition from sections of the Sinhalese community, Bandaranaike abrogated the pact in 1958.

BANK OF CEYLON (BOC). Established in 1939 on the recommendation of the Ceylon Banking Commission as the first major Sri Lankan commercial bank (q.v.). Until 1961 it was jointly owned by the state and private sector when it was nationalized. The original objective of the Bank was to assist Sri Lankan businesses that found it difficult to get funds from the then British-owned banks. BOC, together with the People's Bank, was largely responsible for extending banking facilities to the smaller towns and the rural areas. It also has been in the forefront of more development-oriented commercial banking in the country, especially to promote new industry, and small- and medium-scale businesses. At the end of 1994 it had 337 branches and controlled about one-third of the total commercial bank deposits in the country. The bank has been criticized for making some loans of poor quality, especially under political pressure. The government has also used the bank as an instrument to lend to projects and programs that promote its own developmental goals, although such lending may not be commercially viable. The World Bank (q.v.) has suggested that the BOC should be privatized. There is strong opposition to the proposal from left-wing groups and from a section of the bank employees. As an alternative, the government is considering "restructuring" the bank.

BATTICALOA TAMILS. Sri Lankan Tamils (q.v.) who have traditionally lived in the Batticaloa area in the eastern province. Sri Lankan Tamils of Jaffna origin generally considered themselves to be socially distinct, if not superior, to the Batticaloa Tamils. At the end of 1995 the Tamil population in Batticaloa district was about 290,000.

BIYAGAMA INVESTMENT PROMOTION ZONE (BIPZ). Established in 1989 in a suburb about five miles north of the Colombo city, this is Sri Lanka's second investment promotion zone. BIPZ takes heavy industry that may create environmental problems and also those that require more water and more land space per factory unit. It functions under the Board of Investment (BOI) (q.v.) of Sri Lanka. At the end of 1994 BIPZ had 38 factories in production employing 2,100 workers.

BOARD OF INVESTMENT (BOI). BOI was established in 1992 as the successor to the Greater Colombo Economic Commission (GCEC) (1978-1992). The principal task of BOI as well as its predecessor is to function as a one-stop investment promotion organization. The GCEC's original mandate was to administer the Katunayake Investment Promotion Zone (KIPZ). This later expanded to include other free trade zones that were established in Biyagama (q.v.) and Koggala (q.v.) in the south. The GCEC also had powers to give GCEC status to industries located elsewhere in the country. In 1991 the government decided to make the GCEC the single central authority responsible for promoting export-oriented investment in the formal company sector islandwide. Hence the new name, BOI of Sri Lanka. At the end of 1994 there were 449 industries functioning under BOI approval. It had signed agreements for another 554 new ventures. In 1994 the export production of BOI enterprises totaled Rs 87 billion and they provided employment to 206,000 workers. BOI (GCEC) has been criticized for promoting the garment industry that accounted for 69 percent of the 1994 output. The garment industry relies heavily on imported inputs. Its local value added is only about 30 percent. The current policy of the BOI is to promote only those lines of garment production with a relatively high value added. It also seeks more non garment investments that use more local resources, especially raw materials, to increase the local value added.

BORAHS. A small community of Indian origin numbering not more than a few thousand who have settled down in Sri Lanka. They are found largely in Colombo and its suburbs. Borahs are mostly in business and are a relatively wealthy community.

BUDDHISTS. Except for a very small number of Tamils in the north belonging to depressed castes who have converted to Buddhism, Buddhists in Sri Lanka are almost exclusively Sinhalese. About 92 percent of the Sinhalese are Buddhists. Buddhists account for 69 percent of the population of the country. Sri Lankan Buddhists adhere to the *Heenayana* (Small Vehicle) tradition of Buddhism, which is believed to be closer to the original doctrine of the Buddha than the *Mahayana* (Great Vehicle) tradition. Thus, many Buddhists consider that it is the duty of the country to preserve the Buddhist doctrine and religion in its Sri Lankan form.

BUDGET. The Sri Lanka government budget year is the same as the calendar year. Before 1972 it was from October to September. The budget is traditionally presented in parliament in November by the minister of finance. The 1994 budget amounted to Rs 168 billion, or 29 percent of the gross domestic product (GDP), which is indicative of the significant role that the government plays in the economy. About 23 percent of the budget is set aside for interest payment on the national debt and another 7 percent for pensions. Defense expenditure absorbs

16 percent, transfer payments such as food stamps and payments to cover losses of state enterprises absorb another 13 percent. Salaries (excluding those of the police and armed forces) and other nonsecurity "recurrent" expenditure takes 17 percent, leaving 24 percent for capital projects and other long-term development activity.

C

CABINET. The current (as of February 1996) Sri Lankan cabinet consists of 23 ministers headed by the president. They have a total of 42 ministries including the presidential secretariat and the prime minister's office. Except for the president, all ministers must be members of parliament. In theory, the Sri Lankan cabinet is bound by the principle of collective responsibility. However, there are many instances where this has been breached.

CAPITALISTS. The term capitalist—*dhanapathi* in Sinhalese—has an almost derogatory meaning in Sri Lanka because left propaganda has associated the term with socially unjust exploitation. The perception has changed a little in recent times, partly due to the economic liberalization program (q.v.). Former President Premadasa (q.v.) in particular made an effort to show businessmen in a socially more responsible light. He tried to persuade business to be socially responsible by being good employers fair to workers and to engage in social activities such as the Foster Parents Scheme. He tried to convince the public that wealth creation by individuals was necessary for the greater social good.

CASTE. A caste system has existed both in the Sinhalese (q.v.), and Tamil (q.v.) communities. In the past, caste had an occupational significance with one's job being determined by caste. This is no longer generally true. Modern education has broken the occupational barriers imposed by caste. However, there are certain traditional occupations such as fishing and laundering clothes that are still strongly associated with particular castes. Caste is still significant socially, especially in inter-personal relationships such as marriage where people often prefer to marry within their own caste. Caste also still plays an important role in politics. Political parties generally take into account the caste of a candidate when nominations are given in the belief that candidates belonging to a caste that is strong in a given electorate may have a better chance of winning by mobilizing the "caste vote." In general caste divisions have been more rigid in Tamil society than in Sinhalese society. In the case of the former, this is probably due to the influence of Hinduism that sanctions caste. In the case of the latter, it is probably explained by the influence of Buddhism that does not recognize caste.

CATHOLICS. Catholics account for about 6 percent of Sri Lanka's population. About 5 percent of the Sinhalese, 15 percent of the Sri Lankan Tamils (q.v.), and a similar percentage of the Plantation Tamils (q.v.) belong to this faith. Catholicism was introduced to Sri Lanka by the Portuguese (q.v.) in the 16th century. It took root especially in the coastal areas where the Portuguese presence was particularly felt. The Catholic church came to play, over the years, an influential role in Sri Lanka's school education system. It established an extensive network of schools, especially in the urban centers, that developed a reputation for a quality education. Most of these schools got state funds as subsidies. In the 1950s and the 1960s there was considerable tension between Buddhists (q.v.), and Catholics regarding what the former called "Catholic Action". Buddhists accused the Catholics, especially those in influential positions in the bureaucracy, business, and elsewhere, of favoring their own. Buddhists also viewed the Catholic schools as centers of privilege used by the Catholics to promote Catholic Action and for proselytization. One result of this Buddhist agitation was the takeover of Catholic and other government-assisted but privately managed schools by the state in 1960. The Catholic church responded to Buddhist criticism by trying to attune itself more to the local culture. For example, mass in Latin and English have given way to that in Sinhalese and Tamil in most churches. The Church, especially its more radical younger clergy, has also tried to associate itself with wider social issues such as poverty and environmental degradation that affect the community.

CENTRAL BANK OF SRI LANKA (CB). The CB was established in August 1950 to succeed the Currency Board, which had no effective central banking powers. The CB was created on the basis of a report prepared by John Exter, a central banking expert from the Federal Reserve Bank of New York. He was appointed the first governor of the Bank. Its policy-making body is the three-member monetary board chaired by the governor with the secretary to the treasury (*ex officio*) and one other member appointed by the president as members. The Bank's principal task is the management of monetary policy and to act as the lender of last resort to the banking system. It also functions as the principal financial adviser to the government, manages the government debt, acts as the banker to the government, is the sole authority to issue currency notes and coins used as legal tender, manages the country's foreign currency reserve, and supervises commercial banks and other non-bank financial institutions.

The bank has found it difficult to pursue an independent monetary policy and control interest rates and the volume of bank credit partly due to the unforeseen impact of external events such as commodity price fluctuations on the money supply and partly due to the Bank's obligation to lend to the government to cover its budget deficit. In the 1980s it also failed in its duty to exercise proper control over private finance companies that declared bankruptcy due to financial mismanagement, causing heavy losses to depositors. The Bank has had considerable success in breaking out of the conventional central bank model and undertaking new tasks that promoted more development-oriented finance and lending, especially to the rural sector and to small and medium private industry. The Central Bank (CB) suffered a major blow in January 1996 when a suicide bomber of the Liberation Tigers of Tamil Eelam (LTTE) (q.v.) exploded a bomb at its headquarters in Colombo that destroyed a part of the building, killed several dozen of its staff and injured many more, and temporarily paralyzed its operations.

CEYLON CHAMBER OF COMMERCE (CCC). Established in 1839 by British commercial and planting interests, CCC is the principal body that represents the interest of organized private business in the country. The current membership is about 1,300. It has a strong and well-established secretariat in Colombo. In recent times, with the assistance of USAID and other donors, the Chamber has been developing a program to strengthen its analytical and information-gathering capability to strengthen the role of the private sector in economic policy making.

CEYLON CIVIL SERVICE (CCS). The elite bureaucracy established by the British in 1802. At first it was limited to the British. From the 1850s Sri Lankans were also recruited. CCS officials occupied all the top positions in government until it was replaced by the Sri Lanka Administrative Service (q.v.) in 1963.

CEYLON NATIONAL CONGRESS (CNC). Established in 1919, CNC was to be the umbrella organization to lead the movement for independence from British rule. It initially attracted considerable support. However, in later decades its impact was not felt. One reason was its failure to create a mass base. Another was internal divisions that existed in the ranks of its elite leadership. In particular, many of the Tamil leaders departed from the Congress in the mid 1920s and formed their own organization the *Tamil Mahajana Sabha* to articulate concerns more exclusive to their community. In 1946 the core group that remained in the CNC was absorbed into the newly formed United National Party (UNP) (q.v.).

CEYLON WORKERS CONGRESS (CWC). The CWC is the principal political organization representing the Tamil plantation workers of Indian origin. Established in 1939 under the name Ceylon Indian Congress, it renamed itself in 1951. The CWC has been headed since its inception by Saumiamoorthy Thondaman, the undisputed leader of the plantation Tamil community. The CWC claims a membership of 250,000. It was politically allied with the United National Party (UNP) from 1977 to 1994 when the latter ruled the country. In the 1989 and 1994 parliamentary elections and the 1982 and 1989 presidential elections, it supported the UNP (q.v.) and successfully delivered the bulk of the plantation Tamil vote to UNP candidates. However, in the November 1994 presidential elections it backed the candidature of Chandrika Kumaratunga (q.v.) of the People's Alliance (PA) (q.v.). The CWC, and especially its astute leader Thondaman, is credited with much of the economic, social, and political concessions that the plantation workers have won from the government in the past two decades.

CHELVANAYAKAM, S. J. V. (1898-1977) A lawyer cum politician, he reached the peak of his legal career in 1947 when he was made a King's Counsel. He joined the Tamil Congress (TC) (q.v.) when it was formed in 1944. He won the Kankesanturai seat in parliament in the 1947 general election. He parted company with the TC when its leader G. G. Ponnambalam decided to join the government in 1948. He helped form the Federal Party (FP) that offered itself as the alternative party to the Tamils. In 1952 the FP fared badly in the general elections and Chelvanayakam himself was defeated. However, after language became an issue he and his party came into prominence for advocating the Tamil cause. From 1958 to 1977 he was the undisputed leader of the Sri Lankan Tamils (q.v.). This was particularly remarkable because from the early 1950s he suffered from Parkinson's disease that debilitated him and impaired his speech.

***CHENA* CULTIVATION.** This is the traditional slash-and-burn cultivation that has been practiced in some parts of the country for centuries. Food crops, usually coarse grains or millet, corn and sometimes vegetables are cultivated in *chenas*. The cyclical rotation of land that this system of agriculture involves could, under certain circumstances, be harmful to the environment. It is hard to estimate the actual acreage under *chena* at any given time. However, it probably has declined significantly over the years partly due to the scarcity of suitable land, partly due to the expansion of irrigation for more settled agriculture, and partly due to official discouragement of the practice for environmental reasons.

CHRISTIANS. This term is used in Sri Lanka in two senses. One to mean Christians of all denominations and the other to mean those who are other than Catholic (q.v.). In the former sense, about 7.5 percent of the population are Christians. In the latter sense only about 1.5 percent.

CIVIL DISOBEDIENCE. This form of peaceful protest in the Gandhian tradition has been practiced in Sri Lanka by several opposition groups from time to time. Most notably Tamil political parties adopted this method in the late 1950s to agitate against the "Sinhala Only" (q.v.) language policy of the government.

CIVIL RIGHTS MOVEMENT (CRM). Founded in 1972, CRM is one of Sri Lanka's leading human rights Private Voluntary Organizations (PVOs). In the last 25 years it has played a very active role in voicing public concern over government legislation such as the Prevention of Terrorism Act (q.v.) that was perceived to undermine political and civil liberties and also over alleged violation of human rights (q.v.) by both government troops as well as rebel groups engaged in the ethnic civil war (q.v.).

CLIMATE. Sri Lanka has a tropical climate. The average annual rainfall varies between 2,500 to 5,000 mm in the southwest to less than 1,250 mm in the northwest and southeast. The temperature varies regionally due to altitude but not due to latitude. In the lowlands the mean annual temperature is 27° with a mean daily range of six centigrade. In altitudes above 1,800 meters it drops to 15° centigrade with a mean daily range of ten centigrade. The relative humidity varies from 70 percent during the day to 90 percent at night. Westerly winds (southwest monsoon) prevails from May to September and easterly winds (southeast monsoon) from December to February. From the point of view of comfort the best weather is found in January-February when it is winter in the northern hemisphere.

COCONUT. Coconut *(Cocos nucifera)* is a traditional crop in Sri Lanka from antiquity. Sri Lankans use almost every part of the tree and the nut from the kernel and shell to the husk, leaves, trunk, and root. Coconut products are also an important source of foreign exchange. The coconut tree is found in almost every part of the island. But it grows best on flat land in the "wet" and "intermediate" zones of the island with an evenly distributed annual rainfall of about 2,000 to 3,000 mm. The major coconut areas are the "coconut triangle" north of Colombo and the coastal area to its south. At the end of 1995 about 1.5 million hectares were under coconut. In 1994 the country produced 2.6 billion nuts that accounted for about 4 percent of global production. Approximately two-thirds of the output is consumed domestically and the balance is exported mainly as desiccated coconut. Coconut fiber is also an important product both in domestic industry and exports. In 1994, coconut products yielded 2.4 percent of the country's export earnings.

COLOMBO. Sri Lanka's commercial capital located on the southwest coast of the island. It was a center of some commercial activity as early as the eighth century. However, Colombo developed into a city of some importance from the early 15h century. Its development was accelerated with the arrival of Western powers in the country. The Portuguese and the Dutch constructed a fort. It was during the British period that Colombo acquired its present stature as the preeminent city of the country. It served as the administrative capital for the colonial government. More importantly it was the commercial capital as well. The development of the Colombo port greatly assisted its expansion. In 1981 the Sri Lanka government officially shifted its political capital from Colombo to Sri Jayawardhanapura, a suburb located about seven miles to the east of the city where the new parliament building is located. However, many of the key ministries and other government agencies are still found in Colombo. The current population of Colombo is estimated to be about 1 million

COLOMBO PLAN (C-PLAN). Founded in 1950 by a group of western countries led by the United States of America and Britain to provide technical assistance especially in manpower training to developing countries in Asia. It has a small secretariat in Colombo to service its activities. With the growth of bilateral donors and the multilateral development banks the C-Plan is no longer as important as it was when it was founded. However, it still continues to provide technical assistance to Asian countries including Sri Lanka.

COLOMBO STOCK EXCHANGE (CSE). The CSE is considered, in global terms, one of the emerging markets. It officially came into existence only in December 1985. However, company shares and government securities have been traded in Colombo since the last quarter of the 19th century. From 1904 until its replacement by the Colombo Securities Exchange Ltd. in 1985, the Colombo Brokers Association managed share transactions in Colombo. The CSE is now managed by a nine-member board. As at the end of 1995, CSE had 15 registered brokers and 230 listed companies. CSE has seen a boom in its activity after 1989, following the government's decision to allow foreign investors to buy and sell shares in CSE without any restrictions. The daily turnover of shares rose from an average of Rs 1 million in 1989 to an average of Rs 306 million in February 1994. Since then the market has been sluggish owing to a number of domestic and international factors. From 1990, CSE has become an important source to raise new capital through share issues. In 1994 it raised over Rs 3 billion through 15 new issues. In the last few years it has played an increasingly important role in the privatization of state enterprises by helping to sell their shares to the public.

COLOMBO TAMILS. Refers to Tamils who have lived in Colombo (q.v.) and its suburbs for a long time and are distinguished from "Jaffna" Tamils (q.v.) and "Batticaloa" Tamils (q.v.). There is a Tamil population concentration in Wellawatta, a coastal suburb about five miles to the south of the city center. Colombo Tamils are generally more westernized than their northern counterparts. Traditionally they have had a strong presence in the bureaucracy, mercantile services, and the professions. In 1981 the Tamil population in Colombo was almost 200,000 and accounted for about 20 percent of the city population. Of course, not all Tamils who live in Colombo are permanent residents. A large number are from the north and east who live in the city for employment.

COLONIZATION. The program of state-financed establishment of irrigation-based peasant settlement started in the 1920s and formalized under the Land Development Ordinance of 1935. Sri Lanka's first Prime Minister D. S. Senanayake (q.v.) is recognized as the pioneer of this program. Under colonization the government developed the physical infrastructure including irrigation, roads, schools, and health facilities, provided limited subsidies for housing and other expenses to settlers and leased them state land for small-scale agriculture, mostly rice. Most of the colonization schemes are located in the drier parts of the country, which constituted the venue of a thriving hydraulic civilization in ancient times. Gal Oya, Parakrama Samudra, Minneriya, and most recently the largest of them all, the Mahaveli (q.v.), were some of the more prominent colonization schemes undertaken in the last 50 years. On the positive side these schemes helped, inter alia, the country to produce its own rice (q.v.), reduced the pressure on land in the more densely populated areas of the country, notably the southwest, Jaffna peninsula, and the coastal areas of the east from where most of the settlers came, and reduced the rate of urban growth. However, it is debatable whether the economic returns were commensurate with the massive expenditures incurred. More importantly, the Tamils (q.v.) and Sinhalese (q.v.) got into a serious dispute over the entire program. In the northeast there are only 21 colonization schemes out of a total of about 110 in the entire country. However, Tamils have viewed any Sinhalese settlers in the northeast as an unwarranted state-sponsored intrusion into what they consider as their traditional "Tamil Homeland" (q.v.). The colonization program had almost no impact on the ethnic composition of population in the northern province. However, in the eastern province the ethnic composition changed significantly between the 1920s and the 1980s with a significant increase in the proportion of Sinhalese. The Tamils found this unacceptable. The Sinhalese assert that there is no historical or contemporary reason to set aside the eastern province for the exclusive use of the Tamil community. They believe that they have a legitimate claim to a fair share of the land in that area. This has become a central issue in the current ethnic conflict (q.v.)

COMMERCIAL BANKS. Sri Lanka's first commercial bank, a branch office of a British bank, was established in 1841. This was followed by the establishment of several more, all branch offices of British colonial banks. They primarily catered to the needs of the plantation economy, financing the import-export trade and working capital needs of the plantation companies. The colonial commercial banks generally shied away from lending to the Sri Lankan business community that drew increasingly heavy criticism from the local business and political leaders. In 1939 the colonial government responded to this criticism by establishing the Bank of Ceylon (q.v.) to meet the credit needs of Sri Lankan businesses. In 1950 the Central Bank (q.v.) was established with authority to regulate the commercial banks. The next major event in commercial banking was the nationalization of the Bank of Ceylon and the establishment of the People's Bank in 1961 by the Sirimavo Bandaranaike administration. In the same year, the government also legislated to give a monopoly of all new banking business to these two state banks, thus effectively "nationalizing" the foreign banks by attrition. This legislation was reversed in 1967 by the Dudley Senanayake administration. The banking system was also liberalized in 1978 under the open economy policy of the Jayewardene administration. Foreign banks were permitted to establish branches, and banks were allowed to setup offshore banking units to deal in foreign currency deposits and loans. At the end of 1994, Sri Lanka had 17 foreign banks, four local private banks and two state-owned banks with 875 branch offices, or one per every 20,600 residents. The total volume of bank deposits was Rs 194 billion, or about 37 percent of the gross domestic product (GDP).

COMMUNIST PARTY (MOSCOW) CP(M). Founded in 1943 as the Ceylon Communist Party, it split into two entities when the Soviet Union and China split in 1956 on ideological grounds. Most of the key leaders joined the CP(M) and the party managed to retain the loyalty of bulk of the supporters of the former undivided party. The power of the CP(M) derived primarily from its trade union activity. The party controlled some powerful trade unions in the Colombo port and the transport trade. Although CP(M) advocated revolution, the leaders were entirely willing to operate within a parliamentary democratic framework. Some of its leaders such as Pieter Keuneman were great parliamentarians and made an outstanding contribution to the debates in the house. Its electoral successes were limited to a few seats and after 1977 it has not managed to win a single seat. However, the party was in government from 1970-1975 as a coalition partner in the Sirimavo Bandaranaike administration.

COMMUNIST PARTY (PEKING) CP(P). Born in 1959 as a result of the Sino-Soviet split, CP(P) remained the smaller of the two new communist parties. The party prided itself on its commitment to the proletarian revolution and Maoist ideology. It had a small trade union wing but never succeeded in getting a party candidate elected to parliament.

CONSTITUTION OF 1947. This was the constitution under which Sri Lanka received independence (q.v.) from British rule in 1948. It remained in force until the 1972 first republican constitution (q.v.) was enacted. It gave the country a government in the British Westminster model with a bicameral parliament. The queen (or king) of England was the head of state and was represented by a governor-general resident in Sri Lanka. The cabinet of ministers led by the prime minister sat in parliament. There was no separate provision for fundamental rights. However, provision was made for the protection of minority rights.

CONSTITUTION OF 1972. Known as the first republican constitution, this was prepared by the 1970 parliament when it convened itself as a constituent assembly. The key architect of the document was the Trotskyite minister for constitutional affairs, Colvin R. de Silva (q.v.). The 1972 constitution replaced the 1947 independence constitution (q.v.). The new constitution converted Sri Lanka from a dominion with the queen (or king) of England as the head of state to a republic with a president as the head of state. The senate (q.v.) was abolished, making way for a unicameral parliament. It also included a chapter on human rights (q.v.) but dispensed with the provisions in the 1947 constitution that made special provision for the protection of minority rights. It accorded Buddhism a special status, entitling it to state patronage. To protest these and certain other provisions and also for failing to meet their own demands for Tamil rights, the Tamil political parties in parliament boycotted the proceedings of the constituent assembly. In general the 1972 constitution is perceived to be less "liberal" than the 1947 constitution. The 1972 constitution was replaced in 1978 by the second republican constitution (q.v.).

CONSTITUTION OF 1978. Known as the second republican constitution, this replaced the 1972 constitution (q.v.). The top leadership of the governing United National Party (UNP) (q.v.) led by J. R. Jayewardene (q.v.) were the principal architects of the document. It converted Sri Lanka from a Westminster system of government to an executive presidential system resembling the French "Gaullist" system. The executive president was to be elected in a nationwide election held once every six years. In elections to parliament the "first past the post" system was replaced with a system of proportional representation (q.v.). The 1978 constitution strengthened the provisions for fundamental rights and made Tamil a "national" language. However, it retained the special status granted to Buddhism.

COOPERATIVE RURAL BANKS (CRB). These were established in 1983 with the assistance of the Central Bank (q.v.) to provide credit to the rural sector. The banks are attached to the Bank of Ceylon (q.v.) and the People's Bank that obtain refinance from the Central Bank on concessionaire terms to lend to the CRBs. There were 1,142 such banks at the end of 1994 with Rs 6.4 billion in deposits and Rs 3.2 billion in advances outstanding.

COOPERATIVES. Cooperative credit societies were established in 1911 by the British administration to provide credit to small farmers. Since then, cooperatives have evolved into an elaborate system that covers trade, production, and credit. In principle, cooperatives are supposed to be voluntary organizations that derive their strength from the cooperation of their constituent members. In Sri Lanka, the cooperative movement has always had the assistance and involvement of the government. Cooperatives are governed by legislation, come under a minister, and a separate department is responsible for overall administration and supervision of the system. In 1949 a cooperative federal bank was established as an apex financial institution for the system. That, however, did not make a significant impact. In 1962 the bank was absorbed by the People's Bank that was designated to function as the bank of the cooperative system. The system underwent a major structural change in 1957 when legal provision was made to have multi-purpose cooperative societies (MPCS). The creation of the Cooperative Wholesale Establishment (CWE) in 1958 marked a major reform of the cooperative movement in Sri Lanka. The CWE serves as the apex institution for trade in the cooperative sector. In the period, 1960-1977, cooperatives were used by the government as a principal retail outlet to distribute the subsidized rice ration and other products that were sold at controlled prices or were in short supply.

Economic liberalization in 1977 (q.v.) considerably reduced the role of the cooperatives as a retail outlet. However, they still retain credit functions, especially in rural farm credit, where cooperatives act as the intermediary between the banks and the borrowers. In trade, cooperative retail outlets have reorganized themselves to compete with private traders in the open market. Some production cooperatives have also thrived under the open economy. In emergency situations such as the 1983 July ethnic riots, the government has effectively mobilized the CWE and the cooperative retail stores network to supply essential consumer goods to the public. At the end of 1991 there were 10,747 registered cooperative societies of various types in the country.

COREA, GAMINI (1925-   ) A distinguished Sri Lankan economist and bureaucrat who received his degrees from Cambridge and Oxford. Corea was a senior official in the Central Bank (q.v.) of Sri Lanka and later the chief economic adviser to the Dudley Senanayake administration of 1960-1965. From 1974 to 1984 he was the secretary general of UNCTAD.

COUP OF 1963. The first ever extra-constitutional challenge to the democratically elected government of Sri Lanka, the coup failed in its bid to overthrow the left-of-center government of Prime Minister Sirimavo Bandaranaike (q.v.). The coup was led by a few senior officials from the armed forces (q.v.) and police (q.v.) who were unhappy with the radical "socialist and pro-Buddhist" policies of the government. The coup-makers were largely associated with the Colombo-based, westernized, English-speaking Christian elite sympathetic to the United National Party (UNP) (q.v.). The coup failed when the government, on being informed of the plot, took preemptive action and arrested the plotters. The accused were convicted by the Sri Lankan supreme court (q.v.), but on appeal the sentences were set aside by the Judicial Committee of the Privy Council on the grounds that convictions based on retroactive legislation were a violation of natural justice.

CRICKET. Cricket is the single most popular team sport in the country. Introduced by the English, the game is widely played in the urban areas but of late has spread to more rural communities as well. Cricket is played by schools and clubs at the competitive level. The country gained membership of the International Cricket Conference, the supreme governing body of international cricket in 1981. This has permitted the national team to play the game at the highest ("Test") level against other top cricket playing countries such as England, Australia, India, and the West Indies. Sri Lanka's greatest success in international cricket was achieved in March 1996 when the national team won the Cricket World Cup in the quadrennial one-day limited-over game tournament hosted by India, Pakistan and Sri Lanka. The local game is governed by a Board of Control of Cricket.

D

DAGOBA. The bubble-shaped edifice (also called stupa) constructed by Buddhists as a place of veneration. Usually Buddhist relics are interred in the dagoba. Thuparama in Anuradhapura built by King Devanampiya Tissa (250-210 B.C.) is recognized as the first dagoba constructed in Sri Lanka.

DAHANAYAKE, WIJAYANANDA (1902-) A teacher by profession, Dahanayake entered politics through the teachers' trade union movement. He started his career as an elected official in the Galle Municipal Council in 1939. In 1944 he entered the State Council (q.v.), having won a by-election from the Uva province. He joined the *Trotskyite Lanka Sama Samaja Party* (q.v.) and entered parliament in 1947, winning the Galle seat. With two short breaks, he retained that seat for over 40 years until he retired from politics in 1989. Dahanayake changed his party affiliations regularly. Thus in 1956 he entered parliament as a *Mahajana Eksath Peramuna* (q.v.) member and became the Minister of Education in the Bandaranaike government. When Prime Minister Bandaranaike (q.v.) was assassinated, he briefly took over the premiership as well. However, Dahanayake was always more comfortable as an opposition MP and critic.

DE SILVA, COLVIN R. (1907-1983). A lawyer, historian and politician, de Silva studied at the University College, Colombo, and London University. He combined a lucrative criminal law practice in Colombo with a career in politics. He was a founder member of the *Trotskyite Lanka Sama Samaja Party* (q.v.) and won a seat in parliament on three occasions and lost on another three. He was an excellent debater in parliament. As the Minister for Constitutional Affairs in the Sirimavo Bandaranaike administration of 1977, he played a key role in framing the 1972 first republican constitution (q.v.). In 1982 he contested the presidential election as the nominee of his party but came a poor fifth in a field of five candidates.

DEMOCRATIC UNITED NATIONAL FRONT (DUNF). The DUNF was established in 1991 by a breakaway group of United National Party (UNP) members led by Lalith Athulathmudali (q.v.) and Gamini Dissanayake (q.v.) who were associated with the abortive attempt to impeach (q.v.) President Premadasa (q.v.). The party is committed to liberal democracy. It strongly opposed President Premadasa and his style of administration. Within a short period the party managed to project itself as the credible third force in Sri Lankan southern politics. The assassination of Athulathmudali in April 1993 was a major blow to the DUNF. Nevertheless it polled about 15 percent of the total valid vote in the May 1993 provincial council elections and probably denied outright victories to the ruling UNP in three provinces. On Athulathmudali's demise, Gamini Dissanayake became the undisputed leader of the party. After President Premadasa was assassinated, Dissanayake rejoined the UNP with his followers. On his death at the hands of a Liberation Tigers of Tamil Eelam (LTTE) (q.v.) suicide bomber, DUNF split into two camps. The Dissanayake faction remained with the UNP. The Athulathmudali loyalists under his widow, Srimani, joined the People's Alliance (PA) (q.v.) Mrs. Athulathmudali is a cabinet minister in the PA government.

DEVELOPMENT FINANCE CORPORATION OF CEYLON (DFCC). Established in 1955 as a joint private and state sector venture to provide long-term credit and finance to private industry. It was fully privatized in early 1993. The DFCC has, over the years, financed a significant number of industries, especially in manufacturing. It provides both long-term credit as well as equity capital. At the end of 1994 the total amount of loans outstanding given to industry, mostly manufacturing, stood at Rs 2.7 billion.

DEVOLUTION. A term that has become important in the Sri Lankan political lexicon in recent times because there is almost universal agreement that some form of devolution of power to the Tamil areas is essential to solve the ethnic conflict. Some also recognize that devolution is desirable for other economic and political reasons such as giving local communities a greater voice in the management of their own affairs. However, there is no agreement on the unit of devolution or its degree. The Tamils generally want a unified northeast province to be the unit of devolution. However, there is strong opposition from sizable sections of the Sinhalese and Muslim communities to a permanent merger of the northern and eastern provinces. The Sinhalese are also reluctant to concede more devolved power than what is already found in the provincial council (q.v.) system. In August 1995, the People's Alliance (PA) (q.v.) government proposed a devolution package. It soon became the subject of a heated public debate. In January 1996 the government also produced draft legislation based on the package. From early March 1996, it will be discussed by a parliamentary select committee.

DIAMOND-CUTTING INDUSTRY. Sri Lanka entered the diamond-cutting industry in the early 1980s. At present there are three major firms, all established under the free trade zone, operating in the market. They import, under consignment, uncut diamonds, mainly from South Africa, and export them after cutting and polishing. In 1994 diamond exports amounted to Rs 7.2 billion of which about 7 percent was value added.

DISSANAYAKE, GAMINI (1942-1994). Lawyer cum politician, Dissanayake was one of the 17 United National Party (UNP) (q.v.) candidates who won a seat in the 1970 general elections. He played a key role in the UNP parliamentary group during that period and in helping the party to prepare for and win the 1977 general elections. Dissanayake was rewarded for his loyalty with the Ministry of Lands and Mahaveli Development, a key ministry in the government. His name is closely associated with the gigantic Accelerated Mahaveli Development Program (AMDP) (q.v.) that he helped to implement over a ten-year period from 1978. Dissanayake, together with Lalith Athulathmudali (q.v.), spearheaded R. Premadasa's (q.v.) presidential campaign in 1988. He took the portfolio of Plantation Industries in the Premadasa administration.

Dissanayake was one of the leaders of the group of UNP rebels in 1991 who unsuccessfully attempted to impeach (q.v.) President Premadasa. He was expelled from the UNP and consequently he lost his seat in parliament. He joined Lalith Athulathmudali (q.v.) to form the Democratic United National Front (DUNF) (q.v.). After the latter's assassination, Dissanayake assumed its leadership. Soon thereafter he rejoined the UNP during the time of President D.B. Wijetunga (q.v.). Dissanayake succeeded the latter to the leadership of the party after the defeat of the UNP in the 1994 parliamentary elections. He also became the leader of the opposition and the UNP candidate for the 1994 November presidential elections. He was assassinated by a Liberation Tigers of Tamil Eelam (LTTE) (q.v.) suicide bomber in October of that year at a presidential election rally. Outside politics, one of Dissanayake's notable achievements was to obtain "Test" status for Sri Lanka in cricket (q.v.) in 1982 by securing full membership for the country in the International Cricket Conference, the supreme governing body of international cricket, when he was the president of Sri Lanka's Board of Control of Cricket.

DISTRICT DEVELOPMENT COUNCILS (DDC). DDCs were established in 1981 to devolve power to the districts to satisfy the demand of the Tamil minority for some degree of self-government in the north and east. The scheme failed to satisfy the demands of the Tamils partly because the government failed to speedily transfer effective power from the center to the districts as the Tamil leadership envisaged, and partly because the DDCs did not have adequate financial provision. The DDCs were replaced by provincial councils (q.v.) in 1987.

DIVISIONAL DEVELOPMENT COUNCILS. These were established in 1971 by the Sirimavo Bandaranaike (q.v.) administration to decentralize development work. So funds from the central government budget were allocated to the councils to implement projects that were designed and intended to be executed with grassroots participation. The district political authority overlooked the work of the councils. In general the councils failed to achieve their developmental goals mainly due to poor project selection and shortcoming in implementation.

DOMESTIC DEBT. At the end of 1994 Sri Lanka's domestic debt totaled Rs 249 billion or 48 percent of that year's gross domestic product (GDP) (q.v.). About 8 percent of the domestic debt was held by the central bank (q.v.), 32 percent by the commercial banks (q.v.), and 60 percent by nonbank financial intermediaries. Between 1980 and 1994 the domestic debt has grown almost ninefold. This rapid growth is the result of persistent budget deficits. The government has traditionally captured a large share of private savings to finance its deficit by making it compulsory for savings institutions such as the state-owned National Savings Bank and the government-controlled Employees' Provident Fund (q.v.) and the Employees' Trust Fund (q.v.) to invest their surplus funds in government bonds.

DOMINION STATUS. The constitutional status acquired by Sri Lanka in 1948 when it won independence (q.v.) from the British. As a dominion, the sovereign of England became the head of state of Sri Lanka and the country became a member of the British Commonwealth.

DONOUGHMORE COMMISSION. Appointed by the British colonial administration in 1927 to recommend constitutional amendments, it proposed, inter alia, internal self-government and a legislative body elected by universal franchise. These and other proposals were adopted in 1931 and remained in force until the next major constitutional change took place in 1947-1948.

DUDLEY-CHELVANAYAKAM PACT. An agreement reached in 1965 between Prime Minister Dudley Senanayake (q.v.) of the United National Party (UNP) (q.v.) and S. J. V. Chelvanayakam (q.v.), the leader of the Federal Party. The former promised to meet some of the key demands of the Tamils for language rights and devolution by creating regional councils. The latter promised to support the UNP in parliament to form a coalition government. Senanayake failed to deliver on his part of the deal due to opposition from Sinhalese groups, and the Federal Party left the coalition government.

DUTCH BURGHERS. These are primarily the descendants of the Dutch who came to Sri Lanka in the 16th century. In the 1981 population census they numbered 39,000 and accounted for 0.32 percent of the population. In 1946 they were 0.63 percent of the population. During British rule they enjoyed a privileged position due to their proficiency in English, especially in securing government jobs. However, in the 1950s and the 1960s most of the Burghers left the country permanently in large numbers to settle in Western countries, especially Australia. They were disenchanted with the nationalist policies of the government such as the Sinhala-only (q.v.) language policy. Burghers feared that they would lose their position in society. At the same time, they were attracted by the prospects in Australia and elsewhere that had liberal immigration policies, especially for whites, which many Burghers considered themselves to be.

E

ECONOMIC GROWTH. Sri Lanka's economic growth since independence has been comparatively modest. The gross domestic product (GDP) has grown at an annual rate of about 3 percent, permitting a modest rise in per capita income. The annual growth rate of population has declined from over 2 percent in the 1950s and 1960s to a little over 1 percent in the 1990s, helping to make a greater per capita gain from a given GDP growth rate. Much of the growth has come from agriculture (q.v.), especially rice production, and services. After 1960 manufacturing output expanded a little more rapidly than overall output. However, its contribution to total economic growth has been modest on account of its narrow base. Slow economic growth was partly the result of adverse international economic conditions such as low commodity prices. On the domestic side, bad economic policies such as indiscriminate subsidies and stifling of private enterprise for the sake of "socialism" and poorly managed state enterprises were largely responsible for slow economic growth. Slow economic growth has had several adverse repercussions. Growth was inadequate to create a sufficient number of jobs for the expanding labor force. Living standards rose only slowly. The government found it difficult to expand its tax base to fund the welfare and development programs it wanted.

ECONOMIC LIBERALIZATION. The Jayewardene administration (1977-1988) made a radical departure from the dirigisme economic policies of the preceding 20 years and liberalized the economy after 1977. Inter alia, it removed price controls, cut tariffs, relaxed exchange control, liberalized imports, freed private business from government regulation that stifled enterprise, and encouraged foreign investment. The policy paid off in its first five years in terms of rapid growth, a reduction in the unemployment rate, improved capacity utilization, and export growth in manufactures. It also had some negative effects; jobs were lost in hitherto protected industries that could not compete with cheaper imports, and disparities in income widened. Economic liberalization suffered a severe setback from the ethnic riots of July 1983 (q.v.) and its aftermath. The tourist industry (q.v.) contracted sharply, foreign investment declined, government funds were diverted from development to defense, production in the northeast in particular suffered, and economic growth decelerated. However, from 1991 to 1994 under President Premadasa the economy picked up and the liberalization program entered a new phase. Foreign investment and the tourist industry revived, new manufacturing industries were established, and exports grew rapidly. The government also implemented an ambitious program of privatization of state industries. After 1994 under the People's Alliance (PA) (q.v.) government there has been no significant change in the open-economy strategy. However, economic policy has been clouded by a degree of uncertainty that combined with continuing political instability and violence caused by the ethnic conflict (q.v.), has led to a visible slowdown in economic activity.

ECONOMIC PLANNING. Sri Lanka's first formal economic plan, the Post War Development Plan, was prepared in 1944. It was not a technically sophisticated plan. However, it tried to outline a program of development for an independent Sri Lanka in the postwar period. A more comprehensive investment plan for the government sector was prepared with World Bank (q.v.) assistance in 1952. The S. W. R. D. Bandaranaike (q.v.) administration, inspired by the economic plans of the Soviet Union and India in particular, established a National Planning Commission. The most comprehensive and technically elegant plan ever prepared in Sri Lanka was the Ten Year Plan—1959-1968. It was hailed at that time as a model plan for developing countries. This was followed by the 1972-1976 Five Year Plan. Around the same time, an international team of experts sponsored by the International Labor Office (ILO) produced Matching Employment Opportunities and Expectations, a plan to increase employment in the country. However, none of these documents got fully implemented. Sudden political changes, unanticipated economic difficulties such as sharp drops in commodity export earnings and limited administrative capacity as well as flaws in the plans themselves generally undermined plan implementation. Under the post 1977 open-economy formal planning has been abandoned in favor of a rolling plan of public sector investment that is annually revised. The Ministry of Finance and Planning is responsible for the preparation and implementation of this program.

EELAM. The Tamil name for Sri Lanka. The most widely accepted scholarly view is that the word is derived from the Pali (S)i(ha)la and the Sanskrit (S)i(mha)la. Some have suggested that it may have come from the Tamil word for gold *ila*. It is noted that Tamil texts before the fourth century have used the word *Ilam* for the island. In the last two decades Tamil nationalists have used the term *Tahmileelam* to describe a Tamil cultural-linguistic area in the northeast.

EELAM PEOPLE'S REVOLUTIONARY LIBERATION FRONT (EPRLF). EPRLF was born in 1980 as a result of a split in the Liberation Tigers of Tamil Eelam (LTTE) (q.v.). With the backing of the Indian government, it agreed to participate in the November 1987 northeast provincial council election, which it won, and formed the provincial government. The party professed a socialist ideology that even attracted some Sinhalese with left sympathies. However, the EPRLF provincial government soon fell into disfavor with the Colombo government over issues such as the former's attempt to form an independent military force called Tamil National Army (TNA) with Indian help. Eventually when the EPRLF threatened to declare unilateral independence the government dissolved the northeast provincial council in 1990.

EELAM REVOLUTIONARY ORGANIZATION OF STUDENTS (EROS). EROS was founded in 1980 in Jaffna and functions as an arm of the Liberation Tigers of Tamil Eelam (LTTE) (q.v.). It came into public prominence through a number of bomb explosions, most notably the one in the five-star Oberoi hotel in Colombo and other terrorist attacks in the south.

EMPLOYEES' PROVIDENT FUND (EPF). EPF was established in 1958 to provide a retirement benefit to workers who up to that time did not enjoy such benefits. All employers even with one employee must join the Fund. The employer contributes 10 percent of the gross wage and the employee 5 percent. The Labor Department is responsible for the implementation of the EPF legislation and the Central Bank (q.v.) is responsible for the fund management. At the end of 1994 the EPF had 1.3 million accounts and funds totaling Rs 81.0 billion. Until 1992 by law the EPF was required to invest all its funds in government bonds. Thus it was, and still is, a major source of funding for the public debt (q.v.). However, since 1993 it has begun to invest some of its funds in other debt instruments such as plantation company debentures.

EMPLOYEES TRUST FUND (ETF). Established in 1985 to increase the share of ownership of private enterprise held by the workers. ETF collects 3 percent of the emoluments of employees to be held in trust and returned to them on retirement. The funds are to be invested in stocks and shares. The income and capital growth from such investment is to benefit the contributors to the ETF. In practice, only about 25 percent of the ETF funds are in stocks and shares. The balance has been invested in government bonds and securities. The ETF explains that this is due to lack of good avenues for investment. However, it is also partly due to the fact that as a state-controlled institution it is under pressure to lend to the government to help cover its budget deficit. At the end of 1992 ETF capital funds totaled Rs 5.9 billion of which Rs 1.5 billion were invested in stocks and shares and Rs 3.4 billion in government bonds.

EMPLOYERS' FEDERATION. The premier organization that represents the interests of the employers in Sri Lanka. Established in 1926, its membership consists of the larger private firms. At the end of 1992, it had 345 members. The secretariat of the Federation represents the employers in collective bargaining with trade unions.

ENGLISH LANGUAGE. Introduced by the British to Sri Lanka at the beginning of the 19th century, English serves as virtually the only international language used in the island. Until 1956 it was the sole official language after which Sinhala (q.v.) took its place. In 1978 it was made a national language and in 1988 an official language. English is taught as a second language in schools. A significant percentage of the population especially in the urban areas have some understanding of the language and about 15 percent have a higher level of proficiency. English is the principal language of business in the corporate sector. Scientific and professional degree courses in the universities are mostly taught in English. In government administration it is used to a limited extent.

ENVIRONMENT. Environment has become a major national concern in the last two decades, especially with the reduction of forest cover from an estimated 40 percent of the land area in the late 1940s to about 17 percent in 1990. It is estimated that the country lost approximately 1.4 percent of the total forest area every year in the 1980s. In 1993 officially the country has 56 "nationally protected" areas covering 12.1 percent (8,000 sq. km.) of the total land area. Soil erosion in the catchment areas of the major river systems that feed the irrigation and hydropower network has become a major environmental concern. In general, industrial pollution is a less acute problem although in certain urban areas it is causing concern. Per capita carbon dioxide emissions from industrial processes in 1989 was 0.22 metric tons, less than one-third that of India and well below the Asian average of 1.93 metric tons. The production of methane from anthropogenic sources in 1989 was 540,000 metric tons, again one of the lowest in Asia. The Central Environmental Authority and the Coast Conservation Department are the two principal government agencies that are responsible for the environment. There are a large number of nongovernment organizations that act as pressure groups on environmental issues.

ETHNIC CONFLICT. The current ethnic conflict between the Sinhalese (q.v.) and the Sri Lankan Tamils (q.v.) can be traced back to the pre-independence period when Tamil leaders began to distrust their Sinhalese counterparts and demanded constitutional guarantees of their rights from the British. The conflict became acute in the 1950s when Sinhala (q.v.) was made the "only" official language. Disputes also arose between the two communities over allocation of state agricultural land primarily in the east; the government and the Sinhalese insisted on the right of the latter to what was described as a "fair share" of that land. Tamils opposed such state-aided settlement on the grounds that it would lead to a change in the ethnic composition of the area that they claimed was the "traditional homeland" (q.v.) of the Tamils, a claim that the Sinhalese rejected. The two communities also disputed the share of state sector jobs and university places that each got. The Sinhalese claimed that the Tamils were a minority that was educationally privileged by British colonial education policy and therefore got many more good government jobs and university places than their numbers warranted. Therefore they wanted and got affirmative action to redress the imbalance. The Tamils viewed affirmative action as an unfair device used by Sinhalese-dominated governments to discriminate against them.

Starting in 1956 the country experienced five distinct episodes of ethnic violence (q.v.), and from the early 1980s an ethnic civil war between government troops and Tamil rebels. India's intervention in 1987 through the Indo-Lanka Peace Accord (q.v.) and an Indian Peace

Keeping Force (IPKF) (q.v.) of over 60,000 failed to resolve the conflict. The leading Tamil rebel group the Liberation Tigers of Tamil Eelam (LTTE) (q.v.) controlled the Jaffna peninsula from early 1990 until December 1995 when they were defeated and expelled from that territory by the government in a successful military campaign. However, the LTTE has moved south to Kilinochchi on the mainland. As of early 1996 the situation in the northeast remains unstable. The People's Alliance (PA) (q.v.) government held peace talks with the LTTE from October 1994. The latter broke off negotiations in April 1995 and Eelam War III commenced immediately. While the government troops conducted Operation *Riviresa* to capture Jaffna, the LTTE unleashed several major bomb attacks on civilian targets in Colombo. The government announced a fresh devolution package in August 1995 as a basis for a political settlement. Opinion on the proposal is sharply divided and the prospects for its adoption are less than even.

ETHNIC RIOTS 1956. The first major ethnic riots involving the Sinhalese (q.v.) and the Tamils (q.v.). A peaceful demonstration—*Satyagraha* (q.v.)—by Tamils in Colombo in June of that year against the "Sinhala-only" Official Language Act (q.v.) was violently disrupted by a group who were supporters of the Act. This sparked ethnic clashes in Colombo and elsewhere. The worst affected was the ethnically mixed eastern province where more than 100 deaths were reported. Most of the victims were Tamils (q.v.).

ETHNIC RIOTS 1958. Ethnic passions aroused by the controversy over the "Sinhala-only" language policy (q.v.) and the Bandaranaike-Chelvanayakam Pact (q.v.) that was abrogated in April 1958 led to widespread ethnic clashes in the following month in many parts of the island. Unofficial estimates suggest that several hundreds died and several thousands were made homeless. As in 1956, most of the victims were Tamils. A state of emergency had to be declared to bring the situation under control.

ETHNIC RIOTS 1977. These riots took place in the aftermath of the 1977 general elections. The reasons for the flare-up are not entirely clear. Some suggest that the riots were instigated by politically disgruntled Sinhalese elements chafing under the electoral defeat of the Sri Lanka Freedom Party (SLFP) (q.v.). A series of incidents at the predominantly Tamil Jaffna University campus that led to all the Sinhalese students on the campus leaving alleging harassment from a section of the Tamil students is also cited as another causal factor. The victims of the riots were mostly Tamils (q.v.). Several lost their lives and considerable damage was caused to their property.

ETHNIC RIOTS 1983. The worst of all ethnic riots seen in Sri Lanka, this claimed several hundred lives in one week of July from the 24th to the 29th. There was extensive violence against Tamils (q.v.) living in the south. Property damage was estimated at Rs 953 million. The economy also suffered with a sharp decline in foreign investment and a more than 50 percent drop in tourist arrivals. The riots also marked a watershed both in Sri Lankan politics and also in contemporary Sinhalese-Tamil relations. The militant Tamil groups led by the Liberation Tigers of Tamil Eelam (LTTE) (q.v.) intensified their war to establish an independent Tamil state "Eelam" (q.v.) in the northeast. Tamil members of parliament of the Tamil United Liberation Front (TULF) (q.v.) forfeited their seats in parliament following their refusal to take an oath of allegiance to the Sri Lankan constitution. The ethnic war rapidly escalated after July 1983 and eventually led to the Indo-Lanka Peace Accord (q.v.) and the induction of the Indian Peace Keeping Force (IPKF) (q.v.). The country has yet to recover from the aftermath of the 1983 ethnic violence.

EXCHANGE RATE. Until 1949 the Sri Lankan rupee did not have its own independent exchange rate. It was tied to the Indian rupee. From 1949 until 1977 it followed the fixed exchange rate system established by the International Monetary Fund (IMF) (q.v.). Since 1977 the Sri Lankan rupee has been on a floating peg. Its exchange rate is tied to a basket of currencies dominated by the US dollar. Since 1977 it has depreciated against the dollar by about 270 percent from Rs 15.26 to the dollar to Rs 56.50 per dollar by the end of 1996.

EXECUTIVE PRESIDENCY. Instituted in the 1978 constitution (q.v.), the executive president is elected for a term of six years in a national election. It was the brainchild of J. R. Jayewardene (q.v.), who was also the first holder of that office from 1978 to 1988. He asserted that an executive president independent of parliament was essential to take quick and at times unpopular decisions that were vital for development.

The Sri Lankan presidential system has been criticized for its centralization of power and authoritarian tendencies. Such criticism peaked during the administration of Jayewardene's successor, Ranasinghe Premadasa (q.v.), and led to an impeachment (q.v.) motion being presented to parliament by a group of members of parliament led by Lalith Athulathmudali (q.v.) and Gamini Dissanayake (q.v.), two senior ministers in his own cabinet. Although the motion failed, it encouraged public debate about the suitability of the executive presidency for Sri Lanka. In the 1994 general and presidential elections the People's Alliance (PA) (q.v.) promised to abolish the office if returned to power. However, President Chandrika Kumaratunga, who herself set July 15, 1995 as the deadline for the abolition, has failed to keep her promise.

EXPORT DEVELOPMENT BOARD (EDB). Established in 1982 with the goal of promoting exports (q.v.). The EDB is responsible for overall planning in the export sector, formulating an export policy, and providing assistance to the export sector in general and to particular export industries. It has been successful to some extent in achieving its objective. Sri Lanka's exports outside the three traditional commodities has risen steadily in the past two decades.

EXPORT PROMOTION VILLAGES (EPV). The concept, credited to Lalith Athulathmudali (q.v.), is to develop village-based industries for the export market. This is done with government assistance and usually involves a private-sector company collaborating with a village to purchase and market the product of the village. The village producers in the EPV form themselves into a cooperative to establish the EPV. The program lost its vitality after Lalith Athulathmudali's departure from government.

EXPORTS. The mainstay of the colonial economy was the export of plantation crops, tea (q.v.), rubber (q.v.), and coconut products (q.v.). Today the country has a more diversified export base with garments accounting for 40 percent of gross export earnings. The principal strategy of the liberalized economy (q.v.) is to promote exports. In recent years, USA has been the largest market for Sri Lanka's exports accounting for about one-third of the total, followed by Germany and U.K. each taking about 7 percent to 8 percent of the total.

F

FAMILY PLANNING. In Sri Lanka family planning was introduced in the 1950s by the Ceylon Family Planning Association, a private voluntary organization. In the early stages of its operations it received assistance from Sweden. From the 1960s the government adopted family planning activity as an integral element of its population and health policy. Thus, the provision of contraceptive devices and birth control methods such as vasectomy and tubectomy were made a part of the primary health care system. The current contraceptive prevalence rate of 62 percent in Sri Lanka is the highest in South Asia. Between 1960 and 1993 the country's total fertility rate was halved from 5 to 2.4. Sri Lanka's relative success in this field is due to many factors, including the high literacy rate, especially of women, the support that the family planning program has enjoyed from all the leading political parties over the years, the role played by nongovernmental organizations, and the relatively effective health, welfare, and family planning policies of the state.

FAUNA. Sri Lanka is believed to have about 625 species of terrestrial vertebrates, a thousand varieties of fish in its inland and territorial waters, and a large variety of invertebrates. Among the 84 species of mammals, ten are endemic. Twenty species of birds, about half of the 133 species of reptiles, and 15 amphibians are also endemic to the island. Sri Lanka is annually visited by about 150 species of migrant birds during the period August to April. Some species such as the elephant and leopard are protected by law. There are eight national parks and more than 40 sanctuaries covering about 11 percent of the land area to protect animals.

FINANCE COMPANIES. These are private institutions that collect funds from depositors and lend them to private individuals and businesses. Sri Lanka's first finance company was established in the 1870s. However, they experienced a boom in the 1980s under the open economy (q.v.). The number of finance companies increased from 15 at the end of 1977 to 56 at the end of 1987. After 1987, finance companies began to face difficulties, largely due to financial mismanagement. A large number of them filed for bankruptcy, and depositors lost much of their money. Misuse of funds by the owners and poor supervision by the Central Bank (q.v.), which was the regulatory authority, are responsible for the collapse of several of these institutions. At the end of 1994, 34 finance companies holding deposits worth Rs 6.8 billion remained in business.

FINANCE MINISTRY. Generally considered to be the most powerful ministry in the government on account of the control it exercises over the treasury. It is responsible for the government budget (q.v.), fiscal policy, and the channeling and administration of foreign assistance. In most Sri Lankan administrations the ministry of planning has also been attached to the Finance Ministry. President Kumaratunga (q.v.) holds the finance portfolio in the People's Alliance (PA) administration.

FISHING INDUSTRY. Sri Lanka being a tropical island with rich sources of fish in the sea surrounding it has had a long-established fishing industry. However, in the past several decades it has had to import fish to meet some of its domestic requirements. In the last two decades the local fishing industry has been modernized to a considerable degree with state assistance. Fiberglass boats, outboard motors, and nylon nets have replaced the more traditional paraphernalia. Most fishermen operate on a small-scale using traditional technology. In 1958 the government established a Fisheries Corporation to boost production and marketing of fish. The government also assists inland fishery development. The inland fishery industry suffered a setback in 1991 when the government, in response to protests made by sections of the Buddhist clergy who saw fishing by Buddhists as a violation of Buddhist religious principles, withdrew some of the assistance. But it still provides loans on easy terms to the industry.

FLORA. About 4,000 species and varieties of flowering plants have been identified in Sri Lanka. They belong to 200 families and 1,350 genera. The decline in forest cover, especially in the last three decades, has caused concern about the future protection of many of these species. In recent times a flourishing business has developed in cut flowers such as orchids.

FOOD STAMP SCHEME. This scheme was established in 1978 as the successor to the subsidized rice ration scheme. In that year, food stamps were made available to approximately 70 percent of the population whose monthly family income was estimated to be Rs 300 or less. This number had been gradually reduced to about 50 percent by the end of 1995. In addition to food stamps the recipients were also entitled to kerosene stamps. In 1982 the food stamp scheme cost the government Rs 2.0 billion, or 7 percent of the government budget, which was less than half of the expenses it would have incurred if the previous rice subsidy scheme continued. Since its inception in 1978, the real (purchasing power) value of the food stamps has declined steadily. In 1990 the government introduced the *Janasaviya* scheme (q.v.) designed to gradually replace the food stamp scheme. In 1995 *Janasaviya* was replaced with *Samurdhi* (q.v.). In principle, the beneficiaries of both schemes were to become self-supporting after two years in the scheme. However, in practice, in regard to *Janasaviya,* many of them have returned to the food stamp scheme after two years. It is too early to judge the results of *Samurdhi.*

FOOD SUBSIDIES. Sri Lanka has had an elaborate program of food subsidies for several decades. The mainstay of the program was the supply of a specified amount of rice to all consumers either free or at a subsidized price. It arose from a government rice ration scheme started during the second world war. The ration of two kilos per adult per week and a lesser quantity for children was continued as an entitlement to everyone after the war ended. Gradually the government found it politically difficult to withdraw the ration or to raise the price. Thus a significant subsidy element was built into the scheme as the procurement price rose. The rice subsidy was economically and socially significant for several reasons. It assured the supply of the staple food to everyone. For the poorest 20 percent of the population, the rice subsidy together with the subsidy on wheat flour (including bread) accounted for as much as one-third of the total food budget. However, the subsidy also claimed a substantial proportion of the government budget (q.v.) and eventually became unsustainable. By 1977 about 16 percent of the budget was spent on food subsidies. In 1978 the rice subsidy was replaced with a food stamp scheme (q.v.).

FOREIGN AID. See **PARIS AID CLUB.**

FOREIGN AID. Sri Lanka has been a recipient of foreign assistance since the early 1950s. In fact the meeting that led to the establishment of the Colombo Plan (q.v.), a consortium of Western nations including Japan that provides technical assistance to Asian countries, was held in Colombo in 1950. A Sri Lanka "Paris" Aid Club (q.v.) was established in 1966 under the sponsorship of the World Bank (q.v.). This meets annually in Paris to decide on the quantum and type of aid to be provided for the following year. Aid increased substantially after 1977. Donors have been very supportive of the economic liberalization program (q.v.) launched that year and which still continues. In the last five years, gross annual aid has been about US$ 750 million. The leading bilateral donors are Japan, Germany, the United States, and Britain. The World Bank and the Asian Development Bank have also given substantial assistance. The International Monetary Fund (IMF) (q.v.) has given credit to support the balance of payment (q.v.). Sri Lanka would not have been able to sustain its economy at the current level without aid. About one-third to one-half of all investment is financed with aid funds. The current account deficit in the balance of payment averaging about 5 percent of the gross domestic product (GDP) (q.v.) in the last five years is also met largely with aid funds. However, aid has been criticized for several reasons. The foreign debt (q.v.) amounting to Rs 300 billion at the end of 1994 imposes a repayment burden in foreign currency. Some projects funded with aid money have not yielded sufficient returns. Even the Mahaveli project (q.v.) has been criticized on such grounds.

FOREIGN DEBT. Sri Lanka's foreign debt increased from Rs 35 billion (37.0 percent of gross domestic product (GDP)) in 1982 to Rs 300 billion (57.4 percent of GDP) in 1994 due to heavy borrowing to fund a higher-level of economic activity. About 80 percent of the debt is in long-term loans at low interest obtained from foreign aid (q.v.) sources. However, the remaining 20 percent is more short-term on commercial rates. Sri Lanka has not faced a foreign debt "crisis" as such. The debt service burden (share of export earning devoted to servicing the debt), which stood at 18.1 percent in 1991, declined to 13.0 percent in 1994. Some have criticized foreign borrowing on the grounds that such loans have frequently not been used for purposes with a good payoff in terms of jobs and higher production.

FOREIGN INVESTMENT. Historically much of the growth of the tea (q.v.) and rubber (q.v.) export economy over the last 150 years occurred as a result of foreign investment. However, after independence (q.v.) the country failed to attract foreign investment in any substantial amounts until the late 1970s. Foreign investment shunned the country before 1977 largely because of the official hostility to such investment and the inhospitable policy environment after 1956 that encouraged nationalization and discouraged private enterprise. The policy of the Jayewardene administration (1977-1988) to attract foreign investment paid off in the early 1980s. From a net outflow of US$1.2 million in 1977, it went up to US$63.6 million in 1982. The entire amount was direct investment and not portfolio investment. However, the ethnic war caused a serious setback to it after 1983. After 1989 it has again picked up. The removal of restrictions on portfolio investment in the Colombo Share Market (q.v.) in 1991 gave an added boost. In 1994 direct foreign investment totaled US$195 million and portfolio investment US$65 million. This amount is substantial by Sri Lankan standards but is minuscule compared with, say, foreign investment in Southeast Asian countries such as Thailand. From 1994, largely due to the uncertain investment climate, inflows of private foreign capital to the island has again declined.

FOREIGN POLICY. From independence (q.v.) until 1956 Sri Lanka was known for its pro-western foreign policy under right-of-center United

National Party (UNP) (q.v.) administrations. For that reason, Sri Lanka's admission to the United Nations (U.N.) (q.v.) was opposed for a time by the Soviet Union. From 1956 to 1977, dominated by left-of-center Sri Lanka Freedom Party (SLFP) administrations, the country developed a nonaligned foreign policy that was generally more sympathetic to the Soviet bloc and, at times, quite hostile to western interests. Sri Lanka also played a prominent role in the Non-Aligned Movement (q.v.) (NAM), hosted the NAM summit in 1976 and, as the host country, assumed its chair. The right-of-center Jayewardene administration that came to office in 1977 remained within NAM. However, there was a distinct pro-western shift in policy, partly motivated by the need to attract western aid (q.v.) and foreign private investment (q.v.). The government was successful in getting both. But its pro-western stance provoked the ire of India. In particular, Prime Minister Indira Gandhi viewed the Jayewardene policy as being hostile to India and sought to counteract it by encouraging and assisting the Tamil rebel groups who were fighting against Colombo for an independent state in the north and east of the island. Sri Lanka is still a member of the NAM. However, in the post-Cold War era the anti-western rhetoric of the Sri Lankan left has all but disappeared. The People's Alliance (PA) (q.v.) administration is friendly toward Western powers. In the 1990s Sri Lanka has contributed its share to the promotion of regional cooperation in South Asia through South Asian Association for Regional Cooperation (SAARC) (q.v.).

G

GAL OYA SCHEME. The first major multipurpose irrigation and agricultural development project undertaken in the country. Launched in 1947, the project entailed the tapping of the water of Gal Oya, a small river flowing to the east to irrigate 30,000 acres of rice land, to control floods, and to generate a modest amount of hydropower (q.v.). An economic evaluation prepared in 1968 estimated that the cost benefit ratio of the project was 2:1. However, the study also noted that there were a number of unquantifiable benefits such as an improvement in the quality of life of the farmers, reduction of pressure on land in the densely populated areas of the country from which the settlers came and so forth.

GARMENTS. Garments have replaced tea (q.v.) as Sri Lanka's principal export product. At the end of 1994, 687 garment factories were operating in the country. Together they produce Rs 77 billion worth of export products that accounted for 48 percent of the country's merchandise export earnings. It is estimated that the industry employs over 400,000 workers, mostly women (q.v.). The industry is heavily dependent on imported inputs, especially cloth. Thus the domestic value added, which was only about 30 percent of the gross export earnings in the 1980s, gradually rose to nearly 40 percent by the mid 1990s. The principal market for Sri Lanka's garment is the United States followed by Western Europe. These exports are subject to quotas allocated under the Multi-Fiber Agreement.

GEMS. Sri Lanka is one of the five principal producers of precious stones in the world. It has been renowned from antiquity for its gems, most notably blue sapphires. Cat's eyes, alexandrites, aquamarines, tourmalines, spinels, topaz, garnets, amethysts, and zircon are some of the other valuable stones found in the country.

Gem mining and trading is centered around the town of Ratnapura, which means the "city of gems." Gems are found on the upper layers of the earth (*Illama*), usually between a few meters beneath the surface and 20 meters. The gem-bearing gravel in the mines is washed manually using baskets.

Gem mining, trade, and jewelry making provide employment to about 50,000. Gem exports in 1994 amounted to Rs 3.9 billion, or 2.5 percent of total merchandise export earnings. It is not known how much is smuggled out of the country. The Thais have been prominent buyers in the local gem market since the early 1980s. They have developed a technique of upgrading a cheap stone known as *geuda* into a "blue sapphire" through heat treatment. Since about 1980 Sri Lanka has been trying to develop its own jewelry export business to add more value to its gem exports.

GOONESINHA, A. E. (1891-1967)   A pioneer trade unionist and politician, Goonesinha started his involvement in trade unionism when he was barely out of his teens. In 1915 he formed the Young Lanka League with avowedly radical aims. He was imprisoned by the British in 1915 on suspicion of being involved in the Muslim-Sinhalese riots that year, a suspicion that was baseless. Goonesinha became a keen adherent of Gandhian non-violence. He formed the Ceylon Labour Union to provide the working-class with a radical leadership. He led several strikes in Colombo (q.v.) and became a folk hero to the Colombo working class people. Goonesinha was the principal advocate of universal franchise (q.v.) when the Donoughmore Commission (q.v.) came in 1927. In 1947 he won a seat in parliament and joined the

United National Party (q.v.) government. He lost his seat in 1952 and his attempt to return to parliament in 1956 also was unsuccessful. In the mid 1960s he served as Sri Lanka's ambassador to Indonesia.

GOVIGAMA. The farmer caste among the Sinhalese. In the Sinhalese caste (q.v.) hierarchy they are considered to occupy the top position. They probably account for a little more than half of the Sinhalese population. The *Govigama* caste itself has several subcastes. The most prominent of them is the *Radala,* which is the Kandyan Sinhalese (q.v.) aristocracy.

GRAPHITE. Sri Lanka's graphite (plumbago or black lead) is believed to be one of the purest in the world with a carbon content of 97 percent to 99 percent. The principal deposits are located about 50 km to the east of Colombo. Graphite has been mined in Sri Lanka for over two centuries. In the interwar period it enjoyed a boom. In 1973 the mines were nationalized by the government. They were privatized in 1992. Current annual production fluctuates around 10,000 metric tons. A small quantity is used for the domestic pencil industry. In 1994 Sri Lanka exported graphite valued at Rs 96 million. The principal buyers are Western European countries and the United States.

GREATER COLOMBO ECONOMIC COMMISSION (GCEC). See Board of Investment.

GROSS DOMESTIC PRODUCT (GDP). Sri Lanka's gross domestic product in 1994 was Rs 523 billion (US$10.6 billion). The per capita amount was US$533. This was almost double that of Nepal but only one seventh of that of Malaysia, two other Asian countries with populations similar in number to Sri Lanka's. Sri Lanka's GDP quadrupled between 1970 and the early 1990s. This is a modest achievement compared with Malaysia's, which increased fifteenfold during the same period. It has grown at the rate of about 3.0 percent per annum in the last 25 years. The composition of GDP has changed to some extent in the last two decades after economic liberalization in 1977. The most notable change is the decline in the share of agriculture from about 40 percent in the late 1970s to about 20 percent in the mid 1990s. The share of manufacturing has risen marginally from about 11 percent to 15 percent. The service sector has increased its share from a little under 50 percent to about 60 percent with moderate increases registered by almost all the service industries. The reliability of the Sri Lankan GDP data varies depending on the type and nature of the product and sector. In general, the estimates of export products, services in the formal sector such as banking, insurance, and state services are highly reliable. The quality of estimates of industrial production varies depending on the size, nature, and the composition of firms of the industry. Output of small enterprises and farm output are less reliable estimates.

H

HARTAL OF 1953. A militant civil disobedience campaign launched by the opposition left parties in August 1953 against the policies of the United National Party administration of Dudley Senanayake (q.v.). In particular it protested against the attempt of the government to cut the food (rice) subsidy (q.v.) to the consumer. An islandwide general strike was the key feature of the *Hartal*, which led to some violence.

HINDUS. Sri Lankan Hindus belong to the *Saivite* tradition of Hinduism that is prevalent in South India. They are about 15 percent of the population and are almost entirely Tamil. The Hindu religion and culture have made a strong impact on Sri Lankan life. For example, in most Buddhist temples some Gods of Hindu origin are also worshiped. The *Kataragama Devale* in the south, one of the most popular and venerated places of religious worship in Sri Lanka among Hindus and non Hindus alike, is devoted to the Hindu deity Skanda, who has been "naturalized" as a Sinhalese deity. The Hindus and the Buddhists share the same new year in the month of April. It is also important to point out that the current ethnic conflict between the Sinhalese and the Tamils is not based on a Buddhist-Hindu religious divide. Its origins are largely linguistic, political, and economic. Religion enters it only indirectly through the identity issue.

HOUSING. Sri Lanka's current housing need is estimated to be around 3.1 million units. The number of units that exists approximates this number. About 70 percent are rural dwellings and the rest urban. Approximately 50 percent of the rural houses and about 35 percent of the urban houses do not meet the minimum standards in terms of sanitary facilities and so forth. Thus the current housing stock deficit is about 1.4 million. Largely due to the efforts of the then Housing Minister R. Premadasa (q.v.) the government launched an ambitious housing program in 1978 to build or upgrade 100,000 houses. This was succeeded by a 500,000 housing program in 1982, 1million program in 1986, and a 1.5 million program in 1990. Premadasa's ambition was to provide an adequate house for every family by the year 2000. 1987 was declared the International Year of Shelter by the United Nations based on a proposal he made. He won international recognition for his efforts in this field.

Sri Lanka's housing situation has improved vastly in the last two decades, due partly to state-assisted programs, partly to state policy to encourage private construction, and partly to the greater availability of construction material under the open-economy. However, the program has been criticized for wasteful and high-cost state-funded construction.

Donors such as the World Bank (q.v.) have held the view that investment in housing was not economically very productive. Responding to this criticism the government cut back direct construction and encouraged private construction, especially on a self-help basis in low-income communities under the Village Reawakening (q.v.) schemes. However, it has defended its overall housing policy on the grounds that it pays significant social dividends such as improved health and a better quality of life. The United National Party (q.v.) reaped significant electoral benefits from its housing policy, which is popular among the voters. The People's Alliance (q.v.) government that took office in 1994 is also committed to following a vigorous housing-development program.

HOUSING DEVELOPMENT FINANCE CORPORATION OF SRI LANKA (HDFCSL). Established in 1987 to finance house construction, this is a state-owned institution that is a major source of mortgage loans to individual house builders and to commercial builders. At the end of 1992, HDFCSL had a loan portfolio of Rs 760 million, 65 percent of which was money lent to individual builders.

HUMAN RIGHTS. This has become a major concern in Sri Lanka in the context of the ongoing ethnic strife and political violence in the south connected with the *Janatha Vimukthi Peramuna* (q.v.). International human rights organizations have, from time to time, reported adversely on the human rights record of both the government as well as the Tamil rebels, the Liberation Tigers of Tamil Eelam (q.v.) in particular. Foreign-based groups sympathetic to the Tamil cause have tried to get aid to Sri Lanka suspended on the grounds that the government at times disregarded human rights. The United National Party (UNP) (q.v.) government (1977-1984) responded by establishing a Human Rights Task Force to improve the situation. The People's Alliance (q.v.) administration has appointed, in addition, several presidential commissions to investigate human rights violations during the UNP government. The international human rights community has recognized these as important advances and improvements in the island's human rights conditions, especially after 1993. However, it will be difficult to restore normalcy until the civil war is stopped.

HYDROELECTRIC POWER. Sri Lanka's main source of domestically produced commercial energy. The current installed capacity is about 1,135 mw in 15 hydropower stations that accounts for 82 percent of the nation's total electricity generating capacity. The balance of 250 mw is thermal power. Hydropower accounts for about 20 percent of the total energy consumed (including fuel wood) and for about 60 percent of commercial energy. The Mahaveli Project (q.v.) generates 800 mw of the total hydroelectricity output. It has been estimated that another 870 mw of hydropower remains to be developed making a total of about 2,000 mw.

I

ILMENITE. An estimated 3 million metric tons of proven reserves have been found on the eastern shores in Pulmoddai 60 km north of Trincomalee. It is currently exported in semi-processed form. The export market for this Sri Lankan raw material fluctuates widely. Thus in 1989 exports totaled Rs 229 million but in 1991 only Rs 42 million. In 1994 earnings were Rs 74 million.

IMAGE-HOUSE. Image-houses (*Patimaghara*) were constructed from about the second century A.D. to house images of the Buddha. One of the best preserved of the ancient image-houses is the Thuparama in Polonnaruwa. Galvihare, also in Polonnaruwa, is an excellent example of cave image-houses.

IMPEACHMENT. The Sri Lankan constitution allows parliament to impeach the president for acts of omission and commission on the part of the individual holding that office that it (parliament) deems are not in keeping with the office of president. The first-ever attempt to use this procedure was witnessed in September 1991 when a motion to impeach President R. Premadasa (q.v.) was prepared by a group of rebel ministers and members of parliament in his own party, United National Party (q.v.), led by Lalith Athulathmudali (q.v.) and Gamini Dissanayake (q.v.) with the support of the opposition. The move failed when the speaker of the house refused to table it in parliament.

IMPORTS. Sri Lanka developed an export-import economy under the British. As a small developing economy, its heavy dependence on foreign trade will continue indefinitely. In 1994 Sri Lanka's total imports amounted to Rs 236 billion or 45 percent of gross domestic product (q.v.). Consumer goods accounted for 20 percent, intermediate goods 51 percent (of which oil accounted for one-eighth of the total), and capital goods 29 percent. One of the significant economic achievements of the country in the post-independence period has been the reduction in reliance on rice imports, thanks to the green revolution and peasant colonization (q.v.) programs. However, some basic foods such as wheat flour, sugar, and milk continue to be imported in large quantities. The heavy dependence on imports makes the country vulnerable to global economic convulsions such as oil shocks. In the 1960s and 1970s the government promoted import substitution in manufactures to reduce the reliance on imports. The policy was only a limited success. In the mid 1990s the country's annual import bill has been about 40 percent to 50 percent more than its export earnings. The resulting trade gap is financed largely with foreign aid (q.v.).

INCOME DISTRIBUTION. Sri Lanka has a reasonably reliable set of income distribution data from the *Consumer Finance Surveys* (CFS) of the Central Bank (q.v.) that date back to 1953. According to CFS data, in the 1950s and early 1960s the top 10 percent of income earners took about 50 percent of all household income and the share of the bottom 20 percent was only 5 percent. From the 1960s up to the mid 1970s this changed with the share of the top 10 percent dropping to about 40 percent and the share of the bottom 20 percent rising to 8 percent. The middle-income groups also gained during this period. After the mid 1970s the trend reversed and the present position is roughly the same as it was in the 1950s. The trend toward equality in the 1960s and early 1970s can be attributed mainly to progressive income taxes, government spending programs such as food subsidies (q.v.) more favorable to the poor, and government economic policies that discouraged private enterprise in favor of state enterprise. The trend toward greater inequality after 1977 is largely explained by policies of economic liberalization (q.v.) such as the removal of price controls, rent ceilings, caps on house ownership that boosted income from rents and profit, the higher level of economic activity that boosted the earnings of managers and professionals, reductions in income tax rates, and cuts in government subsidies such as the rice subsidy.

INDEPENDENCE 1948. Sri Lanka gained independence from 150 years of British rule on February 4, 1948. Sri Lanka's road to independence was peaceful, evolutionary, and constitutional. The national leadership led by D. S. Senanayake (q.v.) negotiated the terms and conditions with the British. The Indian independence struggle served as a great source of inspiration and the actual timing was largely determined by Britain's decision to grant India independence in 1947. At independence Sri Lanka became a dominion, acquired membership of the British Commonwealth, established a Westminster form of government with a bicameral parliament and a cabinet of ministers headed by the prime minister. Sri Lanka also signed a defense pact with Britain and allowed the British Air Force and Navy to use bases in the country. Some left political leaders were critical of some of these arrangements and even claimed that the country was not truly independent. In 1972 the Sirimavo Bandaranaike administration gave up celebrating independence on February 4th, and substituted May 22nd, the date on which Sri Lanka was declared a republic (1972), as the independence day. However, in 1978 the Jayewardene administration reverted back to February 4th.

INDIAN TAMILS. Known by several other synonyms including Plantation Tamils, Estate Tamils, Upcountry Tamils and Kandyan Tamils, they account for 5 percent of the population. They came to the country from South India starting in the 1830s as indentured labor to work on the coffee, and later tea (q.v.) and rubber (q.v.), plantations opened by the British. Some also went to work in the principal cities, especially Colombo, mostly in laboring jobs. At first, the Indian Tamils saw themselves largely as temporary migrants. They maintained close connections with South India and traveled back and forth. However, by the 1920s they became a more settled community. In 1922 India prohibited free emigration of Indian workers. Sri Lanka also stopped free immigration from India in 1937. The presence of the Indian Tamils in the tea plantation districts was politically felt in 1931 when they elected a strong delegation to the 1931 state council (q.v.) in the first-ever election in the country held under universal franchise (q.v.). The Sinhalese leadership was alarmed by this development and effectively disenfranchised the majority of them in the Citizenship Act of 1947 by declaring most of them to be stateless. Since then several initiatives have been taken to settle what was called "the Indian Tamil stateless question" (q.v.). By 1990 the issue had been virtually settled with about 500,000 getting Indian citizenship and the balance Sri Lankan citizenship.

The bulk of the Indian Tamils still live on the plantations and work as laborers. Until recent times they were the educationally and socially and, to some extent economically also, the most backward ethnic group in Sri Lanka. However, in the past two decades their economic status as well as social and educational status has improved significantly. The nationalization of the plantations in 1973 and 1975 that made the state responsible for their working and living conditions was one factor that helped. Even more important were their newfound political strength as voters and the astute political and trade union skills of their leader Saumiamoorthy Thondaman (q.v.).

INDIAN TAMIL STATELESSNESS QUESTION. Laborers from South India, mainly Tamil Nadu, were brought to the island by the British starting in the second quarter of the 19th century to work on the coffee and later tea (q.v.), and rubber (q.v.) plantations established by them. The 1911 population census recorded 531,000 Indian Tamils (q.v.) (13 percent of the population). By the late 1920s their number had risen close to about 1 million. At first they were mostly temporary residents who moved back and forth between Sri Lanka and South India. However, gradually they settled in the country permanently. Discussions between the Sri Lankan and Indian governments from 1939 to 1982 attempted to determine the number of Indians living in Sri Lanka who would be entitled to citizenship in the island. These negotiations failed as did negotiations between D. S. Senanayake (q.v.) and the Indian leader, Nehru. Just before independence following the failure of the talks, the Sri Lankan government passed citizenship legislation that effectively made the vast majority of Indian Tamil plantation workers stateless.

Since that time, the issue of citizenship for this group became a major issue in Indo-Lanka relations. In 1964 an agreement was reached between Prime Ministers Sirimavo Bandaranaike (q.v.) of Sri Lanka and Lal Bahadur Shastri of India to resolve the issue. Known as the Sirimavo-Shastri Pact, Sri Lanka agreed to provide citizenship to 300,000 of the stateless Indian Tamils and their natural increases and India agreed to take 525,000 and their natural increase over a 15-year period. A supplementary agreement was later signed by Prime Ministers Sirimavo Bandaranaike and Indira Gandhi in 1974 to absorb a residual number of 150,000 left out by the earlier agreement. Each country agreed to take 75,000 and their respective natural increases. The implementation of the agreement lagged behind schedule. Many were reluctant to return to India. India eventually took only about 506,000 repatriates. The rest were absorbed by Sri Lanka in a series of agreements that were reached between the J. R. Jayewardene administration and the Ceylon Workers' Congress (q.v.) that represented the vast majority of the plantation workers.

INDO-LANKA PEACE ACCORD.   Signed in July 1987 between the Indian Prime Minister Rajiv Gandhi and the Sri Lankan President Junius R. Jayewardene (q.v.), the main goal of the accord was to settle the Sinhala-Tamil ethnic conflict (q.v.).   It made provision, inter alia, for the establishment of a system of provincial councils (q.v.) to devolve power to meet Tamil demands.   The Indian government sent a peace keeping force to Sri Lanka to enforce the agreement.   However, the accord failed.   Provincial councils were established in 1988, including one for the northeast, which the Tamils consider to be their "homeland". However, the Liberation Tigers of Tamil Eelam (LTTE) (q.v.) refused to cooperate and fought the Indian Peace Keeping Force.   The Indians withdrew in March 1990.   The North-East Provincial Council no longer functions.   The war—Eelam War II—between the LTTE and the government forces that resumed in June 1990 continued for over four years until the People's Alliance (q.v.) administration started a round of peace talks with the LTTE in October 1994.   Most would consider the Peace Accord to be defunct now. However, some of the issues it addressed, notably the devolution of power through provincial councils, has left a lasting impression on the Sri Lankan political landscape.

INFLATION.   After World War II, until the mid 1960s Sri Lanka's rate of inflation was very moderate averaging less than 2 percent per annum. This was a period when globally also inflation was very low.   Prices increased moderately in the second half of the 1960s. However, the first oil shock in 1972-1973, together with increases in world food prices around that time, accelerated the annual rate of inflation to over 5 percent. Between 1980 and 1995, the depreciation of the rupee exchange rate after 1977, the second oil shock in 1979, the sharp increase in public and private expenditure following economic liberalization (q.v.), and the growth in defense expenditure pushed the annual rate of inflation into double digits around 15 percent.   Sri Lanka's open economy is vulnerable to external price shocks that are beyond the control of the Sri Lankan authorities. Moreover, the central bank's obligation to take the unfunded portion of government debt undermines the ability of the bank to control inflation by regulating the money supply.   There are three official published indices, the Colombo consumers' price index, the Greater Colombo consumers' price index, and the wholesale price index, as well as the implicit gross domestic product deflator to measure inflation. The first was prepared in 1952 and is no longer very accurate as a measure of inflation. The second, compiled on the basis of a survey in 1985/86 of the bottom 40 percent of households (when ranked by expenditure) is more reliable.

INSURANCE. Sri Lanka's first insurance company was established in 1877 as a branch of a British company. In 1963 the government established the state-owned Insurance Corporation and gave it a monopoly of all new life and general insurance. Thus the private-sector companies slowly wound down their operations. In 1980 the government established a second state-owned insurance company to create a more competitive environment. This policy was soon extended in 1985 to permit private companies to enter the field. As at the end of 1995 there were two state corporations and four private companies in the business engaging a total of 5,300 employees. The private companies largely avoid the less lucrative segments of the market such as motor insurance. The state corporations offer a broader spectrum of services. As at the end of 1994 only 633,000 (7 percent of the over 18 population) life policies were in force. Premium from general insurance for the year totaled Rs 2.4 billion, or 0.4 percent of gross domestic product (q.v.).

INTEGRATED RURAL DEVELOPMENT PROJECTS (IRDPs). Sri Lanka's first IRDPs were started in 1977 in the Kurunegala district in the northwestern province funded by the World Bank (q.v.). Since then 15 more were commenced. The 16 projects had foreign aid commitments totaling Rs 9.9 billion and Sri Lanka government matching funds totaling Rs 1.7 billion. The main goal of the IRDPs is to attempt development with a more decentralized, local, and grassroots focus. It is a need - and community-based approach to rural development. Over a period of 17 years IRDPs have absorbed over Rs 6 billion with mixed results. On the positive side, some genuine rural community needs such as rural roads, small irrigation, community health facilities have been met. On the negative side, none of the IRDPs resulted in any spectacular "take-off" into more sustainable and self-reliant growth in these districts. Critics have pointed to poor planning and selection of projects, heavy expenditure on bureaucracies and corruption and waste as some of the principal shortcomings of IRDPs.

INTERNATIONAL COMMITTEE OF THE RED CROSS (ICRC). ICRC has played an important role in the northeast after the ethnic war accelerated in 1983. It provides medical assistance to hospitals in the region and helps to take care of refugees. ICRC has also acted as an intermediary between the government and the Liberation Tigers of Tamil Eelam (q.v.).

INTERNATIONAL MONETARY FUND (IMF).   Sri Lanka became a member of the IMF in 1955. In 1995 it had 0.06 percent of the total IMF quota and membership in the South Asia group of countries. An official representative of the country holds the position of alternate director of the IMF. The IMF has played a significant role in Sri Lanka's economy, especially after the program of economic liberalization was launched in 1977. The fund has given several loans to the country in return for which the government has had to agree to implement economic stabilization measures including the depreciation of the rupee, cuts in public expenditure and reductions in budget deficits and money supply growth. The last such facility for US\$ 336 million was made available in September 1992 for three years.

INVESTMENT.   Before economic liberalization (q.v.) in 1977, Sri Lanka annually invested about 15 percent of its gross domestic product (GDP). After 1977 until the mid 1980s the ratio increased to 30 percent to 35 percent, largely on account of increased government expenditure on the Mahaveli project (q.v.) and other infrastructure projects. Since then the figure has been around 25 percent. In the last two decades about three-fifths of the country's investment has been funded from domestic savings and the balance from foreign aid (q.v.). In the first half of the 1990s agriculture has taken about 25 percent of the investment, industry 25 percent, infrastructure 30 percent, and services 20 percent. An investment to GDP ratio of 25 percent is reasonable for a developing country in comparative terms. However, the yield on this investment could have been higher than the 5 percent average that the country got in the last decade. Wrong choice of projects, poor implementation, and waste can be cited as major reasons for the relatively low yield.

IRRIGATION SYSTEM.   Sri Lanka developed one of the great civilizations known to the ancient world based on irrigated agriculture. By the fifth century the country possessed a complex irrigation system on the north-central plains. The hallmark of the system was a network of rivers and canals that carried water to an interlinked complex of reservoirs. The system reached its zenith in the tenth century under King Parakramabahu I. The irrigation system proved to be both the principal strength as well as the principal weakness of that civilization. This massive hydraulic system was vulnerable to deliberate destruction by invaders from South India. From the last quarter of the 19th century, the British administration began to rehabilitate the system. This process greatly accelerated after 1935, especially after independence (q.v.). The Mahaveli project (q.v.) is the most notable contribution of the present generation to this long tradition. It is estimated that today Sri Lanka has 105 major reservoirs and over 10,000 minor reservoirs feeding 400,000 ha of rice land.

J

JAFFNA TAMILS. Refers to Tamils in the north of Sri Lanka. Their origins are shrouded in antiquity but there is no doubt that Tamils from South India settled in that part of the country at least just before the tenth century and that by the 14th century had enough strength to form their own kingdom. Except for about 15 percent who are Christians, Jaffna Tamils are largely Hindus in the *Saivite* tradition. Caste has always played an important role in Jaffna society with the *Vellala* (farmer) caste claiming a superior position. In the independence movement some Jaffna Tamils such as Ponnambalam Ramanathan (q.v.) played a key role. However, after independence the Jaffna Tamil political leadership increasingly drifted away from the center of national politics over disputes with the Sinhalese on issues such as language policy (q.v.) and state-sponsored colonization (q.v.) in the northeast. The armed militant Tamil secessionist movement developed in Jaffna peninsular and it remains as the stronghold of the Liberation Tigers of Tamil Eelam (q.v.). Farming has been the traditional occupation of the Jaffna Tamils. However, because of the scarcity of agricultural land in the north, it has been a long established tradition for them to seek employment in the south, especially in Colombo.

JANASAVIYA **SCHEME.** The brainchild of President R. Premadasa (q.v.), the goal of the scheme was poverty reduction. According to the original proposal each *Janasaviya* beneficiary was to receive, in lieu of food stamps (q.v.), a monthly grant of Rs 2,500 for a period of two years. Of this sum Rs 1,450 was to be given each month as a consumption subsidy. The balance Rs 1,050 was to be "saved" for a period of two years and given in a lump sum as a capital grant at the end of the two years to invest in a self-employment project. The consumption grant was actually given to the grantees. However, the capital grant was not given. Instead, at the end of the two-year period, they were paid an interest income on their notional savings. They were also given production loans from state banks on easy terms. Priority was accorded to members of *Janasaviya* families in recruitment to unskilled jobs in government construction projects. Such recruits were paid separately for their work.

Due to budgetary constraints the scheme was not implemented in one round as originally envisaged but broken up into 11 rounds. About 252,000 families who were in the first two rounds had completed their two-year period by the end of 1991. Another 239,000 families were in the scheme at the end of 1994. The total of 291,000 represented about 15 percent of Sri Lanka's households. There is no reliable information to assess the extent to which the scheme succeeded in making the grantees self-reliant at the end of the two-year period. In 1995 the People's Alliance (q.v.) administration replaced the *Janasaviya* with its own poverty-reduction program called *Samurdhi.*

JANASAVIYA **TRUST FUND (JTF).** A US$100 million (Rs 5 billion) trust fund established with World Bank (q.v.) assistance in 1990 to provide financial assistance to Private Voluntary Organizations and local communities undertaking development work with a focus on poverty alleviation. JTF is conceptually linked to the *Janasaviya* Scheme (q.v.). It has four principal project areas; community projects, human development projects, nutritional projects that are given grants, and credit projects. JTF is governed by a board of trustees. Its secretariat distributes loan funds to finance projects approved by the board. Loans varying from Rs 100,000 to Rs 10 million are obtainable for credit projects. The rate of interest currently levied is 15 percent per annum, which is lower than the commercial bank rate for a relatively high-risk, long-term development loan. By the end of 1994, JTF had funded 2,029 rural infrastructure development projects, 324 nutrition projects, and 38,868 micro-enterprises and self-employment projects.

JANATHA VIMUKTHI PERAMUNA **(JVP) (People's Liberation Front).** Established in 1968 under the leadership of Rohana Wijeweera, it professed a Marxist-(Sinhalese) nationalist ideology. Concern for "Indian expansionism" that was perceived as a threat to Sri Lanka's territorial integrity was a major foreign policy issue of the party. The JVP appealed particularly to the rural Sinhalese youth from whose ranks it drew the bulk of its support. It is generally believed that the party was particularly strong among the so called depressed castes in the central and southern parts of the country. Undergraduates drawn from the same social background made the campuses other than those in Jaffna and Batticaloa strongholds of the JVP. It also attracted a large number of young Buddhist monks, especially undergraduate monks.

In the 1970 parliamentary election, the JVP supported the Sri Lanka Freedom Party (q.v.) led coalition. However, it was not satisfied with the scope of the socialist program of the Sirimavo Bandaranaike (q.v.), administration or the speed with which it was implemented. Thus the JVP organized an armed rebellion in 1971 (q.v.), which ended in failure. It is believed that several thousand JVP activists died in these clashes with the armed forces. Almost the entire party leadership that survived the armed confrontation were arrested, convicted, and jailed. The JVP was revived in 1978 after Wijeweera was granted a pardon by President J. R. Jayewardene (q.v.) and released from prison that year. In 1980 the JVP contested the district development council (q.v.) elections. In 1982, Wijeweera, who contested the presidential elections (q.v.), polled 4.2 percent of the total valid votes cast and came third, ahead of Colvin R. de Silva (q.v.), the candidate of the old left.

In 1983 the government accused the JVP of inciting ethnic riots (q.v.) that devastated the country in July of that year and banned the party. The party went underground and organized an anti-government campaign. It gathered momentum especially after the signing of the Indo-Lanka Peace Accord (q.v.) in July 1987 and the stationing of the Indian Peace Keeping Force (q.v.) in the northeast, both of which were hugely unpopular with the Sinhalese. The party relied heavily on its student organization centered on the university campuses for the campaign. Agitation against the private fee-levying North Colombo Medical College (NCMC) was used as the principal rallying issue to mobilize student support. This campaign not only totally disrupted university education in the south for over two years but also gradually spread to the schools. Using the armed wing of the party, *Deshapremi Janatha Viyaparaya* (Patriotic People's Movement), the JVP also began to increasingly use terror tactics against its opponents both in government and opposition. For about 15 months beginning in the third quarter of 1988, the JVP succeeded in almost paralyzing the normal life of the country. Several government offers to the party to negotiate a peaceful settlement with it were rejected by the JVP leadership.

Both the 1988 December presidential election as well as the 1989 March parliamentary elections were held under abnormal conditions due to JVP threats and violent disruptions against the elections. Starting in the last quarter of 1989, the government used its armed forces, police and paramilitary squads to suppress the JVP using counterterror tactics. Wijeweera himself was captured by the army in November 1989 and killed. The same fate befell all but one of the members of the top party leadership. A large number, probably several thousand JVP activists, were killed, and many were taken into custody. Several thousands who were detained have been released following a period of stay in a rehabilitation camp.

The party was revived under a new leadership in 1993. It contested the August 1994 general elections and won one seat from the Hambantota district, a traditional JVP stronghold in the south. The JVP candidate for the 1994 presidential election withdrew in favor of the People's Alliance (q.v.) candidate Chandrika Kumaratunga (q.v.) when the latter promised to abolish the executive presidency if elected.

The JVP, especially in its second reincarnation in the 1980s, has left a lasting impact on Sri Lanka's polity. Inter alia, it focused attention on youth problems. It also further weakened the old left that was already in decline. Its terror campaign and the counterterror of the government were major factors that led to a serious deterioration of the human rights situation in the country.

JATHIKA CHINTANAYA. Meaning "national ideology", the term is used to describe the thinking of those who reject both Marxism and Western liberalism and advocate a more Sri Lankan ideology based on its own history, culture, and values. Gunadasa Amarasekera (q.v.), who is a leading Sinhala novelist and short story writer, and Nalin de Silva, university math professor, are two of the prominent advocates of this line of thinking. Critics of *Jathika Chintanaya* see it as a narrow Sinhalese-Buddhist ideology that is intolerant of a more pluralistic and inclusive modern Sri Lanka.

JAYEWARDENE, JUNIUS RICHARD (1906-1996). Trained as a lawyer, he practiced law for about ten years from 1932 and then abandoned it in favor of a full-time career in politics. He joined the Ceylon National Congress (q.v.) in 1938 and quickly took a leadership role in it. He began to organize the congress along the lines of a political party with countrywide branches. In 1943 he entered the State Council having won a by-election to the Kelaniya seat. One of his more notable initiatives during this period was to get the State Council (q.v.) to adopt the policy of making Sinhala and Tamil official languages in a future independent Sri Lanka. In 1946 he became the Joint Treasurer of the newly formed United National Party (UNP) (q.v.). In the first parliamentary elections in 1947 he retained the Kelaniya seat and became the minister of finance in the new UNP government. He was instrumental in establishing the Central Bank of Sri Lanka (q.v.) in 1950. As the leader of the Sri Lankan delegation to the Japanese Peace Conference of 1951 in San Francisco he made a stirring speech for reconciliation between the warring countries in World War II and generosity toward the vanquished by the victors that won him much acclaim and the lasting gratitude of the Japanese. The latter were particularly generous with aid after 1977 when Jayewardene came to power. From 1953 to 1956 he held the portfolio of agriculture. In 1956 he lost his seat in parliament but was returned in 1960. From 1960 to 1971 he was the deputy leader of the UNP. In the 1965 Dudley Senanayake (q.v.) administration he held the portfolio of minister of state with responsibility for the tourist industry. He took over the party leadership on Dudley Senanayake's death in 1973 and revitalized the party machine.

His major electoral triumph was the landslide victory of the UNP in the 1977 parliamentary elections. In 1978 he replaced the Westminster parliamentary system of government with an executive presidential system under the Second Republican Constitution (q.v.). Jayewardene himself became the first executive president in February 1978. He won the first-ever presidential election in October 1982 and remained the head of state and government until the end of his term in 1988. On relinquishing his position he also retired from politics. In 1977 Jayewardene promised to establish a *Dharmishta* (Just) society under his government. Given the ethnic violence since 1980, corruption in public life, and other obvious shortcomings of his administration, he failed to achieve this lofty objective that he set for himself. However, he made a major positive contribution to national life by instituting radical economic reforms to establish a more open, liberal, and export-oriented market economy (q.v.).

JUDICIARY. The Sri Lanka judiciary is a branch of the central governmental system. It consists of the Supreme Court (q.v.) headed by a chief justice as its apex body with the Courts of Appeal, High Courts, District Courts, and Magistrates Courts functioning as subordinate courts. The last four are courts of the first instance. The High Courts deal with all criminal cases and the District Courts with civil cases. Labor disputes are dealt with by Labor Tribunals.

The Supreme Court consists of the chief justice and not fewer than six and not more than ten judges. The Court of Appeal consists of the president and not fewer than six and not more than 11 other judges. A Judicial Service Commission, consisting of the chief justice and two other judges of the Supreme Court nominated by the president is responsible for the appointment of all judges below the High Court level and for appointment of officials of all the courts.

JVP REBELLION 1971. The first ever mass-based insurrection against the government of Sri Lanka after 1948. It was led by Rohana Wijeweera (q.v.), a then not-well-known young Marxist-nationalist leader who had returned after a period of study at Lumumba University in Moscow. The *Janatha Vimukthi Peramuna* (JVP) (q.v.) supported the victorious left-of-center coalition led by Mrs. Sirimavo Bandaranaike (q.v.) in the 1970 general elections. However, Wijeweera soon began to criticize the Bandaranaike administration for not implementing quickly and in full the socialist program that was promised at the election. The JVP also voiced strong opposition to what it called "Indian expansionism" threatening the territorial integrity of Sri Lanka. Soon the party decided to take over governmental power by violent means. It organized clandestine camps to train and motivate its cadres, mostly undergraduates and young, unemployed youth drawn almost exclusively from the Sinhalese community. The participants at these camps were given five lectures for ideological orientation and rudimentary training in arms.

The JVP launched its attacks on April 5th, 1971 simultaneously in the central and southern parts of the country. The primary targets were the police stations in the provincial towns. The government, which had disregarded intelligence reports of an impending JVP attack, was ill-prepared for battle. Thus several provincial police stations were taken over by the rebels and for a week or more some areas were under rebel control. However, the JVP plans to arrest the prime minister and cabinet members did not materialize. The armed forces remained fully loyal to the government. The opposition also declared support for the government and the powerful left trade unions also backed the government. The military soon launched a strong counterattack with the help of fresh supplies of arms rushed from, among others, India, Pakistan, China, Britain, and the United States of America. The rebellion was crushed in about three weeks. A large number of rebels, perhaps a few thousand, and a small number of military and police personnel were killed in the fighting. Several thousand rebels and their backers were arrested. The vast majority were released after a period of time in a rehabilitation camp. The leaders were put on trial and some, including Rohana Wijeweera, were convicted and sentenced to long periods of incarceration. They were pardoned and released by the Jayewardene administration in 1978. Many of them, including Wijeweera, regrouped and revived the JVP. Wijeweera was a candidate in the 1982 presidential election and the party also contested the June 1981 district council elections. Later it mounted a second JVP armed rebellion (1983-1989) (q.v.) against the government.

The 1971 JVP rebellion pressured the government to implement some radical policies, including the nationalization of privatelyowned tea (q.v.), rubber (q.v.), and coconut (q.v.) plantations and more central government control of the universities (q.v.).

JVP REBELLION 1983-1989. The Jayewardene administration accused the *Janatha Vimukthi Peramuna* (JVP) of instigating communal violence against Tamils in July 1983 and banned the party. It promptly went underground and began to organize antigovernment activity. The JVP campaign began to win the sympathy of sections of the community, especially Sinhalese unemployed rural youth. The latter did not see much benefit accruing to them from the capitalist, market-oriented open economy policies of the government and were attracted by the socialist-nationalist rhetoric of the JVP. As in the 1971 rebellion, the universities became key centers of support for the party. The Indo-Lanka Peace Accord (q.v.) gave additional momentum to the JVP campaign. The JVP fully exploited the widespread dissatisfaction of the Sinhalese public with the terms of the agreement, especially the stationing of the Indian Peace Keeping Force (q.v.) in northeast Sri Lanka. It also mobilized the support of a large section of university students and young Buddhist monks against the establishment of the North Colombo Medical College, a private fee-levying medical college. The JVP conducted antigovernment propaganda charging the government with incompetence and corruption.

The JVP campaign turned increasingly violent after July 1987. A grenade attack against a government parliamentary group meeting killed a junior minister, injured several others and, had it been more effective, would have killed the president and his senior ministers as well. It assassinated one cabinet minister and several government members of parliament, left opposition leaders, a large number of United National Party officials, senior bureaucrats, armed services and police personnel of all ranks and public personalities who were perceived as government supporters or were considered as obstacles to achieving its target to capture state power. The JVP terror campaign reached its peak in the second half of 1988 with the inauguration of the presidential election campaign and continued through the March 1989 parliamentary elections. On several occasions abortive attempts were made to have negotiations between the Jayewardene administration and later Premadasa administration and the JVP to achieve a peaceful settlement. Eventually, led by the powerful and determined state minister for defense Ranjan Wijeratne (q.v.), the government launched a fierce counterattack. Largely using tactics similar to that of the JVP, government forces killed several thousand JVPers and their suspected sympathizers and suppressed the party and its antigovernment campaign. Wijeweera himself and all except one of his central committee members were captured and killed in the process.

The JVP campaign severely disrupted the economy of the south for several years, virtually closed down the southern universities for three years, and generally led to large-scale violations of human rights on both sides.

K

KACHCHATIEVU DISPUTE. A small island located in the Palk Strait to northeast of Sri Lanka. Both India and Sri Lanka claimed ownership of the island. The matter was finally settled in 1972 when Prime Minister Indira Gandhi conceded the island to Sri Lanka. At one time it was believed that there might be oil in Kachchatievu and the surrounding sea. But oil explorations have not yielded any positive results. The island is not inhabited but is used by fishermen from both countries as a transient point. In recent times due to sea activity of the Liberation Tigers of Tamil Eelam and the Sri Lankan navy, attention has again been drawn to the island. Some Indian sources have accused Sri Lanka of harassment of Indian fishermen who go to the area. They want the Indian government to reclaim the island for India.

KACHCHERI. The district-level administration office headed by the government agent. It is a legacy from the British colonial administration. The term "Kachcheri" originated during the time of the "Amildar" experiment under which Malabar officials from India called Amildars established their offices called "kachcheris" in nine areas besides Colombo.

KANDYAN CONVENTION. Signed between the Kandyan leaders who supported the British takeover of the Kandyan kingdom in 1815 and the British colonial administration. The convention provided for, inter alia, Buddhism to be accorded a special place and to be protected by the state. The abortive 1818 Kandyan rebellion against the British was partly motivated by the perception of Kandyan leadership that the British failed to keep the promises in the convention.

KANDYAN KINGDOM. Established in 1469 by King Vickramabahu it became the last bastion of Sri Lankan independence in 1694 when all other centers of political power had collapsed. The Kandyan kingdom lasted for over three centuries until the British invaded in 1815 and ousted Sri Vickrama Rajasingha, the last king of Kandy. The Kandyan kingdom is generally associated with a less-prosperous period of Sri Lankan history and came after the epitome of Sinhala civilization represented in Anuradhapura and Polonnaruwa from about fifth century B.C. to 12th century A.D. However, the Kandyan kingdom had its own moments of military glory in the military victories it scored over invading Portuguese, Dutch, and British armies. It is also associated with some notable works in the creative arts, especially in temple paintings and literature. Its four last kings who were Nayakkars of South Indian extraction came to power due to dynastic reasons. However, they successfully integrated themselves into Sinhala-Buddhist society.

KANDYAN SINHALESE. Refers to about 40 to 45 percent of the Sinhalese population who come from the central highlands and the north-central and eastern plains of the country that formed the Kandyan kingdom (q.v.) in the 16th to the 18th century. The Kandyans, as opposed to the Low Country Sinhalese (q.v.) were less exposed to the influences of the Western colonizers beginning with the Portuguese. They also had lesser educational facilities and more limited business opportunities than the latter. However, in more recent times, they have made considerable progress in almost all areas of national life. This process was greatly assisted by the increasingly prominent positions assumed by Kandyans such as Sirimavo Bandaranaike (q.v.) and D. B. Wijetunga (q.v.) in the national leadership as well as by some major economic development programs such as land colonization (q.v.) and the Mahaveli Program (q.v.) that benefited them.

KARAIYAR CASTE. The caste that is traditionally associated with fishing in the Tamil community. The Liberation Tigers of Tamil Eelam (LTTE) (q.v.) drew a lot of its support, especially in the initial stages of its existence, from this caste. The LTTE leader Prabhakaran (q.v.) is a member of this caste from Velvatiturai.

KARAWA. A major caste group among the Sinhalese who traditionally inhabited the coastal areas were associated with the fishing industry. The Tamil counterparts are known as *Karaiyar*. It is believed that the members of *Karawa* community immigrated to Sri Lanka in 14th or 15th century. Today they are totally integrated into the Sinhalese population. Probably not more than 15 percent of the Sinhalese population, the *Karawa* caste were heavily influenced by the three colonizing powers. Thus a significant proportion of the community is Roman Catholic (q.v.). They also came to occupy a powerful position in the business world. Making use of the superior schools that were established in the coastal areas of western and southern provinces, they also gained access to government and mercantile jobs and professional occupations in large numbers.

KOTELAWALA, SIR JOHN LIONEL (1897-1981). The third prime minister of independent Sri Lanka, Kotelawala was also a soldier and an agriculturist. He was educated in Cambridge and on his return took to managing his properties. Later he joined the Ceylon Light Infantry and rose to the rank of colonel. He entered the State Council (q.v.) in 1931 and became minster of communications and works in the 1936 Council. From 1942-1945 he was a member of the National War Council. He was a founder member of the United National Party (UNP) (q.v.) in 1946. In the 1947 D. S. Senanayake cabinet he was minister of transport and works during which time he modernized the Colombo port. When S. W. R. D. Bandaranaike (q.v.) left the UNP, Kotelawala succeeded him as the leader of the House. He fully expected to succeed D. S. Senanayake to the premiership but was disappointed when he was overlooked in favor of Dudley Senanayake (q.v.).

Kotelawala took over from Dudley Senanayake when the latter resigned in September 1953. Backed by a comfortable majority in parliament (q.v.), he governed the country for two years. His period as prime minister is more noteworthy for some events in international affairs. Sri Lanka gained membership in the United Nations in 1955 when the Soviets dropped its veto against the country. He initiated the 1954 Colombo Coherence of Asian powers that discussed the Indo-China problem. He also participated in the 1955 Bandung conference of Afro-Asian countries. At both conferences he insisted that the representatives should condemn "aggressive communism" as much as they were prepared to condemn "colonialism." In 1956 he dissolved parliament and called for a fresh elections one year ahead of schedule. The UNP led by Kotelawala suffered an ignominious defeat in the polls at the hands of Bandaranaike's *Mahajana Eksath Peramuna* (MEP) (q.v.), winning only eight seats out of 95.

Following his defeat Kotelawala left for England to spend more time on a farm that he owned in that country. In 1959 the UNP opted to invite Dudley Senanayake to assume the leadership of the party. Kotelawala retired from politics in 1960. Kotelawala gifted his residence Kandawala Walauwa to the state to open a national defense academy that has been named after him as the Kotelawala Defense Academy. He was elevated to the rank of general just before he died.

KUMARATUNGA, CHANDRIKA BANDARANAIKE (1945-). She is the fourth executive president of Sri Lanka, having been elected to that office in November 1994. For three months immediately prior to that she held the office of prime minister, having led the People's Alliance (q.v.) to victory in the country's tenth parliamentary elections.

The second child of two Sri Lankan Prime Ministers S. W. R. D. Bandaranaike (q.v.) and Sirimavo Bandaranaike (q.v.), Chandrika Kumaratunga belongs to Sri Lanka's foremost political family. After her primary and secondary education at St. Bridget's Convent, Colombo, an exclusive school for girls, she joined the Sorbonne University, Paris, for a degree in political science. Later she embarked on postgraduate studies in political economy, which she did not complete. She is fluent in three languages, Sinhalese, English, and French.

She returned home from Paris in 1972. In the same year, she was appointed as an additional director of the Land Reform Commission in her mother's administration. From 1976 to 1977 she served as the chairperson of the Janawasa Commission that was also connected to the land reform (q.v.) program of the government. In 1974 she was elected to the executive committee of the Sri Lanka Freedom Party (SLFP) (q.v.) Women's Organization. During this period she was associated with the more radical wing of the SLFP.

In 1978 she married Vijaya Kumaranatunga, a popular Sinhala film actor who held radical left-of-center political views and had political ambitions of his own. He formed his own political party, *Sri Lanka Mahajana Pakshaya* (SLMP) (q.v.), in 1984 and she, having left the SLFP, became one of its vice presidents. The couple played a leading role in forming the United Left Front in the mid 1980s that brought together several of the smaller left parties in the country. Vijaya Kumaranatunga contested parliamentary by-elections twice but was defeated on both occasions. In 1988 he was assassinated by a gunman believed to have been sent by the *Janatha Vimukthi Peramuna* (JVP) (q.v.).

Soon after the assassination of her husband she left for England with her two children, Yasodhara and Vimukthi. The family lived in London for about two years. During her stay abroad she worked as a researcher for the World Institute of Development Economics Research (WIDER) in Helsinki. After her husband's death she assumed the leadership of the SLMP. However, the party soon split, and on her return to Sri Lanka she formed her own party called *Bahujana Nidahas*

Pakshaya. The new party did not survive long and she returned to the SLFP. In 1992 she became a member of its central committee and chief organizer for the Attanagalla electorate, a traditional stronghold of the Bandaranaike family (q.v.). Soon she was in contention with her more right-oriented brother Anura Bandaranaike (q.v.) for the party leadership. She won the battle with the backing of her mother and the left-of-center faction of the party. From that point onward, her political ascendance was meteoric. In May 1993 she led the People's Alliance (PA) to victory in the Western Provincial Council elections and assumed the office of chief minister. She further consolidated her winning streak in politics when she led the PA to a convincing win in elections to the Southern Provincial Council. After parliament was dissolved in June of that year the PA relied on her to lead its general election campaign. The PA won the election but only by a majority of one seat. In August she assumed the office of prime minister and formed a government under President D.B. Wijetunga (q.v.). Three months later she won the presidential election, polling over 62 percent of the total vote, the highest ever percentage polled by a single party or candidate in a national election in Sri Lanka.

Her first two years as president has produced mixed results for the country. Her attempts to make peace with the Liberation Tigers of Tamil Eelam (LTTE) failed and the ethnic war intensified after April 1995. The successful military campaign of the Sri Lankan army that ousted the LTTE from its stronghold in Jaffna in December 1995 is considered as her outstanding achievement to date. Her political package proposing a high degree of devolution for the regions has harnessed international support for her but has failed to gain significant public backing at home. Her economic policies have not produced the growth and jobs promised during the election campaign. She has also failed to keep her promise to abolish the executive presidency by July 15, 1995. Many of her critics find fault with her for poor management skills.

L

LABOR FORCE. In mid 1995 Sri Lanka's labor force was estimated at 6.57 million. Of this number approximately one quarter were female. In the last three decades the labor force grew at an annual average rate of 2.2 percent. In the next three decades it is projected to grow at 2.5 percent per year. From the late 1950s the country has faced a chronic unemployment problem due to the slow growth of the economy. In the mid 1970s about one fourth of the labor force was estimated to be unemployed. Since then the unemployment rate has fluctuated around 15 percent. Youth unrest in the last two to three decades, especially the *Janatha Vimukthi Peramuna* rebellions (q.v.), have been fueled by widespread unemployment, especially among the educated youth.

LAND REFORM. The Sirimavo Bandaranaike administration of 1970-1977 launched a program of land reform in two stages in 1972 and 1975. Land reform was one of the commitments made in the United Front (q.v.) manifesto of 1970. It took an added urgency following the youth revolt of the *Janatha Vimukthi Peramuna* (q.v.) in April 1971. In the first round, under the *Land Reform Law No. 1 of 1972,* the government imposed a ceiling on individual landholdings and acquired the excess land that totaled 228,000 ha. In 1975 under the second stage, the government acquired all company-owned estates that totaled 170,000 ha. Thus the government came to own about one-fifth of the total agricultural land at that time. Approximately 10 percent of the land that was acquired was alienated to the peasantry as small holdings. The balance was managed by two state-owned plantations corporations. In the early 1990s the plantations were handed back to private companies for management.

LANGUAGE POLICY. Sri Lanka's language policy has evolved over a period of three decades. In the 1940s national leaders generally agreed that both Sinhala and Tamil should be official languages in an independent Sri Lanka. This policy changed to a policy of "Sinhala-only" (q.v.) in the mid 1950s as a result of political pressure from Sinhalese nationalist forces. Tamils leaders vehemently protested when the "Sinhala only" language act was passed in parliament in 1956. To ameliorate Tamil concerns, provision was made in the 1958 Tamil Language (Special Provisions) Act (q.v.) for the use of Tamil in official business in Tamil areas and in transactions between Tamil-speaking people and the government. In the 1978 constitution (q.v.) Tamil was made a national language. In 1988, following the Indo-Lanka Peace Accord (q.v.), it was made an official language and English a national language. However, on the one hand, Tamils have regularly criticized the government for not taking adequate practical steps to ensure that its language policy is actually implemented by providing more facilities for the use of Tamil in government business. On the other hand, it has also been pointed out that, whatever the nature of the rhetoric and legislation surrounding this issue might have been, Tamil has always been used in the education system from kindergarten to postgraduate degree level and that in most state activity, including the judiciary, Tamil has always been used to transact business. There is general acceptance among all concerned that English should be the principal international language for education and science, and for commercial and other transactions with the global community.

LANGUAGE PROBLEM. Language has been a principal area of dispute between the Sinhalese and Tamils since the 1940s and was a key factor that led to the current ethnic conflict. Prime Minister S. W. R. D. Bandaranaike (q.v.) acceding to the demand of Sinhalese nationalist forces made Sinhala the only official language in 1956, replacing English. The Tamils opposed the policy and wanted Tamil also to be given parity of status. They feared that otherwise their single most important ethnic marker would be lost and also that they would lose jobs and other economic and educational opportunities due to language discrimination. The language policy (q.v.) of the government has evolved since the 1956 legislation. Now Sinhala and Tamil enjoy formal parity as official languages and English is a national language.

LANKA SAMA SAMAJA PARTY **(LSSP).** Established in 1935, the LSSP (Equal Society Party) adheres to a Trotskyite ideology. It was a member of the Fourth International but broke away in 1964. Its heydays were seen under the leadership of N. M. Perera (q.v.) and Colvin R. de Silva (q.v.). In theory the LSSP advocated revolution of the working-class but in practice the party leaders were parliamentarians par excellence. The party developed a strong trade union base, especially among Colombo city workers in the harbor, transport industry, and the mercantile sector and in some sections of the state and semi-state sectors. The party backed the victorious *Mahajana Eksath Peramuna* (q.v.) coalition of S. W. R. D. Bandaranaike (q.v.) in the 1956 general elections and itself won 15 seats to become the principal opposition party. In 1964 it again gave parliamentary support to the Sirimavo Bandaranaike (q.v.) administration.

In the 1970 general elections the LSSP was a partner in the Sirimavo Bandaranaike-led United Front (q.v.) coalition that won the election. Both Perera and de Silva had cabinet portfolios until the party left the government in 1975. After that date the party has been rapidly losing its political influence. Its trade union base has been eroded by rival unions and by the general decline of the trade unions in the country. The demise of the old leaders weakened the electoral support for the party. The *Janatha Vimukthi Peramuna* (q.v.) also took away some of its potential supporters, especially among the youth. The collapse of socialist regimes, especially that of Yugoslavia, which the

LSSP held up as a model of worker democracy, has also undermined its credibility. The party also split in 1982 with a younger breakaway group setting up a rival *Nava Lanka Sama Samaja Party* (NLSSP) (q.v.) (New Equal Society Party) that claims Trotskyite ideological purity. However, inter alia, its strong advocacy of labor legislation, social welfare measures, support for nationalization and state ownership of enterprises, economic planning, and import substitution industrialization has left a lasting impression on Sri Lanka's public policies in the last half century.

LEGISLATIVE COUNCIL. Established under the Colebrooke-Cameron reforms of 1832, it slowly evolved from being an innocuous advisory body consisting largely of officials to a more influential legislative body with more unofficial and elected members representing different sections of the Sri Lankan community. Some of the principal national leaders such as D. S. Senanayake (q.v.), D. B. Jayatilaka (q.v.), and Ponnambalam Ramanathan (q.v.), who were active in the independence movement, entered political life through this council.

LIBERATION TIGERS OF TAMIL EELAM (LTTE). The LTTE was founded in 1976 by Velupillai Prabhakaran (q.v.). It was the successor to the Tamil New Tigers, a group that was also set by Prabhakaran in 1974. The term "Tiger" was first used in Tamil militant politics in 1961 when an organization called Army of Tigers *(Pulip Padai)* was founded by a group then associated with the Federal Party, the predecessor of Tamil United Liberation Front (TULF) (q.v.). The Army of Tigers withered away when the Federal Party joined the United National Party (UNP) (q.v.) government in 1965.

The original backers of the LTTE were largely drawn from the *Karaiyar* caste in the Velvatiturai area of the Jaffna peninsula. However, now it has a broader social base. Since 1983 it has emerged as the most powerful of the Tamil rebel groups fighting for an independent Tamil state, *(Eelam)*, in northeast Sri Lanka. It has a well-established international network of branch offices in London, Paris, and elsewhere to conduct international propaganda and to raise funds. At the beginning, the party relied heavily on bank robberies and other such blatantly illegal activities for funds. The tradition still continues with money raised through international drug trafficking, extortion from Tamils living in the territory under its control and also from those living abroad. It also receives substantial voluntary contributions from its sympathizers, especially wealthy Tamil expatriates in the West. It is also reported to have profit-making businesses such as shipping. The LTTE also received arms, equipment, and assistance with training from India before 1987. As a part of the July 1987 deal India also gave the LTTE US$2 million. In recent times taxes imposed on the residents and businesses in the territory under control has become a principal source of revenue. The LTTE fighters also continue to capture large quantities of arms, ammunition, and other equipment from Sri Lankan government forces operating in the north and east. It has its own newspaper *Eelanathan.*

The LTTE demands the right of self-determination for the Tamils and its declared goal is *Eelam (q.v.)* However, it has hinted its willingness to settle for something less than total independence. The LTTE has used terror tactics to virtually eliminate all those who have opposed it. It decimated its rival rebel groups in internecine warfare in northeast Sri Lanka and in Tamil Nadu in India. It assassinated several of the traditional Tamil leaders, including the TULF (q.v.) chief Appapillai Amirthalingam (q.v.). It stands accused by India of assassinating the former Indian Prime Minister Rajiv Gandhi, who made an enemy of the LTTE by failing to consult the latter in the 1987 peace accord and later backed the Eelam People's Revolutionary Liberation Front (q.v.). The LTTE is also the principal suspect in the assassination of President Premadasa (q.v.), Ranjan Wijeratne (q.v.), Lalith Athulathmudali (q.v.), Gamini Dissanayake (q.v.), and several other senior Sinhalese political leaders. It has also conducted several terrorist attacks against Sinhalese and Muslim civilian targets to achieve "ethnic cleansing" of the northeast. It is not clear how much popular support the LTTE enjoys in the northeast.

After fighting the Sri Lankan forces from the early 1980s until 1987, the LTTE fought the Indian Peace Keeping Force (q.v.) over the next three years. When the latter evacuated in March 1990, the LTTE took over the Jaffna peninsula. It established a rudimentary administration in the area and ran it until it was ousted from Jaffna city in late 1995 by Sri Lankan forces in Operation *Riviresa.*

The LTTE entered into peace talks with President Premadasa that lasted over 18 months until June 1991. Similar talks were held with President Kumaratunga in 1994-1995. On both occasions the talks were suddenly broken off by the LTTE and war resumed.

As at mid 1996, the LTTE has established itself in the jungles of Kilinochchi on the mainland. They are also moving quite freely in many parts of the eastern province. They are also continuing the random terrorist attacks in the south, mainly in Colombo.

LITERACY. Sri Lanka's functional literacy, defined as being able to read and write, rate for adults (age 15 and over) was 83 percent in 1988. The rate for females was 79 percent and for males 87 percent. In urban areas it was 93 percent, rural 87 percent, and plantations 80 percent. The minimum literacy rate in 1990 was 88 percent. Because of a reasonably good and widely accessible network of schools (q.v.) Sri Lanka took an early lead among developing countries in literacy. In 1901 the rate was 26 percent. At independence it was 58 percent. However, the country has yet to achieve universal primary enrollment that is necessary to wipe out illiteracy. According to the 1981 census 6 percent of males and 7 percent of females in the 5 to 17 age group had never attended school.

LOCAL GOVERNMENT. The Colombo Municipal Council (1865) was the first local body to be established in the country. Since then the system evolved into a four-tier structure consisting of Municipal Councils, Urban Councils, Town Councils, and Village Councils. At independence in 1948 Sri Lanka had a relatively well-developed system of local government covering the entire country. In 1988, Town Councils and Village Councils were replaced by *Pradeshiya Sabhas* (Local Assemblies) (q.v.). The creation of District Development Councils (q.v.) in 1980 and their replacement with Provincial Councils (q.v.) in 1987 was an attempt to end the ethnic conflict (q.v.) by devolving power from the center, especially to meet the demand of the Tamil minority for more self-rule. Two key factors constrain the development of local government and power devolution in Sri Lanka. One is the inability and unwillingness of the center to genuinely transfer power to provincial governments and local bodies. The other is their very limited revenue base. Their powers of taxation are restricted and the bulk of the budgets are funded with grants from the center.

LOW COUNTRY SINHALESE. Those who traditionally lived in the western and southern plain and coastal area are identified by this term. It is estimated that approximately 55 percent to 60 percent fall into this category. In contrast to the Kandyan Sinhalese (q.v.) these people were more exposed to western influence from the 15th century onward. They have been more commercially-oriented and benefited more than the latter from the free enterprise economy under the British. They also had better educational opportunities that permitted them to secure more government jobs. In the country's political leadership also the low country Sinhalese have traditionally played a relatively more prominent role.

M

***MAHAJANA EKSATH PERAMUNA* (MEP).** The MEP (People's United Front) was originally formed as a coalition of parties headed by S. W. R. D. Bandaranaike (q.v.) of the Sri Lanka Freedom Party (q.v.) to fight the 1956 general elections, which it won. Since 1960 it has functioned as a separate political party first led by veteran left leader Philip Gunawardane and from 1980 by his son Dinesh Gunawardane (q.v.). The party economic policy is left-oriented and favors a more statist development strategy. Its social policies advocate more equity. On the ethnic question the party emerges as a strong defender of Sinhalese-Buddhist rights and supports the military campaign to combat what it calls "northern terrorism." The MEP held three seats in the 1989 parliament but failed to win any in the 1994 general elections.

MAHAVELI DEVELOPMENT PROGRAM (MDP). Also known as the Accelerated Mahaveli Development Program (AMDP), this is the single largest development project undertaken in Sri Lanka's history. The total expenditure up to the end of 1994 has exceeded US$1.1 billion. The original UNDP/FAO Master Plan for the project envisaged a period of 30 years for the completion of the project. The construction work of the first headwork in Bowatenna for power and irrigation commenced in 1970 and was completed in 1977. In 1978 the Jayewardene administration accelerated the program of work with the intention of completing it in six years. Five major reservoirs Kotmale, Victoria, Randenigala, Rantambe, and Maduruoya, and six power stations with a total installed capacity of 800 mw were built under the AMDP. These were completed by 1990. The Mahaveli irrigation system is planned to provide water for over 150,000 ha for agriculture to settle about 100,000 farmer families in new farmsteads. This work is still in progress. By the end of 1994, 90,570 families had been settled. About 80 percent of the project funds came from donor sources. By 1993 about half of the country's electricity power output came from Mahaveli. It has also significantly increased the country's capacity to produce rice and other food crops. However, critics have argued that the returns are not adequate for the investment. Some have also noted the possible environmental degradation that could occur as a result of the project.

MALAYS. The Malays are a very small cultural minority who number a few thousand. They originally came to Sri Lanka largely as soldiers of the Dutch army in the 18th century. Some also came to work in minor urban trades. Most of them belong to the Islamic faith. However, they claim a distinct ethnic identity separate from the Muslim (Moor) community on account of their origin in Malaya. In recent years many have migrated to Malaysia.

MARXIST MOVEMENT. Sri Lanka's Marxist movement has a history of over 60 years. In 1935 the Trotskyite *Lanka Sama Samaja Party* (LSSP) (Lanka Equal Society Party) (q.v.) was established. It was followed by the Communist Party (CP) (1943). The Sino-Soviet split affected the latter, which also split into two with one following the Peking line and the other the Moscow line. In the 1960s and later, many other parties with Marxist orientation came to the scene. But with the exception of *Janatha Vimukthi Peramuna* (JVP) (q.v.) none made any impression on Sri Lankan politics.

The Sri Lankan Marxist movement was at its most influential from about 1940 to 1975. The ideas of Marxist leaders such as N. M. Perera (q.v.) and Colvin R. de Silva (q.v.) influenced policy, especially in constitution making and social welfare. The trade unions under the control of the Marxist parties were also powerful and active, especially in the 1950s. The LSSP and the CP helped S. W. R. D. Bandaranaike's *Mahajana Eksath Peramuna* (q.v.) in 1956 and Sirimavo Bandaranaike's Sri Lanka Freedom Party (SLFP) (q.v.) in July 1960 and 1970 to win parliamentary elections by entering into "no contest" pacts. Both the LSSP and the CP were in coalition governments with the SLFP, first in 1962-1964 and later in 1970-1975.

After 1975 the influence and power of the Marxist movement has steadily waned. The growth of the JVP, which posed as a radical Marxist nationalist party was partly responsible for the decline. The weakening of the trade union base of the LSSP and CP, the electoral dependence of the two parties on the SLFP, the success of the United National Party after 1977 in appealing to the youth voters in particular with a more consumer-oriented and practical program of work, the demise of the old and charismatic leaders such as N. M. Perera (q.v.), Colvin R. De Silva (q.v.), and S. A. Wickramasinghe (q.v.), the collapse of the communist regimes in central and eastern Europe were other important factors that led to the decline of the Sri Lankan Marxist movement. In the 1977 general elections, no candidate from a Marxist party won a seat and in 1989 only one was elected. The LSSP and CP have made a comeback as coalition partners of the People's Alliance (q.v.) that won the August 1994 parliamentary elections.

MIDDLE EAST. Sri Lanka's links with the Middle East go back to antiquity when Arab traders used Sri Lanka as an entrepôt. Some traders settled in the island to form a part of the Muslim community (q.v.) that exists today. Today Sri Lanka buys the bulk of its oil from Middle East suppliers, mainly Iran, and exports considerable amounts of tea (q.v.) to several countries in the region. Following the oil boom, Sri Lanka has also become a significant source of labor ranging from house maids (who form the single largest category) and unskilled laborers to skilled engineers, accountants, doctors, and other professionals totaling more than 200,000 at the end of 1994. In foreign policy, Sri Lanka has generally taken a strongly pro-Palestinian position, partly in response to pressures from the local Muslim community. Several Arab countries have developed strong links with the local Muslim community and provide substantial funds for educational, cultural, and other activities of the community.

MINERAL RESOURCES. Sri Lanka is least well endowed with energy minerals. Peat found in a large swamp north of Colombo is one of the few energy minerals (fossil fuel) so far discovered in Sri Lanka. A number of nuclear minerals including thorianite have also been discovered. But none is exploited economically. In the past the search for oil has not yielded any positive result. Sizable quantities of iron ore deposits have been discovered, although no economic use has been made up to now. It is also estimated that the country has beach mineral sand on coastal stretches. The largest located in the northeast near Trincomalee have ilmenite (3 million tons), rutile (6 million tons), and zircon (4 million tons). These are being commercially exploited. The country is relatively best endowed with nonmetallic minerals, graphite (q.v.), clays, feldspar, rock phosphate (apatite), and most notably, precious and semiprecious stones.

MUSLIMS. Muslims also called "Moors" constitute about 7 percent (1.3 million) of the Sri Lankan population. The majority are native speakers of the Tamil language. However, they distinguish themselves as a separate ethnic group on the basis of their adherence to the Islamic faith. About one-third of them are in the eastern province and the rest are scattered in several other parts of the island. Muslims trace their origins to Arab traders and seafarers who came to Sri Lanka over the centuries, especially after the 12th century. However, they have mixed ethnic origins with large numbers immigrating from India. The traders who were almost entirely men married local women and settled down.

N

NATIONAL FLOWER. The national flower of Sri Lanka is "Manel" (*Nymphaea stellata* or *N. Nouchali*). It is indigenous but is also found in India and Tropical Africa.

NATIONAL STATE ASSEMBLY (NSA). The name given to the unicameral parliament created by the 1972 constitution (q.v.). The 1978 constitution (q.v.) replaced it with a House of Representatives. The NSA had 157 members in 1972 and 168 members after the 1977 general elections.

NATIONAL TREE. Sri Lanka's national tree is "Na" (*Mesua ferrea*). It is commonly found in Southeast Asia.

NAVA LANKA SAMA SAMAJA PARTY **(NLSSP).** Founded in 1977 by a young breakaway group of the *Lanka Sama Samaja Party* (LSSP) (q.v.) who were unhappy with the compromises being made by the latter on radical policies, especially in the coalition agreements that the LSSP entered into with the Sri Lanka Freedom Party (q.v.). The NLSSP (New Equal Society Party) advocates a pure form of Trotskyite socialism. It is a member of the Fourth International. The party has one member of parliament, its leader Vasudeva Nanayakkara, in parliament.

NAYAKKAR DYNASTY. The last ruling dynasty of Sri Lanka. Founded in 1739 by Sri Vijaya Rajasingha, who ascended the Kandyan throne, the Nayakkars were of Telugu origin and hailed from Madurai, South India. Nayakkar kings integrated themselves fully into the Sinhalase-Buddhist society. All of them were keen patrons of Buddhism. They adopted the Sinhala language, one of them being a successful poet. The most powerful and successful of the Nayakkar kings was Kirti Sri Rajasingha (1747-1782). Sri Vickrama Rajasingha, the last Nayakkar king, was also the last Kandyan king. He was captured in battle by the British in 1815 during their successful invasion of the Kandyan Kingdom, taken prisoner and exiled to Vellore, India.

NIKAYA. The Buddhist *Sangha (bhikkhu)* (q.v.) establishment is divided into several *nikayas* (sects). These divisions in the island's monkhood first occurred in the first century A.D. At that time the divisions were partly personal and partly ideological, each *Nikaya* having its own interpretation of texts and its own ritual peculiarities. The *Nikaya* divisions today are not connected with the original divisions. The current divisions owe their origins to sources from where the founder monks of the particular *Nikaya* received their "Higher Ordination", the graduation into full-fledged *bhikkhu* status. At present there are three principal sects, namely *Siam, Amarapura,* and *Ramagngna.* To some extent they have a caste basis. For example, traditionally the *bhikkhus* in the *Siam nikaya* come almost exclusively from the farmer caste, traditionally perceived to be the superior caste in Sri Lanka's traditional Sinhalese caste hierarchy.

NONALIGNED MOVEMENT (NAM). Sri Lanka became a founder member of NAM when it was founded in 1956. It hosted the sixth NAM summit in 1976 in Colombo at which the country assumed the chair of the movement until the next summit. The country has played a prominent role in the movement. One of the more notable instances was the attempt by Prime Minister Sirimavo Bandaranaike in 1964 to bring about a negotiated settlement of the Sino-Indian dispute.

O

OFFICIAL LANGUAGE ACT OF 1956. Also known as the "Sinhala-Only Act", it made Sinhala the sole official language, sparking off a major controversy in language policy (q.v.), and creating a language problem (q.v.) between the Sinhalese and the Tamils. It was amended on several subsequent occasions, most notably by the Tamil Language Special Provisions Act of 1958 and the Language Act of 1988.

P

PADDY. See **RICE.**

PAINTINGS. Both religious and secular paintings are to be found in Sri Lankan historical monuments stretching back almost two thousand years. The Sigiriya frescoes (first century A.D.) are the best-known example of secular paintings from ancient Sri Lanka. Several ancient temples have paintings with religious themes. The best-known modern Sri Lankan painter is George Keyt whose works clearly show the influence of Western painters, especially Picasso, but who gave a distinctly oriental—Kandyan/oriental style of lines and flat colors—style to his work. Harry Peiris and Justin Deraniyagala were two other painters of Keyt's vintage who followed a European style. More recent painters such as Senaka Senanayake, Stanley Kirinda, and S. H. Sarath have tried to produce works that are more rooted in the local tradition.

PAKISTAN. Until the ethnic war broke out in the early 1980s Sri Lanka tried to be neutral and evenhanded in its dealings with the traditional South Asian rivals India and Pakistan. However, in the 1971 Bangladesh war, Sri Lanka permitted Pakistan to move troops and supplies via Sri Lanka. But that did not damage Indo-Lanka relations. When India began to assist Tamil separatists after 1983 Sri Lanka gradually began to show more sympathy for Pakistan. Pakistan has assisted Sri Lanka with arms supplies for the military to fight the Tamil separatists. The two countries have generally shared similar views of disapproval of India's attempt to play the role of regional superpower. Pakistan accounted for about 1.3 percent of Sri Lanka's imports and exports in 1994. Among the South Asian countries it is the largest importer of Sri Lankan products.

PARIS AID CLUB. Sri Lanka has been a regular recipient of Paris Aid Club foreign assistance since 1967. The amount of aid received increased substantially after the United National Party (q.v.) came to power in 1977 and the Jayewardene administration decided to liberalize the economy under International Monetary Fund/World Bank guidance. In the mid 1980s some pressure was brought to bear on the Paris club to suspend aid on account of alleged human rights violations against Tamils by the Sri Lankan government. A few of the smaller European donor countries have reduced or withdrawn aid to the government. However, the big donors have continued their support. In the early/mid 1990s the annual gross amount of aid committed by the Paris club had exceeded US$800 million.

PARLIAMENT. From 1947 to 1972 Sri Lanka had a bicameral parliament with a house of representatives and a senate (q.v.). A constitutional amendment in 1971 that abolished the senate converted the system to a unicameral legislature. The house of representatives consisted of members directly elected by the people. Until 1972 there were an additional few appointed by the governor- General on the advice of the prime minister to represent minorities and interest groups that failed to elect representatives to parliament. In each of the 1947, 1952, and 1956 houses the total membership was 101 (95 elected and six appointed). In March 1960, July 1960, 1965, and 1970 it was 157 (151 elected and six appointed). In 1977 it rose to 168, all directly elected. In the 1989 and 1994 parliaments 196 were elected and 29 were appointed from national party lists with each party that polled more than 5 percent of the total national vote getting seats in proportion to the share of the total poll of that party.

Before 1978 the normal life of a parliament was five years. It was raised to six in the 1978 constitution that also introduced a district-based proportional representation system to elect members of parliament. It also abolished by-elections and permitted the party leader to appoint a person to any vacancy that may occur during the life of a parliament.

PARLIAMENTARY ELECTIONS. Parliamentary elections under universal franchise (q.v.) have been held in the country since 1931. There were two breaks in the otherwise regular process. One was the extension of life of the 1970 parliament by two years in 1975 during the Sirimavo Bandaranaike (q.v.) administration. The other was the extension of its life by a full six-year period following a controversial referendum in December 1982 under the Jayewardene (q.v.) administration. Parliamentary elections are conducted by a Commissioner of Elections who, once appointed, can be removed from office before his regular term ends only by impeachment in parliament. This gives the office considerable autonomy. Electoral lists are prepared every year in June based on citizenship, residency and age. Every adult citizen over the age of 18 years fulfilling residency requirements is eligible for registration.

In recent parliamentary elections, with the exception of the 1989 election that was affected by the *Janatha Vimukthi Peramuna* terror campaign, the voter turnout has averaged over 80 percent. Sri Lankan elections generally have been held to be free and fair. The exceptions were the 1982 referendum, the 1988 presidential election, and the 1989 parliamentary elections. The first was discredited by accusations of rigging and other poll malpractice and the other two by widespread violence and alleged poll malpractice. Another negative tendency associated with Sri Lankan parliamentary elections, especially since 1970, has been postelection violence; the perpetrators usually are supporters of the victorious party and the victims those of the defeated parties.

PARLIAMENTARY PRIVILEGES. The Sri Lankan parliament enjoys privileges under Article 67 of the 1978 Constitution and the Parliament (Powers and Privileges) Act. Some have criticized these laws as being antidemocratic for the restrictions that they impose on reporting and commenting on proceedings in parliament and actions of members of parliament.

PARSEES. A small cultural minority of Indian origin in Sri Lanka. They live mostly in Colombo, Kandy, and a few other big towns and are generally engaged in trade.

PEACE CORPS. Sri Lanka was among the first groups of countries to receive Peace Corps volunteers when the scheme was inaugurated by the United States in 1962. Since then, up to the end of 1995 the country has received 276 volunteers. First from 1964 to 1967 and again from 1970 to 1977 the program was stopped by the Sirimavo Bandaranaike (q.v.) administrations. It was resumed by United National Party (q.v.) administrations in both instances. In early 1996, 30 volunteers were serving in the island.

PEOPLE'S ALLIANCE (PA). The current (August 1994 -) ruling party of Sri Lanka, it is a coalition formed in 1993 with the Sri Lanka Freedom Party (q.v.) as the principal constituent party. The other parties in the alliance are *Lanka Sama Samaja Party* (q.v.), Community Party (q.v.), Democratic United National Front (Lalith Wing), *Sri Lanka Mahajana Pakshaya* (Sri Lanka People's Party), Sri Lanka Muslim Congress, Ceylon Workers Congress, and *Desha Vimukti Janatha Party* (National Liberation People's Party). It is led by President Chandrika Kumaratunga (q.v.). The PA won the 1994 August parliamentary elections with 105 seats and the presidential election in November of the same year with 62.28 percent of the vote.

PERAHARA. The annual pageant held in Kandy (q.v.) in July/August. According to legend the pageant was started in the second century by King Gajaba to commemorate his victory in war over a South Indian king. Since then it has evolved into a semireligious festival. It is held to invoke the blessings of the gods on the people of Sri Lanka. The pageant itself consists of groups of traditional drummers, dancers, and other performers together with a large number of gaily decorated elephants that parade the streets of Kandy for about nine days, the first eight in the night and the last during the day. The pageant has five sections. The first and principal section is organized by the *Maligawa* (Temple of the Sacred Buddha Tooth) and the remaining four by the five respective *devalas* (temples) of Kandy. Every year the pageant draws a very large crowd of spectators, including a substantial number of foreign tourists. Traditionally the performers at the *Perahara* gave their time as a service payment to the *Maligawa* and the *devalas*.

PERERA, N. M. (1905-1979). He took his Ph.D. and later D.Sc in political science from the London School of Economics in the early 1930s. While in London he turned to the socialist movement, partly under the influence of his teacher, Harold Laski, a well-known British scholar and radical socialist thinker at that time. On his return to Sri Lanka, for a short period he was on the faculty of the University College in Colombo. However, he soon left that job to take to full-time politics. He was a founder member and leader of the *Lanka Sama Samaja Party* (q.v.) and won one of two seats that the party secured in the 1936 State Council (q.v.) elections. Perera had to cope with two ideologically driven splits in his party in the 1940s. In the early 1940s the British proscribed the party under war regulations and jailed him and several of his colleagues who broke jail and escaped. Perera and his party enjoyed considerable public support for the social work that they did during the Malaria epidemic of the 1930s. They were also in the forefront of the urban working-class movement and trade union movement. These factors gave the party considerable political and electoral strength in the 1950s. Perera was the mayor of Colombo from 1954 to 1956 and the leader of the opposition in parliament (q.v.) from 1956 to 1960.

In 1964 he joined the Sirimavo Bandaranaike (q.v.) administration as minister of finance in a coalition government that lasted only about one year. In 1970 his party was a constituent member of the victorious United Front (q.v.) coalition. Perera became the minister of finance in the new administration. The country underwent considerable economic hardship during the five years that he held the appointment. The first oil crisis and high food import prices made economic management a difficult task for Finance Minister Perera. The weak performance of the Sri Lankan economy that was adversely affected by, inter alia, the first *Janatha Vimukthi Peramuna* rebellion (q.v.) and poorly conceived economic policies made the task even more complicated. Perera left the cabinet when his party left the coalition in 1975. He together with all other candidates of his party lost in the 1977 general elections. In politics he will be best remembered for his outstanding contributions to parliamentary debates and for his impact on social legislation of which he was a passionate advocate. Outside politics he will be best remembered as an avid cricket enthusiast, who for several years was the president of the national governing body of cricket (q.v.).

PIDURUTALAGALA. Rising up to 2,524 meters, Pidurutalagala is the highest peak in the country. It is located close to the resort town of Nuwara Eliya.

PLANTATION TAMILS. See Indian Tamils.

POLICE. The police system was established as early as 1796 by the British. It was elevated to the status of a department of government in 1864. It is charged with the usual tasks of law enforcement. At the end of 1995 the strength of the department, including reservists, is around 80,000. The police is headed by the inspector general of police (IGP) assisted by a large number of deputies in charge of various subjects and geographical ranges. Until 1971 it essentially was a lightly armed civilian agency modeled largely along the lines of the British police. The 1971 *Janatha Vimukthi Peramuna* (JVP) rebellion (q.v.) led to strengthening of the police with more recruits and more modern small arms and equipment. The escalation of the ethnic war in the 1980s and the JVP rebellion of 1983-1989 further strengthened that tendency and converted it into an almost paramilitary force. Most notable is the Special Task Force (STF) of the police that has paramilitary training and is deployed in troubled areas as a counterinsurgency force. In recent times the police have been accused of human rights violations. They have also been the victims of the Liberation Tigers of Tamil Eelam (q.v.) and JVP attacks. Under the provincial council system, the respective provincial administrations have the right to form their own police units. However, this provision has not yet been implemented.

POPULISM. A term used in the country to describe policies and decisions of politicians designed to please the electorate even though they may be beneficial to the country as a whole in the long run. Some of these remain no more than mere election promises. Mrs. Sirimavo Bandaranaike's (q.v.) promise in 1970 to give subsidized rice and Jayewardene's (q.v.) promise in 1977 to give eight pounds of grain per week are examples. However, the term acquired a special meaning during the administration of President R. Premadasa (q.v.). He initiated several schemes including a poverty alleviation program, a school meal program, and a school uniform program that were described as populist. His entire approach to politics has been described as a populist brand of democracy that ignored the elite and appealed to the ordinary masses directly.

PORTUGUESE. In 1505 the Portuguese were the first European power to arrive in Sri Lanka. Soon they wanted to establish control over the Sinhalese and Tamil kingdoms that existed on the island. By the end of that century they were firmly entrenched in the southwestern and northern parts of the island. But several attempts made to conquer the

Kandyan kingdom (q.v.) ended in failure. By 1660 the Dutch (q.v.) ousted the Portuguese and took control of the areas that were under the latter. Portuguese impact was felt mostly in the maritime areas where they were present. The expansion of the cinnamon trade was one aspect. The establishment of the Roman Catholic faith was another. Some of the customs and habits of the Portuguese such as *Baila* music have become a part of the popular culture of the country.

PORTUGUESE BURGHERS. These are distinguished from the Dutch Burghers (q.v.) and are the descendants of the Portuguese who came to Sri Lanka. With the exception of a small community in Batticaloa now also called "Batticaloa Burghers," the Portuguese Burghers have almost disappeared, having been absorbed either by the Dutch Burgher community, or the Sinhalese, or Tamil community. The Batticaloa Burghers speak their own Portuguese Creole and preserve many features of the culture of their ancestors from Portugal.

PRABHAKARAN, VELUPILLAI (1954 -). He is the leader of the most powerful of the Sri Lankan Tamil separatist groups, the Liberation Tigers of Tamil Eelam (LTTE) (q.v.). Youngest of four children in a Jaffna middle-class family, he came from Velvatiturai, a village in the Jaffna peninsula inhabited largely by people of the Karaiyar caste whose traditional occupation is fishing or smuggling. Prabhakaran also belongs to the same caste. He finished high school in Jaffna. His first involvement in politics was in the 1970s through the Tamil Students League and the Tamil Youth League (the youth wing of the Tamil United Liberation Front (TULF) (q.v.)) that organized street protests against the university admissions policy of the Sirimavo Bandaranaike (q.v.) administration and the 1972 Constitution (q.v.). Around this time he was close to the TULF leader Amirthalingam (q.v.), who in 1989 died at the hands of a LTTE assassin. Prabhakaran also cultivated the friendship of Tamil Nadu politicians in the mid 1970s. He turned to terrorism in 1974 when he assassinated the then Sri Lanka Freedom Party (q.v.) mayor of Jaffna Alfred Duriappah, an act that he proudly claims. In 1976 he was involved in a bank robbery to raise money to finance his clandestine political activities. The same year, he founded the LTTE.

He gradually built up the LTTE to make it the most powerful and feared Tamil rebel group. He has ruthlessly eliminated all his rivals, both from within the LTTE as well as from outside, who opposed him or stood in the way of achieving his objectives. India has formally charged him with plotting and ordering the assassination of Rajiv

Gandhi. Since then, assassins belonging to the LTTE are suspected of having killed a large segment of the top Sinhalese political leadership, including President Premadasa (q.v.), Lalith Athulathmudali (q.v.), and Gamini Dissanayake (q.v.), plus a large number of ordinary civilians in a series of terrorist attacks on civilian targets in Colombo and elsewhere. The supporters of Prabhakaran see him as a freedom fighter who is the ultimate embodiment of Sri Lankan Tamil nationalism. His opponents see him as a power-hungry terrorist who wants to impose his authoritarian rule on a hapless people. He and his wife Madivandani have two children, a son and a daughter.

PRADESHIYA SABHA. A system of elected local government bodies (local assemblies) established in 1988 by the Premadasa administration as the basic unit of local government. The members are elected by universal franchise for a period of four years. The unit of administration is a subdistrict but is confined to nonurban areas. There are a total of 258 such assemblies in the island. But 63 of them in the northern and eastern provinces were not functioning as such at early 1996. The primary task of the assemblies is to undertake developmental projects at the grassroots level.

PRAGATHISHEELI. The Sinhala term for "progressive" used to describe views that are of a socialist orientation such as nationalization, greater state control of the economy, and social welfare and opposed to foreign investment, the influence of western and multilateral donors, and so forth. However, following the failure of communist regimes in central and eastern Europe and the acceptance of the market-economy by the Sri Lanka Freedom Party (q.v.) and People's Alliance (q.v.), the term is no longer as fashionable as it was.

PRAKRITS. A mixture of dialects of Sanskrit origin spoken before the fifth century C.E. that formed the basis of the Sinhala (q.v.) language.

PREMADASA, RANASINGHE (1924-1993). Having graduated from high school, Premadasa entered public life through the now-defunct Ceylon Labour Party under the leadership of A. E. Goonesinha (q.v.). He won a seat in the Colombo Municipal Council in 1950 as a Labour candidate and rose to be the deputy mayor in 1954-1955. In the 1956 parliamentary elections as a United National Party (UNP) (q.v.) candidate he contested the *Lanka Sama Samaja Party* (q.v.) leader N. M. Perera (q.v.) and lost. Premadasa helped the UNP leader J. R. Jayewardene (q.v.) reorganize and revitalize the party after its defeat in

1956. In March 1960 he won a seat in parliament from a constituency in Central Colombo (q.v.) that became his political base. He was defeated in the July 1960 elections but won in 1965. He was appointed the parliamentary secretary (deputy minister) of local government and also made the chief government whip. In 1968 he entered the cabinet and quickly made his mark as a skillful administrator. In the 1970 parliamentary elections he won his seat but his party, the UNP, was defeated. Premadasa became the deputy leader of the UNP in 1976 and played a key role in the party's victory in 1977. In the two Jayewardene administrations he served as the prime minister and minister of local government, housing and construction. During this period, his most notable achievements were in housing, supply of drinking water, and the *Gam Udawa* (Village Reawakening) program.

On Jayewardene's retirement, he was the unanimous choice of the UNP to be the party candidate for the presidency. He defeated the Sri Lanka Freedom Party (q.v.) leader Sirimavo Bandaranaike and four others in a contest that was marred by widespread violence provoked by the *Janatha Vimukthi Peramuna* (JVP) (q.v.). His presidency lasted just over three years. On May 1, 1993, while he was busy organizing his party's May Day procession in Colombo close to his private residence, he was assassinated by a Liberation Tigers of Tamil Eelam (LTTE) (q.v.) suicide bomber. President Premadasa was feared for his ruthlessness and intolerance of dissenting opinion. At the same time, he was admired for commitment to hard work and the devotion to his cause. Premadasa was the first non *Govigama* (farmer) (q.v.) caste leader of postindependence Sri Lanka. He practiced a populist brand of politics. During his tenure he succeeded in getting India to withdraw its Peace Keeping Force (IPKF) (q.v.) from Sri Lanka. The JVP rebellion was also crushed within about one year of his assuming office. As president he worked toward two broad objectives. One was to accelerate economic growth through a market-economy. The other was to reduce poverty via targeted interventions.

At the time of his death, his poverty-reduction program called *Janasaviya* (q.v.) was in its first stage. The People's Alliance (q.v.) government discontinued the program in 1995 in favor of its own program. Under Premadasa the economy emerged from the recession of the late 1980s. Premadasa's attempts to find a solution to the ethnic conflict, first by negotiating with the LTTE and later by means of a parliamentary select committee, were not fruitful.

PRESIDENTIAL ELECTIONS. The president is elected by an all-island constituency in an election held in every six years. The single transferable vote method, where each voter is allowed to mark a first, second, and third preference, is used for voting. Any registered voter over the age of 35 who has been a member of parliament or any other registered voter who is nominated by a registered political party can be a candidate. Three presidential elections have been held in the country to date, the first in October 1982, the second in December 1988, and the third in November 1994. On the first two occasions the United National Party (UNP) (q.v.) candidates—Jayewardene and Premadasa, respectively—won obtaining more than 50 percent of the valid votes cast in the first count itself. On the third occasion, Chandrika Kumaratunga (q.v.) of the People's Alliance (PA) (q.v.) won with an unprecedented poll of 62.3 percent of the total valid vote. Given the fact that the Sinhalese-Buddhist account for only 70 percent of the electorate and that their vote traditionally is fairly evenly split between the UNP and Sri Lanka Freedom Party (q.v.), the ethnic and religious minority vote has become a decisive factor in presidential elections. In the first two elections the UNP secured the bulk of the minority vote and in the third, the PA received a majority of that vote.

PREVENTION OF TERRORISM ACT (PTA). Enacted in 1979, it gives extraordinary powers of arrest and detention to the police. Inter alia, the police can detain and keep in custody any person for a period of 18 months without producing the person before a magistrate. Under the ordinary law the police are required to do so within 24 hours of arrest. The PTA has been criticized by human rights activists as an antidemocratic law. The government has defended it on the grounds that extraordinary circumstances require extraordinary laws.

PROPORTIONAL REPRESENTATION (PR). The 1978 constitution (q.v.) introduced proportional representation (PR) in parliamentary elections, replacing the first past-the-post system. PR has also been adopted for provincial council and local authority elections. In parliamentary elections, each administrative district becomes an electorate. Registered political parties and independent groups nominate lists for each district. The voter must vote for one party and may also vote for up to three candidates of his or her choice from that party list. A party must poll a minimum of 5 percent of the valid vote to be qualified for a seat. The total number of seats available for the district is distributed among the parties according to the proportion of the total vote received by each party. The winning party is also given a bonus seat. The winners from each party list are chosen according to the total number of individual preference votes received by the candidates. PR has ensured more balanced representation in parliament and other elected bodies. It has also prevented steamrolling majorities being enjoyed by the governing party as they did in the 1970 and 1977 parliaments, respectively.

PROTESTANTS. Approximately 0.76 percent of the Sri Lankan population are Protestant Christians (q.v.). Many of them are middle-class and urban-dwellers.

PROVINCIAL COUNCILS (PCs). Established as a result of the Indo-Lanka Peace Accord and the 13th amendment to the constitution, PCs replaced the 1981 district development councils as the principal unit of regional government. The main goal of the PC system was to meet the Tamil demand for devolved power in the northeast. Under the Indo-Lanka Peace Accord (q.v.) the northern province and the eastern province were "temporarily" merged to form one council. Elections for all the PCs except that of the northeast were held in June 1988. The Sri Lanka Freedom Party (SLFP) (q.v.) boycotted the elections and the United National Party (UNP) (q.v.) won power in every province. Elections to the northeast PC were held in November 1988 and the Eelam People's Revolutionary Liberation Front (EPRLF) (q.v.) won power. The Liberation Tigers of Tamil Eelam (q.v.) boycotted the election. The northeast council was dissolved by the government in 1990 when the EPRLF tried to declare unilateral independence for the region. Fresh elections are yet to be held. The other PCs ran their full term.

Fresh elections were held in May 1993. The governing UNP won four with an absolute majority, and won a plurality without an absolute majority in two. In the Western provincial council, the largest of the seven, the SLFP won a plurality and formed a government with the support of the Democratic United National Front (q.v.). Chandrika Kumaratunga (q.v.) was elected to public office for the first time in these elections and held the position of chief minister of the Western PC until she became prime minister in August 1994. The PCs have very limited powers of taxation and depend on central government grants for a large share of their budgets. The central government has not handed over to the PCs some of the key functions such as the police that were slated for devolution under the 13th amendment.

PURANA **VILLAGE.** These are the "old" (*purana*) villages that survived the decline of the ancient Sinhalese civilization after about the 12th century A.D. in the northern and eastern planes of Sri Lanka. Most of these villages have now been integrated into new irrigation settlement schemes officially known as "colonization schemes" (q.v.).

R

REBELLION OF 1817-1818. Known as the Kandyan rebellion, it was a last-ditch attempt of the Kandyan aristocracy to oust the British, who they felt betrayed the Kandyans (q.v.) who supported them (the British) in 1815 against the last Kandyan king, Sri Vickrama Rajasingha. In particular the Kandyan leaders were displeased with the manner in which the British administration treated Buddhism for which special state patronage was promised in the 1815 Kandyan convention (q.v.). The rebellion lasted over 12 months. The superior British forces deployed crushed the rebellion and the rebel leaders were punished.

REBELLION OF 1848. A rebellion led by Puran Appu, a pretender to the Kandyan throne. There was some popular support for it on account of the widespread dissatisfaction with the land and other taxes imposed by the British. The rebellion sprang up in some of the less-accessible areas of the Kandyan region but was put down by the British using military force, and its leader was captured and executed.

RICE. Rice *(Oryza sativa)* is the staple food of the Sri Lankans. It has been grown from antiquity. Ancient Sri Lanka's hydraulic civilization that developed a complex irrigation system (q.v.) was based on a rice economy. Rice is cultivated in almost every part of the country except at the highest elevations in the central highlands. In 1934 about 930,000 ha were under the crop. Some of it is rain-fed but the most successful are the dryer north-central and eastern parts of the country that have irrigation. It is almost entirely a small farmer crop with the typical unit not more than one ha. If water is available, two crops *(Maha* and *Yala)* are harvested. From the early 1960s rice production has steadily risen partly due to the impact of the green revolution (adoption of high-yielding varieties and chemical fertilizer under irrigated conditions) and the expansion of area under cultivation via extension of irrigation facilities such as those proved under the Mahaveli scheme (q.v.). At independence Sri Lanka produced only one-third of the rice that was required for domestic consumption. In 1948 at independence the country produced about 460,000 metric tons of paddy per year. In 1994 it was 2.7 million, slightly less than 0.5 percent of world production. This increase has helped Sri Lanka to be almost self-sufficient in rice, a

152 percent increase in population during the intervening period notwithstanding.

RIVERS. The rivers of Sri Lanka radiate from the central highlands. There are 16 rivers that exceed 100 km in length each, but with the exception of the 335 km Mahaveli, the rest are less than 160 km. Many are tapped for irrigation (q.v.) and hydropower (q.v.). The preeminent among them is the Mahaveli Project.

RUBBER. Sri Lanka's second leading cash crop after tea (q.v.). The rubber plant *(Hevea brasiliensis)* was introduced to the island in 1876. It rapidly developed as a cash crop after the turn of the century when the demand for rubber from the automobile industry increased. The area under the crop rose from 800 ha in 1900 to over 60,000 ha by 1910. By the mid 1920s it had risen to 178,000 ha. At the end of 1994 it was 161,479 ha.

Rubber is grown in the southwest quadrant of the island on hill slopes mostly less than 600 m in elevation located in areas receiving at least 2,000 mm of annual rainfall. About two workers are needed per hectare of rubber for tapping.

From 1972-1975 the Sirimavo Bandaranaike administration took over the larger rubber plantations that accounted for 30 percent of the land area. A large proportion of the rubber is in small holdings that are less than 10 ha per unit. In 1994 Sri Lanka's total product was 105 million kg that accounted for a little under 2 percent of world natural rubber production. About 2 percent of the nation's export earnings are from rubber. In the mid 1950s the European Community countries and Pakistan have been the leading buyers of Sri Lankan rubber.

S

SAMAAJAVAADAYA. The Sinhalese term for socialism. Sri Lanka's socialist parties such as the *Lanka Sama Samaja Party* (q.v.), Community Party (q.v.), and the left-of-center Sri Lanka Freedom Party (q.v.), at least before the collapse of communist regimes in central and eastern Europe, expounded a brand of socialism that favored, inter alia, nationalization, import substitution, state intervention, and extensive state-funded social welfare programs. Sri Lankan socialism also discouraged foreign investment, and was unenthusiastic about aid from Western sources. Before the collapse of the Soviet Union and its satellite regimes in central and eastern Europe, this label was practically essential to gain political acceptance in Sri Lanka. For example, even the pro-capitalist United National Party (q.v.) administration of J. R. Jayewardene (q.v.) retained the nomenclature "Democratic Socialist Republic of Sri Lanka" in the 1978 constitution. However, of late the term has lost much of its appeal, partly due to the failure of socialist regimes globally and partly due to the strong appeal of the pro market polices of the Sri Lanka government to a majority of the voters. The People's Alliance (q.v.) and its constituent parties have also abandoned socialism in favor of pro market policies.

SANGHA. The Buddhist order of monks. According to Buddhist tradition both male and female *Sangha* orders were established in Sri Lanka in the third century B.C. during the reign of King Devanampiya Tissa. The current male order is divided into several sects call *Nikayas* (q.v.). A full-fledged female order no longer exists. It is estimated that there are more than 60,000 male members of the *Sangha* in the order today.

SATYAGRAHA. Meaning righteous protest, this is resorted to as a means of "nonviolent" political protest. However, in the Sri Lankan political context, the nuance of the term generally suggests "militant" protest that in practice could mean some violence as well. In point of fact, in almost every instance of a *satyagraha* such as the one in August 1953 to protest the cut in the rice subsidy or the July 1987 protest against the Indo-Lanka Peace Accord (q.v.), some violence has resulted either due to the action of the protesters or the action of the police (q.v.).

SCHOOLS. In ancient Sri Lanka, literacy was acquired largely through the temple and the monastery, a tradition that still continues with temple schools known as *Pirivenas.* Thus many of Sri Lanka's best-known works of classical Sinhala (q.v.) literature have been the work of members of the *Sangha.* Calvinist missionaries who came to the island during Dutch (q.v.) rule in the 18th century established a network of schools with the intention of gaining religious converts. School education expanded rapidly under the British after 1869 when a generous scheme of state funding for private schools was instituted. At the beginning, most of the assistance went to Christian missionary schools, but gradually Buddhist, Hindu, and Muslim organizations also used state subsidies for their own schools. At independence (q.v.) in 1948 the country had 4,537 primary and secondary schools and a literacy (q.v.) rate of 58 percent, one of the highest for a developing country at that time.

At the end of 1994 Sri Lanka had a total of 10,193 government and 567 private primary and secondary schools with a student population of

4.3 million The percentage of children in the six to 11 age group enrolled in schools in 1992 was 107 percent. The secondary school enrollment ratio (12 to 17 age group) is 77 percent. The total teacher population in 1994 was 195,000, yielding a pupil/teacher ratio of 22:1. In 1994 the government spent 7.5 percent (Rs 15 billion) of its total budget on education. On the positive side, the extensive school network has produced a high level of literacy, helped to establish a greater measure of socioeconomic equity, and met some of the manpower requirements of the economy. On the negative side it has been faulted for producing too many graduates without specific skills that are needed for employment in a modern economy.

SENANAYAKE, DON STEPHEN (1884-1952). Senanayake, the first prime minister of independent Sri Lanka, is revered by many Sri Lankans as the "Father of the Nation" for his leadership role in negotiating with the British for the country's independence. Senanayake left school to accept a position as a clerk in government but soon left the job to manage his family properties. He and his two brothers inherited a considerable fortune from their father. The father and three sons entered politics through the temperance movement in the 1910s. Senanayake was jailed by the British for his alleged complicity in the 1915 Sinhalese-Muslim riots. In truth he worked hard, together with his brothers, to prevent the spread of the riots. Senanayake first entered the national legislature in 1924. From that year onward he served the body without a break until his death in 1952. At every election bar the one in 1947, he was returned uncontested. Senanayake quickly established himself as a leader in the nationalist movement, no mean achievement in an arena dominated by lawyers, doctors, and other professionals. This bore testimony to his shrewd judgment and common-sense approach to issues. He shared the leadership in the nationalist movement with D. B. Jayatilaka until 1943 after which he took over. The constitution that Senanayake's advisers drafted for him in 1944 was the one that was adopted by the Soulbury Commission (q.v.) to grant Sri Lanka internal self-government in 1947. From that point it was a minor step to independence and Senanayake, and his colleagues pressured the British administration into granting it in 1948.

Senanayake assumed the premiership in 1947 and held that position until his death in 1952. He took a special interest in the problems of the peasantry and agriculture. He soon developed an expert knowledge and understanding of the subject that made him the automatic choice for the position of minister of agriculture and lands in the 1931 State Council. He also became a member of the Land Commission of 1927 that formulated the land policy that led to the peasant colonization schemes (q.v.). Senanayake was largely responsible for the Land Development Ordinance of 1935 that provided the legal framework for colonization in the last half century. His son, Dudley Senanayake (q.v.), who became prime minister on three occasions, also took a special interest in agriculture, inspired by his father.

SENANAYAKE, DUDLEY SHELTON (1911-1973). Prime minister of Sri Lanka on three occasions, he was educated in Cambridge and was a lawyer by training. Dudley Senanayake came from a political family. He was the elder son of D. S. Senanayake (q.v.), the first prime minister of Sri Lanka. He was an accomplished sportsman in school. In 1935 he returned to Sri Lanka from Cambridge and started a law practice. In 1936 he contested a seat in the State Council elections and won. Following his father's footsteps he also took a special interest in agriculture, securing membership in the State Council committee that dealt with the subject. From 1939 to 1942 he joined J. R. Jayewardene (q.v.) as joint secretary of the Ceylon National Congress (q.v.) to reorganize and revitalize it. In the 1947 election he won the Dedigama seat and entered the cabinet as Minister of agriculture. It was during his tenure that the Gal Oya multipurpose irrigation scheme (q.v.) was completed. Dudley Senanayake succeeded his father to the premiership in March 1952 on the latter's sudden death. He soon dissolved parliament and won a decisive mandate from the electorate in the election that followed.

The economic crisis precipitated by the collapse of Sri Lanka's export commodity prices in the aftermath of the Korean War made the Senanayake administration take some unpopular steps such as a reduction in the consumer rice subsidy. This was exploited by the prime minister's political opponents. About this time his health also failed. Senanayake resigned from the premiership in September 1953 to be succeeded by Sir John Kotelawala (q.v.). Following the United National Party's (UNP) defeat in 1956, Senanayake returned to the UNP in 1959 to resume leadership. The UNP won the largest number of seats for any single party in the March 1960 general elections and formed a minority government. It was defeated in the Throne Speech debate. Parliament was dissolved and in fresh elections the UNP lost to the Sri Lanka Freedom Party (q.v.) led by Mrs. Sirimavo Bandaranaike (q.v.). Dudley Senanayake became the leader of the opposition. In 1965 the UNP won the general elections. During his stewardship as prime minister from 1965 to 1970 he launched a highly successful food production program that substantially raised the output of rice and some other subsidiary food crops. He made a serious bid to solve the ethnic problem by devolving power to a system of regional councils. That, however, failed due to strong opposition from Sinhalese groups. In the 1970 elections the UNP suffered a humiliating defeat that demoralized Senanayake. He never recovered from it. Between 1970-1972 the leadership of the party shifted to J. R. Jayewardene almost by default. Senanayake died on April 13, 1973 after a brief period of ill health. He will be best remembered for his contribution to Sri Lanka's agricultural development and for his commitment to liberal democracy.

SENATE. The upper house of the bicameral parliament (q.v.) that Sri Lanka had from 1947 to 1972. Fifteen of the 30 members were elected by secret ballot of members of parliament and the other 15 were appointed by the governor-general on the recommendation of the prime minister each for a six-year term. In principle, the Senate was meant to provide an opportunity for persons distinguished in their own fields but were unwilling or unable to enter the hustings to make a contribution to public life. The Senate had only delaying powers over legislation; a finance bill could be delayed up to one month and any other up to one year. The main purpose was to prevent the government from rushing through legislation without adequate public debate. The 1947-1948 constitution required that the minister of justice be from the Senate. In her first administration (1960-1965) Prime Minister Sirimavo Bandaranaike (q.v.) was a member of the Senate. She abolished the Senate in her second administration.

SINDHIS. Another very small cultural minority of Indian origin that also live largely in Colombo and engage themselves in various business pursuits.

SINHALA. The language of the Sinhalese people. Originating from a mixture of spoken dialects (Prakrits) of Sanskrit origin, Sinhala as a distinct language developed from about the fifth century C.E.

SINHALA CINEMA. The first Sinhala film was *Kadavunu Poronduwa* (Broken Promise) produced in 1950. Since then the Sinhala cinema has developed along two distinct lines. One, largely aimed at the box office and popular entertainment, has closely followed the popular Indian Hindi cinema produced in Bombay. The majority of the Sinhala films that are produced fall into this category. The second category of films deal with more serious themes. Lester James Peiris pioneered this tradition in Sri Lanka.

SINHALA CREATIVE WRITING. The Sinhala creative writing — short story, novel, and verse — has undergone significant change since the times of Martin Wickremasinghe who is considered the first serious creative writer, to publish his works in the 1950s. Some of his works such as the novel *Gam Peraliya* dealt with social change. Others such as *Viragaya* dealt with personal introspective themes. The more recent works have been heavily influenced by contemporary socioeconomic and political problems facing Sri Lankan society and by postmodernist works from the West. Thus sexual exploitation of females, ethical problem, and workers who go to West Asia have become popular themes for writers such as Somaweera Senanayake, Ranjith Dharmakeerthi, and Weerapokune Uparatane and Monica Ruwanpathirana, who rank among the leading contemporary Sinhala creative writers.

SINHALA DRAMA. E. R. Sarachchandra's *Maname* produced in 1956 is considered as the first work in modern Sinhala drama. It was inspired by the folk drama tradition. His pioneering production established one principal strand of contemporary Sinhala dramatic form. However, the Sinhala drama today is more pluralistic. Productions with political themes such as state oppression and those that deal with social issues such as exploitation of women have become popular. It is a "theater with a purpose". Some critics see such productions as being forceful but lacking in finesse.

SINHALA MAHA SABHA. An organization founded by S. W. R. D. Bandaranaike (q.v.) in 1932 to mobilize radical Sinhalese nationalist forces first in the struggle for independence and later to achieve Sinhalese nationalist goals such as making Sinhala the official language. It also served as a useful forum for Bandaranaike to achieve his personal political ambitions and formed an important part of the *1956 Mahajana Eksath Peramuna* (q.v.) coalition.

SINHALA ONLY. The language policy in the 1956 Official Language Act (q.v.) that made Sinhala the only official language replacing English. This policy is held largely responsible for the alienation of Tamils who demanded that the Tamil language be given parity of status. In 1958 legislative provision was made for the use of Tamil in official business. In practice, there was never a Sinhala-only policy in the literal sense. For example, education from kindergarten through university was available in the Tamil medium. Tamil speakers transacted much of their business with the state in that language. However, Tamils generally believe that the government language policy severely discriminated against them. The 1972 Constitution (q.v.) that enshrined Sinhala as the official language is cited as an example. In the 1978 Constitution (q.v.) Tamil was made a national language and in 1988 an official language. Nevertheless, some sections of the Tamil community complain, with some justification, that facilities are inadequate to implement the full use of Tamil as an official language.

SINHALA-MUSLIM RIOTS OF 1915. Started in Kandy as the result of a dispute between the Sinhalese and the Muslims over the question of a Buddhist street pageant passing a mosque beating drums. The incident simply brought to a head the pent-up adversarial feelings that each community harbored toward the other induced largely by economic rivalry. The communal clashes resulted in several deaths and extensive damage to property belonging to both communities. The British administration reacted by incarcerating leading Sinhalese political leaders.

SINHALESE. The people of Sri Lanka who are native speakers of the Sinhala (q.v.) language. About 74 percent (13.5 million at the end of 1995) of the Sri Lankan population (18.2 million) are Sinhalese. They traditionally trace their origins to migration from West Bengal about 2,500 years ago. However, historical evidence suggests a more mixed origin with migrants from many parts of India settling on the island over a period of years. During the course of time inter-marriage between the immigrants and the Proto-Austroloid native *Vedda* (q.v.) population would have taken place. In time they developed their own language— Sinhala (q.v.)—and culture, adopted Buddhism as the predominant religion in the third century B.C., and established an advanced agricultural civilization based on a sophisticated irrigation system (q.v.). The height of the ancient Sinhalese civilization was achieved in the period first century B.C. to the 12th. Today the Sinhalese dominate the island's politics and are engaged in a bitter ethnic battle with the Sri Lankan Tamils in the north. The Sinhalese are generally known as a community who are easygoing and very hospitable.

SINHALESE-BUDDHIST. Sinhalese Buddhists constitute about 69 percent (12.6 million at the end of 1995) of the Sri Lankan population. There is a debate among scholars about the nature of Sinhalese-Buddhist nationalism. Some assert that it is an exclusive nationalism that does not accommodate the non-Sinhalese-Buddhist sections of society. This attitude is identified as a major causal factor of the current ethnic conflict. Some others reject that argument and point out that the Sinhalese-Buddhists historically have been a very tolerant and accommodative community. According to them, Sri Lanka's dominant culture being Sinhalese-Buddhist is a historical given that is unavoidable. Minorities must adjust to that fact while the Sinhalese-Buddhists must reach out to the minorities and accommodate their special needs. In reality it is hard to lump all Sinhalese-Buddhists under either of these categories. There are different shades of opinion on the kind of relationship that they should have with minorities and the nature of the polity that the country must nurture.

SOULBURY COMMISSION. A British-appointed three-person commission led by Lord Soulbury that came to Sri Lanka in 1944 to examine the prospects for granting independence (q.v.) to the country. It recommended granting of independence and also provided the basic framework for the 1947 constitution (q.v.).

SOUTH ASIAN ASSOCIATION FOR REGIONAL COOPERATION (SAARC). Founded in 1985, SAARC is the regional association that is designed to promote cooperation among the South Asian countries. It has a secretariat located in Kathmandu, Nepal. Sri Lanka's President Premadasa (q.v.) was elected to chair the group in 1991 and it was Sri Lanka's turn to host the summit in 1992. However, it had to be postponed on two occasions, once due to the inability of the King of Bhutan to attend the meeting and, on the other, the inability of the Indian Prime Minister Narasimha Rao to attend. On both occasions many observers felt that it was an attempt on the part of India to snub Sri Lanka's President Premadasa whose relations with India were rather shaky. SAARC has achieved very little by way of regional cooperation. The rules of the Association preclude bilateral issues being discussed at SAARC forums. India insists on adhering to this rule to prevent the smaller member countries from bringing up bilateral disputes with India and ganging up against it. This prevented Sri Lanka from raising its dispute with India over the latter's assistance to the Tamil rebels in SAARC. Moves are afoot to establish a South Asian Preferential Trading Arrangement (SAPTA). To date SAARC has yielded very little tangible benefits to Sri Lanka.

SOUTH ASIAN FEDERATION GAMES (SAF). SAF is the South Asian regional umbrella sports body. As a member nation, Sri Lanka hosted the fourth SAF Games in 1992 in Colombo.

SPICES. From antiquity Sri Lanka was renowned for its spices. Indian, Greek, and Roman traders and later Arab, Portuguese (q.v.), and Dutch (q.v.) traders were attracted to the island by its spices. The principal spices are cinnamon, pepper, cloves, cardamom, and nutmeg with a total area of about 40,000 ha. All are cultivated in the wet southwest quadrant of the country. In 1994 together spices earned about Rs 2 billion in foreign exchange, accounting for 1.3 percent of total exports.

SRI LANKA. Meaning the resplendent island, this has been the traditional name of the country from antiquity. The word Lanka is also found in an ancient Indian language called Mundari that does not belong to any of the main language groups of the Indian sub-continent. Until 1972 when the name Sri Lanka was officially adopted in the 1972 Constitution (q.v.), it was known as Ceylon, the name adopted by the British.

SRI LANKA ADMINISTRATIVE SERVICE (SLAS). This is the principal arm of the government bureaucracy and replaced the Ceylon Civil Service (q.v.) in 1963. SLAS officers occupy almost all the middle and senior positions in government. The 1995 cadre is 3,550. The bulk of the SLAS officers are recruited through an open competitive examination and an interview open to graduates. A smaller number is recruited from among the ranks of the senior clerical grades.

SRI LANKA FREEDOM PARTY (SLFP). Founded in 1951 by S. W. R. D. Bandaranaike (q.v.), the SLFP is one of the two major political parties in Sri Lanka. The party was the principal constituent of the April 1956-1959 *Mahajana Eksath Peramuna* (q.v.) government. Following Bandaranaike's assassination in September 1959, his widow Sirimavo R. D. Bandaranaike (q.v.) took over the party leadership that she still holds 36 years later. The SLFP again governed the country between July 1960 and March 1965 and between May 1970 and July 1977 sometime with the support of Marxists (q.v.). In August 1994 it was returned to power as the principal party of the People's Alliance (PA) (q.v.). Traditionally the principal source of electoral support for the party comes from the rural Sinhalese-Buddhists (q.v.) and the urban lower-middle and working-class. However, as a constituent party of the PA it attracted extensive minority support, especially in the 1994 presidential election won by its candidate Chandrika Kumaratunga (q.v.).

Traditionally SLFP policies have broadly been nationalist and left-of-center favoring nationalization and state control of key sectors and subsidized social welfare programs. Its landmark legislations include the Official Languages Act of 1956 (q.v.) and the nationalization of

Western petroleum distribution companies (1962) and plantations (1972/5). For the 1994 parliamentary elections and presidential election the party together with the PA revamped its economic policies in favor of a market-oriented strategy. The foreign policy of the SLFP has traditionally been somewhat anti-Western. In the current post-Cold War environment this too has been modified and the party is more favorably disposed toward the West. However, it continues its strong support for the Non-Aligned Movement (q.v.).

For a long time the party's efforts to regain power was hampered by the absence of an acceptable successor to replace Mrs. Bandaranaike (80) (q.v.). The issue was resolved when Anura Bandaranaike (q.v.), the son of Mrs. Bandaranaike, who gave leadership to the right-wing of the SLFP left the party in 1991 to join the United National Party (q.v.). Chandrika Kumaratunga, one of the two daughters of Mrs. Bandaranaike, rejoined the party in 1990. She had the support of the left-wing of the party and became the de facto leader of the SLFP. She led the party to a series of victories at the polls that started with the Southern Provincial Council elections in 1993 and culminated in her own victory in the 1994 November presidential election.

SRI LANKA MAHAJANA PAKSHAYA (SLMP). Founded in 1984 as a radical socialist party by the actor-turned-politician Vijaya Kumaranatunga. Kumaranatunga's wife, Chandrika (q.v.), who is the second daughter of Mrs. Sirimavo Bandaranaike (q.v.) was a key figure in the SLMP (Sri Lanka People's Party) until she left it in 1990 to form her own party *Bahujana Nidahas Pakshaya* following the assassination of her husband, suspected to be the work of a *Janatha Vimukthi Peramuna* (q.v.) gunman. After 1990 the SLMP split into two factions. One, under Ossie Abeygunasekera, got increasingly associated with President Premadasa (q.v.) and the United National Party (q.v.). The other joined the People's Alliance (q.v.) as one of its constituent parties.

SRI LANKAN TAMILS. This term is used to describe the 12 percent (2.2 million at the end of 1995) of the country's population who are Tamil speakers (excluding Muslims (q.v.) who are also Tamil speakers) and are natives of the north and east. About two-thirds of the Sri Lankan Tamil community live in that part of the country and the balance in the south, largely in Colombo. They trace their ancestry to immigrants from South India in antiquity. Thus they are to be distinguished from the Indian Tamils (q.v.) in Sri Lanka who came to the country after about 1825. The Sri Lankan Tamils had their own kingdom in Jaffna for a limited period of time from about the 13th century to the 17th. They developed a strong Hindu Tamil culture. From the 1920s Sri Lankan Tamil leaders were an integral element of the national leadership that led the movement for independence from British rule. However, they gradually drifted away over language (q.v.) and other policies that affected the Tamil community. From the late 1970s Tamil separatist groups, the Liberation Tigers of Tamil Eelam (q.v.) in particular, have been engaged in a bloody civil war with the Sri Lankan government. Sri Lankan Tamils are generally perceived to be a hardworking and thrifty community.

SRI PADA (ADAM'S PEAK). With a height of 2,243 meters this is the fifth highest mountain peak in Sri Lanka. It is located in the central highland tea (q.v.) growing area and is the source of origin of some of Sri Lanka's major rivers including the Mahaveli. Thus it is of critical importance to the ecology of the country. It also has great religious significance to Sri Lankan Buddhists (q.v.) and Christians (q.v.). The latter believe that Adam lived somewhere in the vicinity of the peak, hence its Anglicized name. Buddhists believe that Buddha on His third visit to the country visited the peak and left his footprint. Hence the Sinhalese name for the peak *Sri Pada* (Resplendent foot). Buddhists go on a pilgrimage to climb the mountain every year in large numbers between December and May. A Buddhist shrine is found on the summit of the mountain.

STATE COUNCIL. The legislature established on the basis of a proposal made by the Donoughmore Commission (q.v.), it functioned from 1931 to 1947 until its replacement by a parliament (q.v.). The state council consisted of 61 members of whom 50 were elected from territorial constituencies by voters exercising universal franchise, eight nominated and three were state officials. The council also acted as an executive body by dividing itself into seven executive committees in charge of different subjects. The chairperson of each committee became the minister responsible for the subject concerned.

STATE RELIGION. Sri Lanka has no state religion. However, both the 1972 Constitution (q.v.) as well as the 1978 Constitution (q.v.) state that Buddhism shall be accorded the "foremost place" and that " —it shall be the duty of the State to protect and foster the Buddha *Sasana,* while assuring all religions the rights granted (by the Constitution)."

SUPREME COURT. The supreme court is the highest appellate court of the land. It is headed by the chief justice and has no fewer than six and not more than ten other judges. All supreme court judges including the chief justice are appointed by the president. Once appointed they cannot be removed without an impeachment motion passed in parliament.

T

TAMIL CONGRESS (TC). The TC was founded in 1944 under the leadership of G. G. Ponnambalam (q.v.), the father of the present leader Kumar Ponnambalam. It entered the United National Party-led government of D. S. Senanayake (q.v.) in 1947, and G. G. Ponnambalam held the cabinet portfolio for trade and commerce. It left the government in 1950 in a dispute over language policy. The TC split in 1949 with a more radical Tamil nationalist group led by S. J. V. Chelvanayakam (q.v.) forming the Federal Party (q.v.). By the mid 1950s the former had lost its position as the leading Tamil political party to the latter. The current TC leader Kumar Ponnambalam unsuccessfully contested the 1982 presidential election. The TC has no visible public support base at present and currently has no members in parliament.

TAMIL EELAM LIBERATION ORGANIZATION (TELO). Founded in 1977 as the political wing of the Tamil Eelam Liberation Army, TELO developed close links with India, especially the Indian intelligence agency Research and Analysis Wing.

TAMIL HOMELAND. Sri Lankan Tamils (q.v.) claim that the northeast constitutes their homeland. This is strongly disputed by the Sinhalese. The Tamil claim is based primarily on two arguments. One is the historical fact that there was an independent Jaffna kingdom in the north from about the 13th century to the 17th century. The other is the demography of the area in the early part of this century when Tamils were in a majority in the north as well as in the east.

The Sinhalese (q.v.) generally concede that the north has been traditionally inhabited by Tamils. However, they reject similar claims made for the east. It is pointed out that historically the east was a part of the Kandyan (q.v.) kingdom until the Dutch (q.v.) took over the maritime provinces in the 18th century. Demographically, in the early part of this century, Tamil settlements in the east were largely limited to a thin strip of land along the seacoast. In the interior there were scattered old Sinhalese villages (*purana* villages) (q.v.) that were remnants of an older Sinhalese civilization that had disappeared several centuries ago. Therefore some Sinhalese claim that the east is a traditional Sinhalese homeland. At present about 40 percent of the population of the province is Muslim (q.v.), who also stake a claim to the area. Thus the large majority among the Sinhalese and Muslims adhere to the notion that the east has always been an area of mixed ethnicity and is therefore not the exclusive homeland of any one ethnic group. In any event many Sinhalese argue that no part of Sri Lanka could be set aside as a homeland for one ethnic group.

TAMIL LANGUAGE (SPECIAL PROVISIONS) ACT OF 1958. This was passed to provide for the use of Tamil in administration and the judiciary. However, Tamils continue to point out that the government has failed to fully implement the act.

TAMIL LITERATURE AND ARTS. In the late 1950s and 1960s Sri Lankan Tamil creative writers spoke of a Sri Lankan Tamil literature as opposed to a South Indian Tamil literature. However, the South Indian tradition was too strongly felt to achieve a total escape from it. Moreover, Western creative arts also exerted a strong influence on Tamil literature and creative arts in Sri Lanka.

In drama, dialogue mixed with music and song in the Indian tradition were the most popular form. From the 1950s until the early 1980s some of the younger Tamil dramatists experimented with adaptations of Western plays by writers such as Bretch and Tennessee Williams. Plays with social themes that condemned caste or the dowry system were also produced.

In poetry, Tamil writers in the late 1950s and early 1960s made an attempt to establish a Sri Lankan tradition that was independent of the South Indian tradition. Tamil newspapers regularly published the "free" verse compositions of these writers.

Newspapers were the main avenue of publication for Sri Lankan Tamil short-story writers also. Tamil novelists and other creative writers in the 1960s and 1970s were also influenced by socialist and nationalist ideas. Influenced by Western literature they also experimented with the spoken idiom and more contemporary themes. These led to debates with the traditionalists who wished to adhere to the classical South Indian forms. Since 1983 the ethnic war has affected Tamil literature and creative arts. Many writers have left Sri Lanka permanently. In Jaffna the Liberation Tigers of Tamil Eelam has encouraged the production of plays and writings with political themes.

TAMIL SEPARATIST MOVEMENT. The conceptual origins of Tamil separatism can be traced back to the 1950s when C. Suntheralingam, a Tamil academic and a cabinet minister in the 1947 D. S. Senanayake (q.v.) administration, in a letter to Prime Minister S. W. R. D. Bandaranaike (q.v.) expressed the view that it was no longer possible for the Tamils and Sinhalese to live as one nation and mooted the idea of an independent Tamil *Illanka* (Ceylon).

The current, more violent phase of the separatist movement originated in the Tamil politics of the 1970s. In particular, the Tamil Student League and the Tamil Youth League, the youth wing of the principal Tamil political party Tamil United Liberation Front (q.v.), got rapidly radicalized in the 1970s in response to what it perceived were discriminatory policies of the Colombo governments and the failure of the traditional Tamil leadership to find solutions to Tamil problems through the regular political process. By the early 1980s there were a number of Tamil separatist groups fighting the Sri Lankan government forces in guerrilla warfare. However, after the July 1983 ethnic riots (q.v.), the Liberation Tigers of Tamil Eelam (LTTE) (q.v.) emerged as the principal separatist group. They and other groups developed bases in Tamil Nadu and enjoyed the hospitality of the Tamil Nadu government and politicians. Several of these groups also received assistance with arms and training from the Research and Analysis Wing (RAW), the secret service of the Indian government. The internecine warfare in the separatist movement that took place in the 1980s resulted in the LTTE practically wiping out its rival groups from Jaffna. Several of the latter moved to Colombo and have joined the mainstream political process.

TAMIL UNITED LIBERATION FRONT (TULF). Formed in 1976 as an umbrella political party led by the Federal Party (FP) (q.v.), and including Tamil Congress (q.v.) and the Ceylon Workers Congress (q.v.). The TULF effectively replaced the FP as the leading Tamil political party. Its 1976 Vadukkoddai convention resolution calling for a separate Tamil state was included in the 1977 party election manifesto. In the northern province the party polled 60 percent of the valid vote cast and won all 14 seats, and in the east it polled 42 percent of the vote and four out of nine seats that it contested. It emerged as the largest opposition party in parliament, and the TULF leader Appapillai Amirthalingam (q.v.) became the leader of the opposition. TULF members of parliament forfeited their seats en bloc in 1983 when they refused to take an oath of allegiance to Sri Lanka as required by the 13th amendment to the constitution. After July 1983 most of the TULF leaders went into exile in Madras. Several of them, including

Amirthalingam, were assassinated by the LTTE. They won ten seats in the 1989 general elections but only five in the 1994 elections. The TULF no longer wields the influence that it once enjoyed in Tamil and Sri Lankan national politics.

TEA. Sri Lanka's best-known export product. Tea *(Camellia sinesis)* was introduced to Sri Lanka by the British in the 1860s as a commercial plantation crop. By the turn of the century over 162,000 ha had been brought under the crop. By 1948 this had risen to over 200,000 ha. The current extent is 220,000 ha. Tea is grown on mountain slopes in the southwest quadrant (wet zone) of the island, which receives a well-distributed and reliable rainfall of over 1,900 mm per year. The elevations range from above 1,200 m for "high-grown" teas (33 percent of the total area), to below 600 m for "low-grown" teas (29 percent) and elevations in between for the "mid-grown" teas.

Tea was the principal source of income and wealth in the colonial economy and still occupies an important place in the economy. Until the tea plantations were nationalized in 1972-1975, the industry was largely in the hands of the private-sector. For the next two decades the larger estates were run as state enterprises. In the early 1990s they were handed over to private management companies. Starting in 1995 there was a move to sell them back to the private-sector. In 1993 Sri Lanka's tea output was 232 million kg (12 percent of world output). The island is the world's preeminent tea exporter and the second largest black tea producer after India.

Until the mid 1980s tea was Sri Lanka's leading export accounting for as much as 35 percent of total export earning. In 1994 this was down to 13.2 percent (Rs 21 billion). The bulk of the product is sold at the Colombo Tea Auction. The Middle East has been the biggest market in recent years accounting for about half of total exports.

TEMPERANCE MOVEMENT. Founded in the late 19th century by Christian organizations to discourage the use and spread of alcohol, it was taken over by Buddhist leaders in the early years of the 20th century and converted to a broader campaign against "Westernization" and "Christianization" that were seen as the reasons for the spread of alcohol consumption. The Temperance Movement served as a forum for the revival of Sinhalese Buddhist nationalism. Anagarika Dharmapala (q.v.) was one of its most prominent leaders.

TERRORISM. A controversial term in the Sri Lankan context. The government and sections of the Sinhalese public generally view Tamil separatist groups, especially the Liberation Tigers of Tamil Eelam (LTTE) (q.v.), who resort to violence as "terrorist" organizations. The groups themselves and probably the majority of the Tamils view them as "liberation fighters". Before Rajiv Gandhi's assassination, India also viewed almost all these groups as such. However, after the assassination, for which several LTTE men including the Tiger leader Prabhakaran (q.v.) himself have been indicted in Madras, the Indian and the Tamil Nadu governments as well as many other sections of the Indian community view them, particularly the LTTE, as terrorists. Between 1993 and early 1996 the LTTE lost much of the international sympathy it enjoyed previously when it assassinated several Sri Lankan leaders and bombed civilian targets causing heavy casualties.

TESAVALAMAI. A code of civil law that is applied in northern Sri Lanka in the Tamil community. The principal laws under this system relate to personal law and land law.

TOOTH RELIC. The Tooth Relic of the Buddha now housed in the *Sri Dalada Maligawa* in Kandy is an object of great veneration to the Buddhists of Sri Lanka and elsewhere. It was brought to Sri Lanka in the fourth century A.D.

TOURISM. Sri Lanka has enormous potential as a tourist destination. It has, among other things, a tropical climate, lush green vegetation, excellent beaches, several sites of historical and cultural interest, and a people who are well known to be hospitable toward guests. In the last two decades the government and the private sector invested heavily in developing a physical infrastructure for the industry. As a result the country has a relatively good network of hotels and other facilities. It is also competitive in terms of price for an Asian tourist destination. Most of the tourists who come to Sri Lanka are from Western Europe. In 1993 Sri Lanka received a little over 405,000 tourists. This number is still less than the 410,000 achieved in 1982 before the ethnic conflict (q.v.) intensified but is a significant improvement on the numbers recorded between 1984 and 1990. The industry has generated about 50,000 jobs. In 1994 the country earned Rs 11 billion in foreign exchange from the industry. The future of the industry will depend much on political stability and bringing to an end the current ethnic conflict (q.v.).

U

UNITED FRONT (UF). The coalition led by the Sri Lanka Freedom Party (SLFP) (q.v.) that won the 1970 general elections. It formed a left-of-center government that lasted until 1975 when the *Lanka Sama Samaja Party* (q.v.) and Communist Party (Moscow) (q.v.), who were the minor partners, left the government. The UF implemented several programs of a radical nature, most notably the nationalization of plantations (land reform) and more state control and takeover of trading. The UF anticipated substantial foreign assistance from socialist countries that did not materialize. The first Organization of Petroleum Exporting Countries oil crisis (1972-1973) and sharp increases in prices of imported foods and domestic policy failures made its economic stewardship a difficult one. Eventually failures in economic policy contributed to the heavy electoral defeat of the SLFP and its erstwhile coalition partners in 1977.

UNITED NATIONAL PARTY (UNP). Formed in 1947 under the leadership of D. S. Senanayake (q.v.) as the successor to the Ceylon National Congress. It was originally associated with the traditional aristocratic elite and the English-educated Westernized elite of the country. However, under J. R. Jayewardene's (q.v.) leadership (1971-1988) it gradually shed this image and under Premadasa (1979-1993) (q.v.) it acquired a more populist "party of the common man/woman" image. It probably has the best political machine among the country's major political parties. However, as in all other Sri Lankan political parties there is not much internal democracy within the party.

The UNP has governed the country from 1947 to 1955, 1965 to 1969, and from 1977 to 1994. It is the principal right-of-center political party in Sri Lanka. Party policy has always favored market-oriented economic policy. Its foreign policy has traditionally been pro-Western although the country has remained in the nonaligned movement under its administrations as well. The UNP prides itself on achieving a peaceful transfer of power from Britain in 1948 under D. S. Senanayake's leadership. Its land-settlement policies have been largely responsible for the large irrigation and peasant colonization schemes (q.v.) in the "dry zone" (q.v.) of the country. The 1977 UNP government reversed the socialist and statist economic policies of the previous Sri Lanka Freedom Party (q.v.) administrations and launched a liberal market-oriented capitalist development strategy. Its social policies are committed to the provision of basic human needs but state subsidies are subject to more means testing. Both in 1965-1970 as well as in 1977-1994 the party tried to evolve a more accommodative policy toward the Tamils but failed to come up with a lasting solution to the ethnic conflict (q.v.). But its alliance with the Ceylon Workers Congress (q.v.) between 1977 and 1994 helped to bring the Indian Tamil (q.v.) community in the plantations to the mainstream of national politics. In 1994, after 17 years in office, it lost both the parliamentary elections as well as the presidential election to the People's Alliance (q.v.). Widespread corruption among some members of the government and the desire of the voters for "new faces" were two of the principal reasons for the defeat.

UNITED NATIONS (UN). Sri Lanka became a member of the UN in 1955. It took seven years after independence to obtain membership because of Soviet opposition on the grounds that Sri Lanka was a pro-Western country. Sri Lanka's position at the UN on major international issues has been influenced largely by domestic factors. During the Cold War period, in general, when the United National Party (q.v.) has been in power, the voting has been pro-Western and when the Sri Lanka Freedom Party (q.v.) has been in power more anti-Western. Both regimes have generally voted with the Arabs on the Israel-Palestine issue. Between 1955 and 1993 Sri Lanka received US$137 million in assistance from the United Nations Development Program and another US$32 million from other UN agencies.

UNIVERSAL FRANCHISE. Sri Lanka was one of the first colonies ruled by any European power to get a universal franchise. It was proposed by the Donoughmore Commission in 1931. Until 1958 the qualifying age was 21 but since that year it has been 18. Universal franchise has partly been credited for the relatively advanced state of human development — high literacy rate and high life expectancy rate — in Sri Lanka. Mass pressure via elections has made the political decision makers more responsive to mass aspirations, especially in the provision of health, education, and other basic human needs.

UNIVERSITIES. At the end of January 1996 Sri Lanka had 12 full-fledged state universities and three affiliated university colleges with a total student population of 25,000 and an Open University for distant education with a student enrollment of about 20,000. One of the regular universities is a technological institution. The rest offer a mix of subjects. The universities are unable to meet the demand for places which has far outpaced availability. There are two private institutions that grant degrees of foreign universities to which they are affiliated.

UNIVERSITY ADMISSIONS. There are approximately 6,000 first-year places available annually in Sri Lanka's eight universities. About 150,000 candidates compete in the General Certificate of Education-Advanced Level (GCE-AL) examination for these places, and about 50,000 obtain the minimum qualifications for admission. Competition is most intense in the science-based professional courses such as medicine and engineering.

Until 1970 admissions were based on merit in terms of the raw marks obtained. Under that system in 1969 approximately 50 percent of the places in medicine and engineering were taken by Sri Lankan Tamil candidates, who were only about 13 percent of the country's population. The Sinhalese demanded affirmative action to cut the Tamil share and increase their own. The government initially responded by introducing different cutoff points for the different media. In effect this required the Tamil medium students to secure higher marks than their Sinhala medium counterparts. Following widespread protest this was replaced with a system of media-wise standardization (abandoned in 1977) and quotas for districts based on population size and preferential quotas for "backward" districts. Within each district, places were allocated on merit. Admission based purely on merit (raw marks) based on an island-wide list was limited to about one-third of total admissions.

The district and national shares have undergone change from time to time. Under the current system 40 percent are taken on the basis of an all-island merit list, 55 percent on the basis of district-wise merit lists with each district getting a quota proportional to its population, and 5 percent from "backward districts." This system has stabilized the Sinhalese share at about 75 percent and the Tamil share at about 20 percent. Candidates from Colombo (mainly Sinhalese) and Jaffna (almost entirely Tamil) suffered and those from the more rural districts gained. The Sinhalese viewed it as a fair correction of an imbalance. The Tamils viewed this as another instance of discrimination against them by the Sinhalese-dominated government. This is believed to have been a major contributory factor that alienated the northern Tamil youth, who took up arms against the government.

UNTOUCHABLES (JAFFNA). The depressed caste groups in the Jaffna Tamil community. They were generally relegated to doing menial jobs such as scavenging. Until recent times many Hindu temples would not allow them to enter the premises for worship. A significant number have converted to Buddhism in response to this situation.

UPAWASA. Hunger strike, which is resorted to from time to time by various protesters. In the 1950s a university professor and a member of parliament resorted to this method to pressure the government to adopt the Sinhala-only (q.v.) language policy. In 1989 a Liberation Tigers of Tamil Eelam (q.v.) leader in Sri Lanka government custody went on a hunger strike to protest his detention and died.

V

VADAMARACHCHI OPERATION. A military operation ("Operation Liberation") launched in the Vadamarachchi area of the Jaffna peninsula by Sri Lankan troops against the Liberation Tigers of Tamil Eelam (q.v.) in May-June 1987. The government troops achieved a quick and decisive breakthrough and there was some expectation that they may even be able to reach Jaffna town. The Indian government intervened at this point by indicating to Colombo that it would not tolerate a decisive military victory of the government over the Tamil rebels. The government was forced to stop the campaign in early June and consider negotiation with the rebels using India as an intermediary that eventually culminated in the Indo-Lanka Peace Accord (q.v.) signed in July.

VEDDAS. The aborigines of Sri Lanka who inhabited the island prior to the arrival of immigrant settlers from India. The bulk of them were absorbed into the mainstream. However, pockets of the *Vedda* community survived until very recent times. They spoke a dialect that was a mixture of their own original language and Sinhalese (q.v.) and Tamil (q.v.). Originally they were hunter/gatherers. But over the years many took to settled agriculture. One of the last *Vedda* communities was dismantled by the Mahaveli development program (q.v.). Nevertheless, there are several thousand people on the northern and eastern areas who claim *Vedda* ancestry.

VELLALA CASTE. The farmer caste in the Sri Lankan Tamil (q.v.) community. Traditionally they have dominated Jaffna society and politics. However, the ascendance of the Liberation Tigers of Tamil Eelam (q.v.) with strong affiliations to the *Karaiyar* caste has changed this situation significantly.

VEREENIDGE OOST-INDISCHE CAMPAGNIE (VOC). Known as the Dutch East India Company, VOC was the agency of the Dutch government that managed its colonies in Asia. VOC came to Sri Lanka in 1556 and administered the maritime area of the country that it took over from the Portuguese. VOC left the country in 1796 when it handed over its Sri Lankan territory to the British East India Company.

VIPLAWAYA. The Sinhalese term for revolution, it has been a popular term in the Sinhalese political lexicon especially among radical youth groups such as the *Janatha Vimukthi Peramuna* (q.v.).

W

WALAWWA. A traditional residence of the old Sinhalese aristocracy, these are scattered in many parts of southern Sri Lanka, especially in the Kandyan (q.v.) area. Some are considered to be architecturally important.

WICKRAMASINGHE, RANIL (1949-). The leader of the opposition in the tenth parliament of Sri Lanka, he comes from an elite family that has been influential in Sri Lankan politics for many years. Having studied at Royal College, one of the country's most prestigious schools for boys, he entered the University of Colombo and read for a law degree. In 1972 he was admitted as an advocate of the supreme court. While practicing law he joined the United National Party (UNP) (q.v), which was then in opposition. In 1977 he was returned to parliament on the UNP ticket as its youngest member of parliament. He was appointed the deputy minister of foreign affairs in the new J. R. Jayewardene (q.v.) administration. Later he entered the Jayewardene cabinet as the minister of education, youth affairs and employment. In the 1990 Premadasa (q.v.) administration he held the industries portfolio.

In May 1993 he succeeded D. B. Wijetunga as the prime minister. In October 1994, following the assassination of the then leader of the opposition Gamini Dissanayake (q.v.), he assumed that position as well as the leadership of the UNP.

WIJETUNGA, D. B. (1922-). The third executive president of Sri Lanka, he assumed office on the death of President Ranasinghe Premadasa (q.v.) in May 1993. After graduating from high school, Wijetunga took a position as a minor official in the Department of Cooperative Development. He showed early signs of leadership skills when he organized the first union in the department. His political career began in 1947 when he accepted the post of private secretary to A. Ratnayake, one of the most prominent political figures in the country at that time.

He unsuccessfully contested the 1956 elections as a United National Party (UNP) (q.v.) candidate. He again lost in the March and July 1960 general elections but won in 1965. From 1965 to 1970 he was a back-bencher in parliament. He was considered a good constituency member of parliament. However, he lost in the 1970 elections. Wijetunga worked hard for the revival of the UNP in the early 1970s and returned to parliament in 1977. In the Jayewardene (q.v.) administration he first held the portfolio of information and broadcasting and later that of post and telecommunication. In 1989 he decided to retire from national politics. Premadasa (q.v.) persuaded him to change his mind and Wijetunga was returned to parliament in the 1989 parliamentary elections. Premadasa appointed him the prime minister and also gave him the finance portfolio. Later he also held, in addition to the above, the labor portfolio and the position of state (deputy) minister of national security.

In May 1993 when President Premadasa was assassinated Wijetunga assumed the office of executive president in accordance with the constitution. He did not contest the 1994 presidential election and retired from active politics. The Wijetunga presidency was welcomed in many quarters, especially by those who did not like the authoritarian style of Premadasa. A mild-mannered person, Wijetunga preferred a more collegial and open style of administration.

WIJEWEERA, ROHANA (1943-1989). Leader of the *Janatha Vimukthi Peramuna* (JVP) (q.v.). He founded the party on his return from the Soviet Union in the late 1960s where he studied for a degree at the Patrice Lumumba University. He was convicted and imprisoned for his role in the abortive insurrection of the JVP in 1971. On his release from prison in 1978, he reorganized the JVP and entered mainstream politics. He contested the 1982 presidential election and polled 3.5 percent of the vote, ahead of the veteran *Lanka Sama Samaja Party* (q.v.) Colvin R. de Silva (q.v.). He went underground after the JVP was proscribed by President Jayewardene (q.v.) in 1983. He was believed to have led the JVP terror campaign of 1988-1989 that virtually paralyzed the normal life of the country outside the northeast. The JVP campaign collapsed rapidly following his arrest in November 1989 by the security forces. At the time of the arrest he was living with his family disguised as a planter cum businessman. He died while in the custody of security forces, but the exact circumstances of his death have never been made public.

WOMEN. Sri Lankan women constituted 50 percent of the population at the last (1981) census. For a low-income developing country, Sri

Lankan women have achieved a relatively high level of human development. Their life expectancy at birth is 74 years, maternal mortality rate is 80 per 100,000 live births, the total fertility rate is 2.5, adult literacy rate is 85 percent, and the average age at marriage is 24. In nonagricultural employment, Sri Lankan women's average wage has been shown to be 90 percent of that of men, the fourth highest among a sample of countries that included both developed and developing. However, there are significant differences in these numbers when women are differentiated by residence (urban, rural, and plantation), income and social class (low, middle, and high-income) and ethnicity. About 36 percent of the women in the working age group are in the labor force. However, this number underestimates the actual contribution of women to national income because women who work in the informal sector, especially in rural agriculture, are usually not counted in formal surveys and censuses. In politics Sri Lanka produced the first woman prime minister of the world, Sirimavo Bandaranaike (q.v.), in 1960. In the People's Alliance (q.v.) government both the president and the prime minister are women. However, women are grossly under-represented in political office at almost every level below that from cabinet (q.v.), to parliament (q.v.) to provincial councils (q.v.) and *pradeshiya sabhas* (q.v.)

WORLD BANK. Sri Lanka became a member of the International Bank for Reconstruction and Development, better known as the World Bank in 1955. Between 1955 and 1995 the bank has lent US$2.1 billion into the country for various developmental activities. About 1.9 billion (90 percent) of this amount has come as 61 credits from the International Development Association (IDA) the soft lending affiliate of the World Bank that assists the low-income member countries. This amounts to about 0.6 percent of total global World Bank lending and about 2.4 percent of IDA lending. The latter is much higher than Sri Lanka's share of 0.6 percent of the IDA country total population.

Since 1977 the bank has played a key role in Sri Lanka's economic reform program by making available structural adjustment loans. The World Bank has been instrumental in making significant changes in Sri Lanka's extensive welfare schemes and subsidy programs. Currently it supports a poverty-alleviation program by funding a US$100 million trust fund. It also played a major role in funding the multibillion dollar Mahaveli power and irrigation development project (q.v.). Critics of World Bank activities in Sri Lanka have faulted it for forcing the government to make sharp cuts in the welfare programs for the poor and for disregarding the adverse long-term environmental implications of some of the projects that they have funded.

Y

YOUTH COMMISSION. A presidential commission appointed by the Premadasa (q.v.) administration in 1990 to study and report on youth grievances and possible solutions to them. This was primarily a response of the government to the political crisis associated with the second *Janatha Vimukthi Peramuna* rebellion of 1984-1989 (q.v.). The commission held extensive public hearings and produced a report that contained many specific proposals to solve youth problems. A few of them, most notably the one to have a minimum quota of nominees under the age of 35 in all local government elections, have been implemented.

APPENDIX 1

Table 1

Sri Lanka: Area by Districts, 1996
(including inland waters) (sq. km)

District	Total Land Area
Colombo	699
Gampaha	1,387
Kalutara	1,598
Kandy	1,940
Matale	1,993
Nuwara Eliya	1,741
Galle	1,652
Matara	1,283
Hambantota	2,609
Jaffna	1,025
Mannar	1,996
Vavuniya	1,967
Mullativu	2,617
Kilinochchi	1,279
Batticaloa	2,854
Ampara	4,415
Trincomalee	2,727
Kurunegala	4,816
Puttalam	1,372
Anuaradhapura	7,179
Polonnaruwa	3,293
Badulla	2,861
Moneragala	5,639
Ratnapura	3,275
Kegalla	1,693
Sri Lanka	65,610

Source: Department of Census and Statistics, *Statistical Pocket Book (annual)*

Table 2
Sri Lanka: Population, 1945-1995

Year	Population (,000s)	Year	Population (,000s)
1945	6,650	1971	12,608
1946	6,854	1972	12,861
1947	7,037	1973	13,091
1948	7,244	1974	13,284
1949	7,455	1975	13,496
1950	7,678	1976	13,717
1951	7,876	1977	13,942
1952	8,074	1978	14,184
1953	8,290	1979	14,471
1954	8,520	1980	14,738
1955	8,723	1981	14,988
1956	8,929	1982	15,189
1957	9,165	1983	15,417
1958	9,388	1984	15,599
1959	9,625	1985	15,837
1960	9,896	1986	16,117
1961	10,168	1987	16,361
1962	10,443	1988	16,587
1963	10,646	1989	16,806
1964	10,903	1990	16,993
1965	11,164	1991	17,247
1966	11,439	1992	17,405
1967	11,703	1993	17,600
1968	11,992	1994	17,900
1969	12,252	1995	18,112
1970	12,516	1996	18,366

Source: Sri Lanka Department of Census and Statistics, *Statistical Abstracts,* Annual

Table 3
Sri Lanka: Crude Birth, Death, and Infant Mortality Rates,
1945-1993

Year	Birth Rate	Death Rate	Infant Mortality Rate
1945	35.9	21.5	140
1950	39.7	12.4	82
1955	37.3	10.8	71
1960	36.6	8.6	57
1965	33.1	8.2	57
1970	29.4	7.5	53
1975	27.8	8.5	44
1980	28.4	6.2	35
1985	24.6	6.2	23
1990	22.0	6.0	18
1993	20.0	6.0	17

Source: *Annual Report of the Registrar General on Vital Statistics, Sri Lanka;* The World Bank, *World Tables 1993*

Table 4
Sri Lanka: Life Expectancy at Birth and Total
Fertility Rate, 1970-1993

Year	Life Expectancy	Fertility Rate (%)
1970	64.7	4.3
1975	66.0	3.9
1980	68.1	3.5
1985	69.8	2.9
1990	70.8	2.5
1993	72.0	2.4

Source: The World Bank, *World Tables* (Annual), Washington, D.C.: The World Bank

Table 5
Sri Lanka: GNP per Capita (US$), GDP Growth Rate
and Annual Inflation Rate (%), 1970-1994

Year	GNP/capita (US$)	GDP Growth Rate (%)	Inflation Rate(%)
1970	180	3	4.8
1971	190	2	4.8
1972	190	-2	4.5
1973	220	10	8.7
1974	250	4	12.0
1975	290	7	7.1
1976	290	4	3.3
1977	300	5	1.3
1978	260	5	12.9
1979	260	6	11.4
1980	260	6	25.6
1981	300	6	18.4
1982	330	8	13.8
1983	340	5	14.1
1984	370	5	16.4
1985	390	5	1.2
1986	410	4	8.1
1987	410	1	7.5
1988	420	3	14.0
1989	430	2	11.4
1990	470	6	22.0
1991	500	5	11.6
1992	540	4	11.6
1993	600	7	11.7
1994	650	6	9.4
1995	713	5	8.4

Source: The World Bank, *World Tables 1993*, Washington,
D.C.: The World Bank; Central Bank of Sri Lanka, *Annual Reports*

Table 6
Sri Lanka: Export, Import, and Terms of Trade, 1970-1993
(U.S. dollars in millions; index: 1987=100)

Year	Export	Import	Terms of Trade Index
1970	331.6	386.6	143
1971	323.7	328.1	132
1972	323.4	336.4	118
1973	410.2	429.7	135
1974	519.7	688.1	102
1975	557.7	744.6	99
1976	565.2	552.1	125
1977	760.3	701.1	167
1978	843.9	942.1	130
1979	977.7	1,449.2	119
1980	1,043.0	2,035.4	104
1981	1,007.5	1,803.8	95
1982	994.8	1,769.9	96
1983	1,051.8	1,788.4	109
1984	1,435.5	1,847.4	128
1985	1,246.2	1,786.3	103
1986	1,159.2	1,831.6	101
1987	1,326.0	2,021.3	100
1988	1,463.7	2,210.6	94
1989	1,506.3	2,087.5	93
1990	1,888.9	2,631.5	89
1991	2,629.4	3,861.5	87
1992	2,486.9	3,469.7	90
1993	2,896.0	4,227.0	

Source: The World Bank, *World Tables 1993*, Washington, D.C.:
The World Bank

Table 7
Sri Lanka: Direct Foreign Investment and Foreign Debt
1970-1993 (U.S. dollars in millions)

Year	Direct, Foreign Investment	Foreign Debt
1970	0.3	433.2
1971	0.3	517.7
1972	0.4	551.9
1973	0.5	629.2
1974	1.3	781.2
1975	0.1	815.5
1976	--	929.7
1977	1.2	1,132.1
1978	1.5	1,372.8
1979	46.9	1,553.8
1980	43.0	1,841.4
1981	49.3	2,234.6
1982	63.6	2,625.4
1983	37.8	2,884.3
1984	32.6	2,993.1
1985	24.8	3,540.0
1986	29.2	4,079.8
1987	58.2	4,748.1
1988	43.6	5,201.1
1989	17.7	5,172.5
1990	42.6	5,844.1
1991	43.8	6,546.9
1992	121.0	6,401.1

Source: The World Bank, *World Tables 1993*, Washington, D.C.:
The World Bank

Table 8
Sri Lanka: Social Indicators

	c.1971	c.1980	c. 1990
Primary School Enroll Ratio (total)	99	103	107
Primary School Enroll Ratio	94	100	106
Secondary School Enroll Ratio	47	55	74
Population per Physician	5900	7000	5500
Illiteracy Rate			
Total	22	13	12
Female	27	20	17
Percentage of Married Females (age 19-49) Using Birth Control Method	--	--	62
Adults Who Smoke	--	--	25
Population (%) with Access to:			
Health Services	--	--	93
Safe Drinking Water	--	--	60
Sanitation	--	--	50
Share (%) of Total Income Received by			
Poorest 40% of Households	19.2	--	13.5
Richest 10% of Households	28.9	--	43

Source: The World Bank, *World Development Reports and World Tables (Annual)* Washington, D.C.: The World Bank

APPENDIX 2

GOVERNORS-GENERAL

Sir Henry Monck-Mason-Moore	1948-1949
Viscount Soulbury	1949-1954
Sir Oliver E. Goonetilleke	1954-1962
William Gopallawa	1962-1972

PRESIDENT

William Gopallawa	1972-1978

EXECUTIVE PRESIDENTS

J. R. Jayewardene	Feb. 1978 - Jan. 1990
R. Premadasa	Jan. 1990 - May 1993
D.B Wijetunge	May 1993 - Nov. 1994
Chandrika Kumaratunga	Nov. 1994 -

APPENDIX 3

PRIME MINISTERS

The Rt. Hon. D. S. Senanayake	Sep.	1947 -	Mar. 1952
Dudley S. Senanayake	Mar.	1952-	Oct. 1 1953
The Rt. Hon. Sir John Kotelawala	Oct.	1953 -	Apr. 1956
S. W. R. D. Bandaranaike	Apr.	1956 -	Sep. 1959
W. Dahanayake	Sep.	1959 -	Mar. 1960
Dudley Senanayake	Mar.	1960 -	Jul. 1960
Mrs. Sirimavo R. D. Bandaranaike	Jul.	1960 -	Mar. 1965
Dudley S. Senanayake	Mar.	1965 -	May 1970
Mrs. Sirimavo R. D. Bandaranaike	May	1970 -	Jul. 1977
J. R. Jayewardene	Jul.	1977 -	Feb. 1978
R. Premadasa	Feb.	1978 -	Jan. 1990
D. B Wijetunge	Jan.	1990 -	May 1993
Ranil Wickremasinghe	May	1993 -	Aug. 1994
Chandrika Bandaranaike Kumaratunga	Aug.	1994 -	Nov. 1994
Mrs. Sirimavo R. D. Bandaranaike	Nov.	1994 -	

APPENDIX 4

General Elections

	UNP		SLFP		Others		Total
	Votes (%)	Seats	Votes(%)	Seats	Votes(%)	Seats	Seats
1947	40.3	42	-	-	59.7	53	95
1952	44.0	54	15.5	9	40.5	32	
1956	27.9	8	-	-	72.1	87	
1960 (March)	29.4	50	21.3	47	49.3	54	151
1960 (July)	37.6	30	33.7	75	28.7	46	
1965	39.4	66	30.3	41	33.3	44	
1970	37.9	17	36.9	91	25.2	43	
1977	50.9	140	27.9	8	19.4	20	168
1989	50.7	125(110+15)	31.9	67	17.4	33	225
1994	44.1	94	48.6	105	7.3	26	

Presidential Elections

	UNP Votes (%)	SLFP Votes (%)	Others Votes (%)
1982	52.9	39.1	8.0
1988	50.4	45.0	4.6
1994	35.9	62.3	1.8

BIBLIOGRAPHY

INTRODUCTION

The purpose of the bibliography is to help its user identify sources for further information on Sri Lanka in topics ranging from its history and culture to contemporary politics and economic development. Given the limitations of space, we have generally selected the more recent material. We were also deeply conscious of the importance of covering different viewpoints and opinions, especially, on the more controversial issues in politics and economics.

The bibliography has been divided into several sections. The order of division follows a systematic sequence that takes the user from general works of reference to geography, history, culture, society, politics, and economic development. Each of these themes is divided into subthemes for easy reference. However, a work listed under one heading may have relevant material to another. As a rule we included such publications under the principal theme that they dealt with.

The final section of the bibliography has a list of Sri Lankan newspapers and periodicals. In regard to the latter, we have been highly selective with a bias toward those that have an educational content.

GENERAL WORKS

Works of Reference

Associated Newspapers of Ceylon Ltd. *Ferguson's Sri Lanka Directory*. Colombo: The Associated Newspapers of Ceylon Ltd., (Annual). 1859-

Central Bank of Ceylon. *Annual Report*. Colombo: Central Bank of Ceylon. 1950-

-----. *Economic and Social Statistics of Sri Lanka*. Colombo: Central Bank of Ceylon, (Annual).

-----. *Survey of Ceylon's Consumer Finances*. Colombo: Central Bank of Ceylon, (Published periodically).

Department of Census & Statistics. *Statistical Pocket Book*. Colombo: Department of Census & Statistics, (Annual).

Department of Census & Statistics. *Statistical Abstract of the Democratic Socialist Republic of Sri Lanka*. Colombo: Department of Census & Statistics, (Annual). 1949-

Europa Press. *Australasia and the Far East*. London: Europa Press, (Annual).

Peebles, Patrick. *Sri Lanka: A Handbook of Historical Statistics*. Boston: G. K. Hall, 1992.

Survey Department. *National Atlas*. Colombo: 1988.

University Grants Commission. *Statistical Hand Book*. Colombo: University Grants Commission, (Annual).

Wimalaratne, K. D. G. *Personalities of Sri Lanka. A Biographical Study. 1490-1990 A.D.*. Colombo: Ceylon Business Appliances Ltd., 1994.

-----. *Directory of Dates and Events, Sri Lanka (Ceylon) (543 B.C. - 1984 AD)*. Colombo: Trumpet Publishers, 1988.

Travel and General Description

American Women's Association. *Colombo Handbook*. Colombo: American Women's Association, 1991.

Anthonis, Ravindralal. *Sri Lanka, Insight Guides*. New York: Prentice Hall, 1987.

Baker, Samuel W. *Eight Years in Ceylon*. Dehiwala, Sri Lanka: Tisara Publishers, 1983.

Bandaranayake, Senake. *Sri Lanka Island Civilization*. Colombo: Lake House Bookshop, 1978.

Barrow, George Sir. *Ceylon: Past and Present*. London: John Murray, 1857.

Brohier, Richard Leslie. "Ceylon, Poetry, Pageantry, Romance" in *Plate's Ceylon Annual*, No. 23, 1939.

-----. *Discovering Ceylon*. Colombo: Lake House Investments Ltd., 1973.

-----. *Ceylon, the "Wonderland of the East," A Representative Selection of the Finest Scenery in the Island*. Colombo: Cargills Ltd., n.d.

Cordiner, James. *A Description of Ceylon*. Dehiwala, Sri Lanka: Tisara Publishers Ltd., 1983.

Davy, John. *An Account of the Interior of Ceylon and of its Inhabitants with Travels in that Island*. Dehiwala: Tisara Publishers Ltd., 1983.

De Silva, Andrew G. *Ceylon Beckons: A Guide to Tourists*. Colombo: Alliance Publishers, 1952.

Elliot, C. Brooke and A. L. Martin. *The Real Ceylon, No. 1, Travel in Ceylon*. Colombo: H.W. Cave, 1924.

-----. *The Enchanted Isle*. Colombo: Ceylon Government Press, 1950.

Gibson, Ashley. *Cinnamon and Frangipani*. London: Chapman and Dodd, 1923.

Goonetileke, H.A.I. *Images of Sri Lanka Through American Eyes: Travellers in Ceylon in the Nineteenth and Twentieth Centuries*. Colombo: United States Information Service, 1983.

Grossman, Susan. *The Serendipity of Sri Lanka*. London: Harpers and Queen, 1977.

Hulugalle, H. A. J. *Ceylon of the Early Travellers*. Colombo: Multipaks (Ceylon) Ltd., 1965.

Insight Guides. *Sri Lanka*. Hong Kong: APA Productions (HK) Ltd., 1983.

Jayekody, Marcelline Fr. *In Search of Ceylon*. Colombo: Associated Newspapers of Ceylon, 1964.

Jennings, Sir William Ivor. *Ceylon and its People*. Colombo: Ceylon Daily News Press, 1942.

Knox, Robert. *An Historical Relation of the Island Ceylon*. Dehiwala, Sri Lanka: Tisara Publishers Ltd., 1989.

Marshall, Henry. *Ceylon: A General Description of the Island and its Inhabitants*. London: William H. Allen. 1846; Kandy: Kandy Printers, 1954, New ed.

-----. *Seeing Ceylon in Vistas of Scenery, History, Legend and Folklore*. Colombo: Lake House Investments Ltd., 1965.

Spittel, Richard Lionel. *Far-off Things: Treating of the History Aborigines, Myths and Jungle Mysteries of Ceylon*. Colombo: Colombo Apothecaries Co. Ltd., 1933.

Thambimuttu, Paulinus. *Ceylon - The Garden Island of Asia, Lands and People*. New York & Toronto: Grolier Society, 1957.

Tressider, Argus John. *Ceylon: An Introduction to the "Resplendent Land"*. Princeton, N.J.: Van Nostrand, 1960.

Vijayatunga, Jinadasa. *Island Story*. Madras: Oxford University Press, 1949.

Watkins, Michael. *Ceylon - When its Tuesday or Christmas, Other Places.*, Ipswich (Suffolk): East Anglian Magazine Ltd., 1973.

Woolf, Leonard Downhill. *All the Way. An Anthology of the Years 1919-1939*. London: Hogarth Press, 1967.

Bibliographies on Sri Lanka

Alwis, N. A. W. A. T. *University of Peradeniya: Index to theses 1942-1992*. Peradeniya: University of Peradeniya, 1993.

De Silva, C. R. and Daya de Silva. *Sri Lanka (Ceylon) since Independence (1948-1976)*. Hamburg: Institute of Asian Affairs, 1978.

-----. *Sri Lanka since Independence: A Reference Guide to the Literature*. New Delhi: Navrang, 1992.

Goonetileke, H. A. I. *A Bibliography of Ceylon: A Systematic Guide to the Literature on the Land, People, History and Culture Published in the Western Languages from the Sixteenth Century to the Present Day:* 5 volumes. Zug, Switzerland: Inter Documentation Co., 1970-1983.

Siddhisena, K. A. P. *Bibliography - The Demography of Sri Lanka*. Colombo: Lake House Printers and Publishers, 1981.

GEOGRAPHY

Agrarian Research and Training Institute (ARTI). *The South-East Dry Zone of Sri Lanka*. Colombo: ARTI, July 1993.

Cook, Elsie. *Ceylon, Its Geography, Its Resources and Its People*. London: Macmillan & Co., 1931.

Cooray, P. G. *An Introduction to the Geology of Ceylon*. Colombo: National Museum of Ceylon, 1967.

De Alwis, K. A. and C. R. Panabokke. *Handbook of the Soils of Sri Lanka*. Colombo: Paper presented at the 3rd Annual Sessions of the Soil Science Society of Ceylon, 3rd July 1972.

Department of Census and Statistics. *The Ceylon Economic Atlas*. Colombo: Ceylon Government Press, 1969.

Government of Sri Lanka. *Report of the Land Commission, 1987, Sessional Paper III*. Colombo, Department of Government Printing, 1990.

Kalpage, F. S. C. P. D. and A. W. R. Joachim. *Bibliography of Soils and Related Sciences of Ceylon.* Compiled by M.W. Thenabadu. Colombo: Soil Science Society of Ceylon, 1973.

Peiris, G. H. *Development and Change in Contemporary Sri Lanka: Geographical Perspectives.* Kandy: International Centre for Ethnic Studies, 1996.

-----. "The Physical Environment" in K. M. de Silva (Ed.). *Sri Lanka, A Survey.* London: C. Hurst, 1979, 3-30.

Rupasinghe, M. S., Dissanayake, C. B., and D. G. A. Perera (Eds.). *The Sri Lankan Geuda.* Kandy: Institute of Fundamental Studies, 1994.

HISTORY

General

Arasaratnam, S. *Ceylon.* Englewood Cliffs, N.J.: Prentice-Hall, 1964.

De Silva, Chandra Richard, *Sri Lanka: A History.* New Delhi: Vikas Publishing House, 1987.

De Silva, K. M. (Ed.). *Sri Lanka, A Survey.* London: C. Hurst & Co., 1977.

De Silva, K.M. *A History of Sri Lanka.* London: C. Hurst, 1981.

De Silva, Nimal. *Kandy: A Cultural Guide to World Heritage City.* Deveco Designers & Publishers (Pvt.) Ltd., 1994.

Ludowyk, E. F. C. *The Story of Ceylon.* London: Faber, 1962.

-----, and M. le M. Scrivenor. *Sri Lanka, Land, People and Economy.* London: Heinemann, 1981.

Nicholas, C. W., and S. A. Paranavitana. *A Concise History of Ceylon.* Colombo: University of Ceylon Press, 1961.

Paranavitana, S (Ed.). *The University of Ceylon, History of Ceylon*, Vol. I (Parts 1 & 2). Colombo, University of Ceylon Press, 1959-1960.

Wimalaratne, K. D. G. *Personalities of Sri Lanka. A Biographical Study. 1490-1990 A.D.* Colombo: Ceylon Business Appliances Ltd., 1994.

Prehistory

Deraniyagala, S. U. "Prehistoric Sri Lanka: 1885-1980" in P. L. Prematilleke, W. T. P. Gunawardana and R. Silva (Eds.). *P. E. P. Deraniyagala Commemoration Volume*. Colombo: Lake House, 1980, 152-207.

-----. *The Prehistory of Sri Lanka: An Ecological Perspective, Memoir*. Volume 8, Part 1. Colombo: Department of Archaeological Survey, 1992.

-----. "The Prehistory of Sri Lanka: An Outline" in Rutnam, James, A. R. B. Amarasinghe and S. J. Sumanasekera Banda (Eds.). *Festschrift. 1985*, Colombo: UNESCO, 1985, 14-21.

Ancient History

Geiger, Wilhelm (Ed.). *The Mahavamsa*. London: Pali Text Society, 1958.

-----. *A Short History of Ceylon: From the 5th Century B.C. to the 4th Century A.D.* Calcutta: Thacker, 1931.

Gunawardana, R.A.L.H. *Robe and Plough. Monasticism and Economic Interest in Early Medieval Sri Lanka*. Tucson: Arizona. University of Arizona Press, 1979.

-----. "The People of the Lion: The Sinhala Identity and Ideology in History and Historiography." *Sri Lanka Journal of the Humanities*, 5 (1&2). 1979, 1-36.

Guruge, Ananda W. P. *Mahavamsa: The Great Chronicle of Sri Lanka.* Colombo: Associated Newspapers of Ceylon, 1989.

Liyanagamage, A. *The Decline of Polonnaruwa and the Rise of Dambadeniya (Circa 1180-1270 A.D.).* Colombo: Department of Cultural Affairs, 1968.

Mendis, G. C. *Ceylon Today and Yesterday: Main Currents of Ceylon History.* 2nd ed. Colombo: Associated Newspapers of Ceylon, 1963.

Parker, H. *Ancient Ceylon.* New Delhi: Asian Educational Services, 1992.

Ragupathy, P. *Early Settlements in Jaffna: An Archaeological Survey.* Madras: Surdarson Graphics, 1987.

Modern History (post-1505)

Abeyasinghe, T. *Portuguese Rule in Ceylon, 1594-1612.* Colombo: Lake House, 1966.

De Queyroz, F. (Translated by S. G. Perera) *The Temporal and Spiritual Conquest of Ceylon.* Colombo: Government Press, 1930.

De Silva, C. R. *The Portuguese in Ceylon, 1617-1638.* Colombo: H. W. Cave & Co., 1972.

De Silva, K. M. (Ed.). *History of Ceylon,* Vol. III. Peradeniya: University of Ceylon, 1973.

----- (Ed.). *History of Sri Lanka,* Vol. II. Peradeniya: University of Peradeniya, 1995.

De Silva, Colvin R. *Ceylon Under the British Occupation,* 2 vols. Colombo: Colombo Apothecaries Press, 1950.

Dewaraja, Lorna S. *The Kandyan Kingdom of Ceylon 1707-1760.* Colombo: Lake House Investments Ltd., 1972.

Duncan, James S. *The City as Text: the Politics of Landscape Interpretation in the Kandyan Kingdom.* Cambridge: Cambridge University Press, 1990.

Goonewardena, K.W. *The Foundation of Dutch Power in Ceylon, 1638-1658.* Amsterdam: Netherlands Institute for International and Cultural Relations, 1958.

Heidemann, Frank. *Kanganies in Sri Lanka and Malaysia: Tamil Recruiter-cum-foreman as a Sociological Category in the 19th and 2oth Century.* Munchen: Ahacon, 1992.

Jennings, Sir Ivor, and H. W. Tambiah. *The Dominion of Ceylon.* London: Stevens, 1952.

Ludowyk, E. F. C. *The Modern History of Ceylon.* London: Weidenfeld and Nicolson, 1966.

Mendis, G. C. *Ceylon Under the British.* Colombo: Apothecaries Co. Ltd., 1952.

-----. (Ed.). *The Colebrooke Cameron Papers,* 2 vols. Oxford: Oxford University Press, 1956.

Nadesan, S. *A History of the Upcountry Tamil People in Sri Lanka.* Colombo: Nandalal Publication, 1993.

Navasivayam, S. *The Legislatures of Ceylon, 1928-1948.* London: Faber and Faber, 1950.

Nicholas, C. W., and S. Paranavitana. *A Concise History of Ceylon.* Colombo: Ceylon University Press, 1961.

Peebles, Patrick. *Sri Lanka: A Handbook of Historical Statistics.* Boston, Mass.: G. K. Hall & Co., 1982.

Powell, G. *The Kandyan Wars: The British Army in Ceylon, 1803-1818.* London: Leo Cooper, 1973.

Vimalananda, Tennakoon. *Buddhism in Ceylon under the Christian Powers and the Educational and Religious Policy of the British Government in Ceylon 1797-1832.* Colombo: M.D. Gunasena, 1963.

Vittachi, Tarzie. *Emergency '58. The Story of the Ceylon Race Riots.* London: Andre Deutsch, 1958.

Wesumperuma, Dharmapriya. *Indian Immigrant Plantation Workers in Sri Lanka: A Historical Perspective 1880-1910.* Colombo: Vidyalankara University Press, 1986.

Wijesekera, Nandadeva. *Contacts and Conflicts with Sri Lanka.* Colombo: Nandadeva Wijesekera, 1986.

CULTURE

Art and Architecture

Affate, Francesco. *Indian Art and the Art of Ceylon, Central and Southeast Asia.* (Ed. Jean Richardson). London: Octopus Books, 1972.

Amunugama, Sarath. "An Introduction to Kandyan Painting." Peradeniya: *Ceylon University Magazine - First Term 1958-59,* 4-10.

Archer, W. G. "Painting in Ceylon" in S. Paranavitana. *Ceylon, Paintings from Temple, Shrine and Rock.* 1957, 5-15.

Bandaranayake, Senake Dias. *Sinhalese Monastic Architecture.* Leiden: E. J. Brill, 1974.

-----. *The Rock and Wall Paintings of Sri Lanka.* Colombo: Lake House, 1986.

Collins, Charles Henry. "Art in the New Ceylon." *New Lanka,* 1 (4), July 1950.

Coomaraswamy, Ananda Kentish. *The Arts and Crafts of India and Ceylon.* London and Edinburgh: T. N. Joulis, 1913.

-----. *Art and Swadeshi.* Madras: Ganesh, n.d. (1910?).

-----. *Medieval Sinhalese Art.* Gloucestershire: Essex House Press, 1908.

De Fonseka, Lionel. *On the Truth of Decorative Art: A Dialogue between an Oriental and an Occidental.* London: Greening, 1912.

De Silva, Minette. "Architecture in Sri Lanka. Third Century B.C. to Present Day" in Sir Banister Fletcher (Ed.) *The History of Architecture.* London: University of London, The Athlone Press, 1975.

Devendra, Don Titus. *Classical Sinhalese Sculpture, 300 B.C. to A.D. 1000.* London: Alec Tirant, 1958.

Dharmadasa, K. N. O. "Drama, Film and Music" in K. M. de Silva (Ed.). *Sri Lanka: A Survey.* Honolulu: University Press of Hawaii, 1977.

Dolapihilla, Punchibandara. "Sinhalese Music and Minstrelsy" in Ralph Pieris (Ed.). *Some Aspects of Traditional Sinhalese Culture.* 1956, 34-35.

Fernando, C. M. *An Album of Ceylon Music.* Colombo: George J. A. Skeen, Government Printer, 1904.

Godakumbura, Charles Edmund. *Architecture of Sri Lanka.* 2nd ed., Colombo: Department of Cultural Affairs, 1976.

-----. *Sinhalese Architecture.* Colombo: Ceylon Government Press, 1963.

Goonetileke, L.P. *Art in Ceylon: 43 Group and the Contemporary Scene C.F.R.,* 5 (16), 5 Dec. 1952.

Gunasinghe, Siri. *An Album of Buddhist Paintings from Sri Lanka (Ceylon) (Kandyan Period).* Colombo: National Museums of Sri Lanka, 1978.

Halpe, Ashley. "Painting and Sculpture" in K. M. de Silva (Ed.). *Sri Lanka: A Survey.* Honolulu: University Press of Hawaii, 1977.

Lewie, J. Pensy. *Tombstones and Monuments in Ceylon.* Colombo: 1913.

Longhurst, Arthur Henry. *The Development of the Stupa.* Colombo: Ceylon Government Press, 1936.

Manjusri, L. T. P. *Design Elements from Sri Lankan Temple Paintings.* Colombo: Archaeological Society of Sri Lanka, 1977.

Ministry of Cultural Affairs. *Cultural Treasures of Sri Lanka.* Colombo: Sri Lanka Government Press, 1973.

Mudiyanse, Nandasena. *The Art and Architecture of the Gampola Period, (1341-1415 A.D.).* Colombo: M. D. Gunasena, 1965.

Narada Maha Thera. *The Buddha and His Teachings - Illustrated with Paintings from Buddhist Temples in Sri Lanka.* Colombo: The Lever Brothers Trust, 1987.

Navaratnam, K. *Development of Art in Ceylon.* Colombo: Ceylon Printers, 1955.

Nell, Andreas. "The Origin and Styles of Ancient Ceylon Architecture." *Journal of the Royal Asiatic Society (Ceylon Branch),* 26 (71), 1918.

Paranavitana, Senarat. *Art of the Ancient Sinhalese.* Colombo: Lake House Investments Ltd., 1971.

Perera, Noeyal. *The Decorative Art of Ceylon. C.T.,* 10 (2). February 1961.

Pertold, Otakar. *The Ceremonial Dances of the Sinhalese.* Dehiwala: Tisara Publishers Ltd., 1973.

Pieris, Ralph. *Some Aspects of Traditional Sinhalese Culture - A Symposium.* Peradeniya: University of Ceylon, 1956.

Prematilleke, L. *Sri Lankan Bronzes (Buddhist and Hindu).* Colombo: National Museum, 1986.

Ravenhart, R. *Ceylon: History in Stone.* Colombo: Lake House Publishers, 3rd ed., 1981.

Salgado, B. Victor *Elements of Sinhalese Art.* Kandy: Gamini Printing Works, 1955.

Sansoni, Barbara. *Viharas and Verandas of Ceylon.* Colombo: Lake House Publishers & Printers Ltd., 1978.

Sarachchandra, E. R. *The Sinhalese Folkplay and the Modern Stage.* Colombo: Ceylon University Press Board, 1953.

-----. *Folk Drama of Ceylon.* Colombo: Department of Cultural Affairs, 1966.

Schroeder, Ulrich Von. *The Golden Age of Sculpture in Sri Lanka.* Hong Kong: Visual Dharma Publications Ltd., 1992.

Seneviratne, Anuradha. *Kandy - An Illustrated Survey of Ancient Monuments.* Colombo: Ministry of Cultural Affairs, 1984.

Seneviratne, John M. "The Sinhalese and their Contribution to the Art and Culture of the World" in *United National Party Independence Day Souvenir*, February 4, 1949.

Smith, Arthur Vincent. *A History of Fine Art in India and Ceylon from the Earliest Times to the Present Day.* Oxford: Clarendon Press, 1911.

Wickramasinghe, Martin. *Buddhism and Art.* Colombo: M. D. Gunasena, 1972.

Sinhala Language, Literature and Linguistics

Auery, John. "The Language of the Veddhas." *American Antiquarian and Oriental Journal.* 9 (3) March, 1887.

De Silva, K. M. "Language Problems: The Politics of Language Policy" in K. M. de Silva (Ed.). *Governance of Sri Lanka.* New Delhi: Konark, 1993.

-----. *Religion, Nationalism and the State in Modern Sri Lanka.* (USF Monographs in Religion and Public Policy; No. 1). Florida: University of South Florida, 1986.

-----. "Ethnicity, Language and Politics: The Making of Sri Lanka's Official Language Act No. 33 of 1956." *Ethnic Studies Report*, 9 (1), January 1993, 1-29.

Dharmadasa, K. N. O. "Language and Sinhalese Nationalism." *Modern Ceylon Studies*, 3 (2), 1972, 125-143.

-----. "Diglossia, Nativism and the Sinhalese Identity in the Language Problem in Sri Lanka." *International Journal of the Sociology of Language, 13, 1977, 21-32.*

-----. "Language Conflict in Sri Lanka." *Sri Lanka Journal of the Social Sciences*, 4 (2), December 1981, 47-70.

-----. *Language, Religion and Ethnic Assertiveness: The Growth of Sinhalese Nationalism in Sri Lanka.* Ann Arbor: Michigan University Press, 1992.

Disanayaka, J. B. *Introducing Sri Lankan Language. Sinhala A Unique Indo-Aryan Language.* Colombo: M. H. Publications, 1994.

-----. *The Structure of Spoken Sinhala, Vol. One. Sounds and Their Patterns.* Maharagama, Sri Lanka: National Institute of Education, 1991.

----. *Sinhala Tamil English Trilingual Writing.* Colombo: S. Godage & Brothers, 1992.

Geiger, W. *Etymological Glossary of the Sinhala Language.* Colombo: Royal Asiatic Society, Ceylon Branch, 1941.

Godakumbura, Charles. *Sinhala Literature.* Colombo: Colombo Apothecaries, 1955.

-----. *A Grammar of the Sinhalese Language.* Colombo: Royal Asiatic Society, Ceylon Branch, 1938.

Government of Ceylon. *Final Report on the Commission on Higher Education in the National Languages, Sessional Paper 10.* Colombo: Government Press, 1956.

Gunasekera, Abraham Mendis. *A Comprehensive Grammar of the Sinhalese Language.* Colombo: Government Press, 1891.

Jayaweera, Swarna. "What Schools Could Do Towards Promoting National Unity." *Journal of the National Education Society of Ceylon*, IV (1), 1956.

-----. "Language and Colonial Educational Policy in Ceylon." *Modern Ceylon Studies*, 2 (2), 1971, 151-169.

Kearney, Robert. *Communalism and Language in the Politics of Ceylon*. Durham, N.C.: Duke University Press, 1967.

Reynolds, C. H. B. (Ed.) (trans. by W. G. Archer *et al.*). *An Anthology of Sinhalese Literature up to 1815*. London: Allen and Unwin, 1971.

-----. *An Anthology of Sinhalese Literature of the Twentieth Century*. Kent: Paul Norbury, 1987.

Roberts, Michael (Ed.). *Collective Identities, Nationalisms and Protest in Modern Sri Lanka*. Colombo: Marga Institute, 1979.

Russel, Jane. "Language, Education and Nationalism. The Language Debate of 1944." *The Ceylon Journal of Historical and Social Studies*, (CJHSS) new series VIII (2), 1982, 38-64.

Sarachchandra, E. R. "Ludowyk and Sinhala Theatre" in A. Halpe (Ed.). *Honouring E. F. C. Ludowyk*. Colombo: 1984.

Tambiah, S. J. "The Politics of Language in India and Ceylon." *Modern Asian Studies*, 3, 215-240.

Walatara, Douglas. *The Teaching of English as a Complementary Language in Ceylon*. Colombo: Lake House Investments, 1965.

Wickramasinghe, Martin. *Sinhalese Literature*. Colombo: Gunasena, 1949.

-----. *Sinhala Language and Culture*. Dehiwala, Sri Lanka: Tisara Publishers Ltd., 1975.

Tamil Language, Literature & Linguistics

Agesthialingom, S., and S. V. Shanmugam. *The Language of Tamil Inscriptions, 1250-1350 A.D.* Annamalainagar: Annamalai University, 1970.

Ambikaipakan, S. *Some Landmarks in the History of Tamil Literature in Ceylon.* Mallakam: Thuruwakal Press, 1974.

Dharmadasa, K. N. O. "Literacy Activity in the Indigenous Languages" in K. M. de Silva (Ed.). *Sri Lanka: A Survey.* London: C. Hurst, 1977.

Indrapala, Karthigesu. "Language and Literature in the 19th & 20th Centuries II. Tamil Language and Literature." *University of Ceylon History of Ceylon*, Vol. 3, 1973.

Kailasapathy, K. "Ceylon and its Contribution to Tamil" in S. Sanmuganathan (Ed.). *Souvenir of the Pageant of Lanka.* Colombo: Associated Newspapers of Ceylon, 1948, 39-51.

-----. "A Century of Tamil Poetry in Sri Lanka." *Radio Times*, 25 (27), October, 1973.

-----. "Tamil Studies in Sri Lanka." *News Letter of the Society for South India Studies*, Massachusetts: Dept. of Religion, Williams College, Williamstown, November 1977.

-----. "Cultural and Linguistic Consciousness of the Tamil Community" in *Ethnicity and Social Change in Sri Lanka.* Colombo: Social Scientists' Association, 1985.

-----., and A Sanmugadas. *Tamil.* Colombo: Dept. of Cultural Affairs, n.d.

Karunathilake, W. S., and S. Suseendirajah. "Pronouns of Address in Tamil and Sinhalese: A Sociolinguistic Study." *International Journal of Dravidian Linguistics*, 4 (1), January 1975.

-----., and S. Suseendirajah. "Phonology of Sinhalese and Sri Lanka Tamil. A Study in Contrast and Interference." *Indian Linguistics: Journal of the Linguistic Society of India*, 34 (3), September 1973.

Sivakumaran, K.S. *Contemporary Tamil Writing in Sri Lanka.* Colombo: Vijaya Luckshmi Book Depot, 1974.

Somasundaram Pillai, J. *Two Thousand Years of Tamil Literature.* Tinnevelly: South India Saiva Siddhanta Works Publishing Society, 1959.

Thananjayarajasingham, S. "The Tamil Diglossia Situation in Sri Lanka." *Ceylon Historical Journal*, 25 (1-4), October 1978.

Vaiyapuri Pillai, S. *History of Tamil Language and Literature.* Madras: New Century Book House, 1956.

Zvelebil, Kamil V. *Tamil Literature.* Weisbaden: O. H. O. Harrasowitz, 1974.

English Language, Literature and Linguistics

Collin-Thome, Percy, and Ashley Halpe (Eds.). *Honouring E.F.C. Ludowyk: Felicitation Essays.* Dehiwala, Sri Lanka: Tisara Publishers, 1984.

Gooneratne, M. Y. *English Literature in Ceylon 1815-1878.* Dehiwala, Sri Lanka: Tisara Publishers, 1968.

Ludowyk, E. F. C. "The Eighteenth Century Background of Some Early English writers on Ceylon." *Ceylon Historical Journal*, III (3 and 4), January and April 1964, 268-274.

-----. "Writing in English in Ceylon." *Adam International Review*, 367-369, 1972, 22-28.

Obeyesekere, Ranjini, and Chitra Fernando (Eds.). *An Anthology of Modern Writing from Sri Lanka.* Michigan: Association for Asian Studies, Inc., University of Michigan, 1981.

SOCIETY

Anthropology

Amunugama, Sarath. *Notes on Sinhala Culture.* Colombo: Gunasena, Reprint, 1990.

Ariyapala, M. B. *Society in Medieval Ceylon.* Colombo: Department of Cultural Affairs, 2nd ed., 1968.

Brow, James. *Vedda Villages of Anuradhapura.* Seattle: University of Washington Press, 1978.

Carrithers, Michael. *The Forest Monks of Sri Lanka: An Anthropological & Historical Study.* Delhi: Oxford University Press, 1983.

Chandraprema, C. A. *Ruhuna: A Study of the History, Society and Ideology of Southern Sri Lanka.* Nugegoda, Sri Lanka: Bharat Publishers, 1989.

Codrington, H. W. *Ancient Land Tenure and Revenue in Ceylon.* Colombo: Ceylon Government Press, 1938.

David, Kenneth Andrew. "The Magul Poruwa or Customary form of Sinhalese Marriage." *Spolia Zeylanica,* 30 (2), 1965.

De Munck, Victor C. *Seasonal Cycles: A Study of Social Change and Continuity in a Sri Lankan Village.* New Delhi: Asian Educational Services, 1993.

Dharmadasa, K. N. O. "Creolization, Legend and History: An Aspect of the History of the Veddas of Ceylon." *Sri Lanka Journal of Humanities,* 1 (1) June, 1975.

-----. and S. W. R. de A. Samarasinghe. *The Vanishing Aborigines: Sri Lanka's Veddas in Transition.* Kandy: International Centre for Ethnic Studies, 1990.

Dissanayake, J. B. *The April New Year Festival.* Colombo: Pioneer Lanka Publications, 1993.

Geiger, W. *The Culture of Ceylon in Medieval Times.* Weisbaden: Otto Harrasowitz, 1960.

Kapferer, B. *A Celebration of Demons: Exorcism and the Aesthetics of Healing in Sri Lanka*. Bloomington: Indiana University Press, 1983.

Leach, E. R. *Pul Eliya: A Village in Ceylon*. Cambridge: Cambridge University Press, 1961.

Morrison, Barrie, M. P. Moore, and M. U. Ishak Lebbe. *The Disintegrating Village: Social Change in Rural Sri Lanka*. Colombo: Lake House, 1979.

Navaratnam, C. S. *Vanni and the Vanniyas*. Jaffna: Eelanadu Ltd., 1960.

Obeyesekere, Gananath. *Land Tenure in Village Ceylon*. Cambridge: Cambridge University Press, 1967.

-----. *Medusa's Hair*. Chicago and London: University of Chicago Press, 1981.

-----. *The Cult of the Goddess Pattini*. Chicago and London: University of Chicago Press, 1984.

Paranavitana, Senarat. *The God of Adams Peak*. Ascona, Switzerland: Artibus Asian Publications, 1958.

Peiris, Edmund. "Marriage Customs and Ceremonies of Ceylon." *Journal of the Royal Asiatic Society, Ceylon Branch*, n.s. 8 (1), 1962.

Perera, Jayantha. *New Dimensions of Social Stratification in Rural Sri Lanka*. Colombo: Lake House Press, 1985.

Pertold, Otakar. *The Ceremonial Dances of the Sinhalese: An Inquiry into Sinhalese Folk Religion*. Dehiwala, Sri Lanka: Tisara Publications Ltd.

Raghavan, M. D. "The Ahikuntikayas." *Spolia Zeylanica*, 27 (1), 1953.

Ratnapala, Nandasena. "Some Observations on the Kandyan Sinhalese Kinship System." *Man*, 3 (3), September 1968.

-----. *Folklore of Sri Lanka*. Colombo: State Printing Corp., 1991.

Seligmann, C. G., and Brenda Z. Seligmann. *The Veddas*. Oosterhout: Anthropological Publications, 1969.

Seneviratne, H. L. *Rituals of the Kandyan State*. Cambridge: Cambridge University Press, 1978.

Southwold, M. *Buddhism in Life: The Anthropological Study of Religion and the Sinhalese Practice of Buddhism*. Manchester: Manchester University Press, 1983.

Spittel, Richard Lionel. *Vanishing Trails: The Last of the Veddas*. Bombay: Oxford University Press, 1950.

Stirrat, R. L. *On the Beach: Fishermen, Fishwives and Fishtraders in Post-Colonial Lanka*. Delhi: Hindustan Publishing Corporation, 1988.

Thananjayarajasingham, S. "Notes on the Telengu Gypsies of Ceylon." *Journal of the Anthropological Society of India*, 8 (2), October 1973.

Weerakoon, R. *Sri Lanka's Mythology*. Colombo: Samayawardhana Printers, 1985.

Wirz, Paul. *Exorcism and the Art of Healing in Ceylon*. Leiden: Brill, 1954.

Yalman, Nur. *Under the Bo Tree*. Berkeley: University of California Press, 1967.

Population and Demography

Abeykoon, A. T. P. L. *Demographic Aspects of Manpower in Sri Lanka*. Colombo: Ministry of Plan Implementation, 1973.

-----. *Ethno-Religious Differentials in Contraceptive Accessibility and Use in Sri Lanka*. Colombo: Ministry of Plan Implementation, 1987.

Abeyratne, O. E. R., and C. H. S. Jayewardene. *Family Planning in Ceylon*. Colombo: Colombo Apothecaries Co. Ltd., 1968.

Attanayake, Chandra. "The Theory of Demographic Transition and Sri Lanka's Demographic Experience." *Vidyodaya Journal of Arts, Science & Letters.* 12, 1984.

Caldwell, John et.al. "The Role of Traditional Fertility Regulations in Sri Lanka." *Studies in Family Planning,* 18 (1), 1987, 1-21.

Dangolla, Nimal. "Fertility Control Policies of Sri Lanka." *Sri Lanka Population Digest,* 3, 1987.

Demographic Training & Research Unit. *Demographic Atlas of Sri Lanka.* Colombo: University of Colombo, 1980.

Department of Census and Statistics. *Sri Lanka Demographic and Health Survey, 1987.* Columbia, Md.: Institute for Resource Development, 1988.

Jones, Gavin W., and S. Selvaratnam. *Population Growth and Economic Development in Ceylon.* Colombo: Hansa Publishers, 1972.

-----., and A. K. Kayani. *Population Growth and Education Progress in Ceylon.* Colombo: Caxton Printing Works, 1971.

Korale, R. B. M. *Demographic Trends and Projects. Proceedings of the First Annual Sessions of the Organization of Professional Associations.* Colombo: 6-9 October, 1988.

Langford, C. M. "The Fertility of Tamil Estate Workers in Sri Lanka." *World Fertility Survey Scientific Report, No. 31.* Coorburg: International Statistical Institute, 1982, 23-24.

Ministry of Plan Implementation. *World Fertility Survey: Sri Lanka.* Colombo: Ministry of Plan Implementation, 1978.

Rao, S. L. N. "Mortality and Morbidity in Sri Lanka" in *Population Problems of Sri Lanka.* Colombo: Demographic Training and Research Unit, University of Ceylon, Colombo, 1971, 55-78.

Ratnayake, Kanthi et.al. *Fertility Estimates of Sri Lanka Derived from the 1981 Census.* Colombo: Aitken Spence, 1984.

Sarkar, H. K. *The Demography of Ceylon*. Colombo: Ceylon Government Press, 1957.

Siddhisena, K. A. P. *Bibliography - The Demography of Sri Lanka*. Colombo: Lake House Printers and Publishers, 1981.

-----. *Family Composition and Infant and Child Mortality in Sri Lanka*. Ph.D. thesis: Michigan University, 1989, Unpublished.

Selvaratnam, S., and S. A. Meegama. "Towards a Population Policy for Ceylon." *Marga*, 1 (2), 1971.

University of Sri Lanka. *Population Problems of Sri Lanka - Proceedings of a Seminar*. Demographic Training and Research Unit, Colombo: University of Sri Lanka, 1976.

Weerasooria, W. *Population Redistribution Policies and Measures in Sri Lanka*. Colombo: Government Press, 1982.

Social Conditions

Aserappa, Antony F. *A Short History of the Ceylon Chetty Community and Various Facts of General Interest*. Colombo: Catholic Press, 1930.

Banks, Michael. "Caste in Jaffna" in Leach, E. R. (Ed.). *Aspects of Caste in South India, Ceylon and Northwest Pakistan*. Cambridge: Cambridge University Press, 1960, 61-77.

Bawa, Ahamades. "The Marriage Customs of the Moors of Ceylon." *Journal of the Royal Asiatic Society, (Ceylon Branch)*, X, 1988.

Ellawala, Hema. *Social History of Early Ceylon*. Colombo: Department of Cultural Affairs, Government of Ceylon, 1969.

Evers, H. D. *Monks, Priests and Peasants: A Study of Buddhism and Social Structure in Central Ceylon*. Leiden: E. J. Brill, 1972.

Gold, Martin. *Law and Social Change: A Study of Land Reform in Sri Lanka*. New York: Nellen, 1977.

Government of Sri Lanka. *Report of the Presidential Commission on Youth, Sessional Paper, No. 1.* Colombo: Government Press, 1990.

Gunatilake, Godfrey. *Children in Sri Lanka: A Status Report.* Colombo: UNICEF, 1987.

Hettiarachchy, Tilak. *History of Kinship in Ceylon up to the 4th Century A.D.* Colombo: Lake House Investments, 1972.

Hettige, Siri T. *Wealth, Power and Prestige: Emerging Patterns of Social Inequality in a Peasant Context.* Colombo: Sri Lanka Ministry of Higher Education, 1984.

Jayah, M. Murad. *The Sri Lanka Malays: A Brief Historical Sketch.* Colombo: Muslim Development Fund Sri Lanka, 1976.

Jayaraman, R. *Caste Continuities in Ceylon.* Bombay: Popular Prakashan Private Limited, 1975.

Kearney, Robert N., and Barbara Diane Miller. *Internal Migration in Sri Lanka and Its Social Consequences.* Boulder: Westview Press, 1987.

Mauroof, Mohammed. "Muslims in Sri Lanka: Historical, Demographic and Political Aspects." *Journal of the Institute of Muslim Minority Affairs*, 1 (2&3), 1981.

McGilvray, D. B. "Dutch Burghers and Portuguese Mechanics: Eurasian Ethnicity in Sri Lanka." *Comparative Studies in Society & History*, 24, 1982, 235-263.

Paranavitana, Senarat. *Sinhalese and the Patriots, 1815-1818.* Colombo: Colombo Apothecaries, 1950.

Peiris, G. H. "Changing Prospects of the Plantation Workers of Sri Lanka" in S. W. R. de A. Samarasinghe and Reed Coughlan (Eds.). *Economic Dimensions of Ethnic Conflict.* London: Pinter Publishers, 1991, 156-193.

Pfaffenberger, Bryan. *Caste in Tamil Culture.* New Delhi: Vikas Publishing House Pvt. Ltd., 1982.

Pieris, Ralph (Ed.). *Sinhalese Social Organization - The Kandyan Period.* Colombo: University of Ceylon Press, 1956.

Raghavan. M. D. *India in Ceylonese History, Society and Culture.* Bombay: Indian Council for Cultural Relations, Asia Publishing House, 2nd ed., 1969.

-----. *Tamil Culture in Ceylon.* Colombo: Kalai Nilayan Ltd., 1972.

Rajapakse, Sampson. *Mudaliyar - A Memoir with a Sketch of the Salagama Sinhalese, Their Chiefs and Clans.* Colombo: H. W. Cave, Printer, 1912.

Roberts, Michael. *Caste Conflict and Elite Formation.* Cambridge: Cambridge University Press, 1982.

-----. *People In-between: The Burghers and the Middle Class in the Transformations within Sri Lanka, 1790s-1960s.* Ratmalana, Sri Lanka: Sarvodaya Press, 1989.

Robinson, Marguerite S. *Political Structure of a Changing Sinhalese Village.* Cambridge: Cambridge University Press, 1975.

Ryan, Bryce. *A Sinhalese Village.* Florida: University of Miami Press, 1958.

-----. *Caste in Modern Ceylon: The Sinhalese System in Transition.* New Brunswick, N.J.: Rutgers University Press, 1953.

Schwarz, W. et.al. *The Tamils of Sri Lanka.* London: Minority Rights Group, 1986.

Sharma, K. L. *Society and Polity in Modern Sri Lanka, South Asian Studies Series 17.* New Delhi: South Asian Publishers Pvt. Ltd., 1988.

Shukri, M. A. M. *Muslims of Sri Lanka: Avenues to Antiquity.* Beruwala: Jamiah Naleemia Institute, 1986.

Stirrat, Roderick Lennox. "The Social Organization of Fishing in a Sinhalese Village." *Modern Ceylon Studies,* 6 (2), July 1975.

Tiruchelvam, Neelan. *The Ideology of Popular Justice in Sri Lanka: A Socio-Legal Inquiry*. New Delhi: Vikas Publishing House, 1984.

UNICEF-Colombo. *Sri Lanka: The Social Impact of Economic Policies During the Last Decade - A Special Study*. Colombo: UNICEF, 1985.

Weeratunge, Nireka. *Aspects of Ethnicity and Gender among the Rodi of Sri Lanka*. Colombo: International Centre for Ethnic Studies, 1988.

Wickramanayake, D. "The Caste System in Sri Lanka" in W. A. Veenhoven (Ed.). *Case Studies on Human Rights and Fundamental Freedoms - A World Survey, Vol. 2*. The Hague: Martinus Nijhoff, 1975.

Wijesekera, Nandadeva. *The Sinhalese*. Colombo: Gunasena, 1990.

Wijesinghe, C. A. *The Sinhalese Aryans*. Colombo: W. E. Bastian, 1922.

Religion

Abeyasingha, N. *The Radical Tradition. The Changing Shape of Theological Reflection in Sri Lanka*. Colombo: The Ecumenical Institute, 1985

Adikaram, E. W. *Early History of Buddhism in Ceylon*. Colombo: Gunasena, 1953.

Ames, Michael. "The Impact of Western Education on Religion & Society in Ceylon." *Pacific Affairs*, 40 (1-2), 1967.

Amunugama, Sarath. "Anagarika Dharmapala (1864-1933) and the Transformation of Sinhala Buddhist Organization in a Colonial Setting." *Social Science Information*, 24 (4), 1985.

Ananda Guruge Felicitation Committee. *Ananda: Essays in Honour of Ananda W. P. Guruge*. Colombo: Felicitation Volume Editorial Committee, 1990.

Azeez, A. M. A. "Islam in Ceylon." *Voice of Islam*. Karachi, III (9).

Balasooriya, Somaratne, Andre Bareau et al. *Buddhist Studies in Honour of Walpola Rahula*. London: Gordon Fraser, 1980.

Bond, George D. *The Buddhist Revival in Sri Lanka: Religious Tradition, Reinterpretation and Response*. Columbia: University of South Carolina Press, 1988.

Carter, John Ross (Ed.). *Religiousness in Sri Lanka*. Colombo: Marga Institute, 1979.

Casperz, P. "The Role of Sri Lanka Christians in a Buddhist Majority System." *The Ceylon Journal of Historical & Social Studies*, n.s. 4, 1974, 104-10.

Collins, Steven. *Selfless Persons, Imagery & Thought in Theravada Buddhism*. Cambridge: Cambridge University Press, 1982.

de Silva, K. M. "Hinduism and Islam in the Post-Independence of Sri Lanka." *Ceylon Journal of Historical & Social Studies*, IV (1&2), December-January 1970.

De Silva, Lynn A. *The Problem of the Self in Buddhism & Christianity*. Colombo: Study Centre for Religion & Society, 1975.

Don Peter, W. L. A. "The Catholic Presence in Sri Lanka through History, Belief and Faith" in John Ross Carter (Ed.). *Religiousness in Sri Lanka*. Colombo: Marga Institute, 1979.

Gombrich, Richard F. *Buddhist Precept and Practice: Traditional Buddhism in the Rural Highlands of Ceylon*. Oxford: Oxford University Press, 1971.

-----, and Gananath Obeyesekere. *Buddhism Transformed: Religious Change in Sri Lanka*. Delhi: Motilal Banarsidass Publishers Pvt. Ltd., 1988.

Houtart, F. *Religion and Ideology in Sri Lanka*. Colombo: Hansa Publishers, 1974.

King, Winston. *Theravada Meditation: The Buddhist Transformation of Yoga*. University Park: Pennsylvania State University Press, 1980.

Mackeen, Abdul Majid. "The Religious Practices of Muslims in Sri Lanka in Manifestation and Meaning" in John Ross Carter (Ed.). *Religiousness in Sri Lanka*. Colombo: Marga Institute, 1979.

Malalgoda, K. *Buddhism in Sinhalese Society 1750-1900*. Berkeley: University of California Press, 1976.

Mirando, A. H. *Buddhism in Sri Lanka in the 17th and 18th Centuries*. Dehiwala, Sri Lanka: Tisara Publishers Ltd., 1985.

Navaratnam, K. *Studies in Hinduism*. Jaffna, Sri Lanka: 1963.

Neill, S. *A History of Christian Missions*. Harmondsworth: Penguin, 1964.

Obeyesekere, G. "Social Change and Deities: The Rise of Bhakti Religiosity in Buddhist Sri Lanka." *Man*, 12, 1977.

Paranavitana, S. "Pre-Buddhist Religious Beliefs in Ceylon." *Journal of Royal Asian Societies (Ceylon Branch)*, XXXI (82), 1929.

Pfaffenberger, B. "The Kataragama Pilgrimage: Hindu-Buddhist Interaction and its Significance in Sri Lanka's Polyethnic Social System." *Journal of Asian Studies*, 38, 1979.

Phadnis, Urmila. *Religion & Politics in Sri Lanka*. London: C. Hurst Publishers, 1976.

Rahula, Walpola. *History of Buddhism in Ceylon*. Colombo: Gunasena, 1956.

-----. *The Heritage of the Bhikku: A Short History of the Bhikku in the Educational, Cultural, Social and Political Life*. New York: Grove Press, 1974.

Siriwardene, R. (Ed.). *Equality and the Religious Traditions of Asia*. London: Frances Pinter, 1987.

Smith, B. (Ed.). *Religion and the Legitimation of Power in Sri Lanka.* Chambersburg, Pa: Anima Books, 1978.

Stirrat, R. L. *Power and Religiosity in a Post-Colonial Setting: Sinhala Catholics in Contemporary Sri Lanka.* Cambridge: Cambridge University Press, 1992.

Tambiah, S. J. *Buddhism Betrayed? Religion, Politics and Violence in Sri Lanka.* Chicago and London: The University of Chicago Press, 1992.

Wickremeratne, Ananda. *Buddhism and Ethnicity in Sri Lanka: A Historical Analysis.* New Delhi: Vikas Publishing House, 1995.

Wilson, D. K. *The Christian Church in Sri Lanka.* Colombo: Study Centre for Religion and Society, 1975.

Women

Abeywardena, Padmini. *Women and Credit in Sri Lanka.* Colombo: CENWOR, 1993.

Amarasuriya, Nimala R. *Technologies in Use by Women in Household and Economic Activities.* Colombo: CENWOR, 1992

Andersshon, Claes Axel. *Women's Participation in the Construction Industry in Sri Lanka.* Colombo: International Labour Organization, 1991.

CENWOR. *Integrating Women in Development. Integrated Rural Development Programmes.* Colombo: CENWOR, 1990.

CENWOR. *Shadows and Vistas: On Being a Girl Child in Sri Lanka.* Colombo: CENWOR, 1993.

CENWOR. *Proceedings of the Fourth National Convention on Women's Studies.* Colombo: CENWOR, 3-6 March 1994.

-----. *Facets of Change: Women in Sri Lanka. 1986-1995.* Colombo: CENWOR, 1995.

-----. *Facing Odds: Women in the Labour Market.* Colombo: CENWOR, 1995.

-----. *Women, Political Empowerment and Decision-Making.* Colombo: CENWOR, 1995.

Department of Census and Statistics. *Women & Men in Sri Lanka.* Colombo: 1995.

Dewaraja, Lorna (Ed.). *Growth and Development of the Sri Lanka Federation of University Women 1941-1991.* Colombo: SLFUW, 1991.

Government of Sri Lanka. *Women's Charter (Sri Lanka).* Colombo: Ministry of State for Women's Affairs, 1993.

Harris, Elizabeth J. *The Gaze of the Coloniser: British Views on Local Women in the 19th Century.* Colombo: Social Scientists Association, 1994.

Jayaweera, Swarna. *Women, Education and Training.* Colombo: CENWOR, March 1993.

-----., and Thana Sanmugam. *Women in the Rubber Sector in Sri Lanka.* Colombo: CENWOR, 1993.

Kiribamune, Sirima, and Vidyamali Samarasinghe (Eds.). *Women at the Crossroads: A Sri Lankan Perspective.* Kandy: International Centre for Ethnic Studies, 1990.

Perera, Pearl. *Rights of Women in Buddhism.* Colombo: the author, 1993.

Samarasinghe, L. K. Vidyamali, Sirima Kiribamune, and Vijaya Jayatilake. *Maternal Nutrition and Health Status of Indian Tamil Female Tea Plantation Workers in Sri Lanka.* Washington, D.C.: International Center for Research on Women, Research Monograph No. 8, 1991.

-----. "Access of Female Plantation Workers in Sri Lanka to Basic Needs Provisions" in Momsen, Jane and Vivian Kinnaird (Eds.) *Different Voices, Different Faces: Gender and Development in*

Africa, Asia and Latin America. London: Routledge & Kegan Paul, 1993.

-----. "'Puppets on a String': Women's Wage Work and Empowerment among Female Tea Plantation Workers of Sri Lanka." *Journal of Developing Areas,* April 1993.

-----. Sri Lanka Federation of University Women. *Women Engineers in Sri Lanka.* Colombo: Sri Lanka Federation of University Women, 1992.

Svendsen, Dian Seslan, and Sujatha Wijetilleke. *Navamaga: Training Activities for Group Building, Health and Income Generation.* Colombo: Women's Bureau of Sri Lanka, 1983.

Thiruchandran, Selvy (Ed.). *Images.* Colombo: Women's Education and Research Centre, 1994.

Uyangoda, Jayadeva. *Life under Milk Wood: Women Workers in Rubber Plantations. An Overview.* Colombo: Women's Education and Research Centre, 1995.

Education

Anon. "Buddhist Temple Education in Ceylon." *Maha Bodhi,* 19 (19), September 1911.

Ariyadasa, K. D. *Management of Educational Reforms in Sri Lanka.* Paris: UNESCO Press, 1976.

Bastian, Sunil. "University Admission and the National Question" in *Ethnicity & Social Change in Sri Lanka.* Colombo: Social Scientists Association, 1985.

De Saram, Don David. "Education: An Era of Reforms." *Asian Survey,* 13 (12) December, 1973.

De Silva, C. R. "Sinhala-Tamil Relations and Education in Sri Lanka: The University Admissions Issue -The First Phase, 1971-7" in Goldmann, Robert B. and A. J. Wilson (Eds.). *From Independence* to Statehood - Managing Ethnic Conflict in Five African and Asian States. London: Frances Pinter (Publishers), 1984, 125-146.

De Silva, Kingsley M. "The Universities of the Government in Sri Lanka." Minerva. A Review of Science, Learning and Policy, 16 (2) Summer, 1978.

-----. "University Admissions and Ethnic Tension in Sri Lanka" in Goldmann, Robert B. and A. J. Wilson (Eds.). From Independence to Statehood - Managing Ethnic Conflict in Five African and Asian States. London: Frances Pinter (Publishers), 1984, 97-110.

-----. "A University Grants Commission in a South Asian Setting: The Sri Lanka Experience." Higher Education. 13 (5), October 1984.

-----. "An Annual Survey of The Universities of Sri Lanka." The Commonwealth Universities Yearbook. London: The Association of Commonwealth University. (Annual)

-----. "The Sri Lankan Universities from 1977 to 1990: Recovery, Stability and the Descent to Crisis." Minerva, 1989.

-----, and G. H. Peiris (Eds.). The University System of Sri Lanka: Vision and Reality, Kandy: International Centre for Ethnic Studies, 1995.

De Silva, Chandra Richard, and Daya de Silva. Education in Sri Lanka 1948-1988: An Analysis of the Structure and a Critical Survey of the Literature. New Delhi: Navrang, 1990.

Diyasena, W. Pre-vocational Education in Sri Lanka. Paris: UNESCO, 1976.

Don Peter, W. L. A. Fr. Education in Sri Lanka under the Portuguese. Colombo: The Colombo Catholic Press, 1978.

Fernando, M. R. Financing of Education. Colombo: Sri Lanka Economic Association, 1993.

Gnanamuttu, George A. Education and the Indian Plantation Worker in Sri Lanka. Colombo: Wesley Press, 1977.

Government of Ceylon. *Education in Ceylon: A Centenary Volume.* Colombo: Ministry of Education, 1969.

Government of Sri Lanka. *An Introduction to the Open University of Sri Lanka.* Colombo: Ministry of Higher Education, 1980.

Government of Sri Lanka. *Some Indicators and Projections Relevant to First and Second Level General Education.* Ministry of Education, December 1986.

Gunawardana, R. A. L. H (Ed.). *More Open Than Usual? An Assessment of the Experiment in University Education at Peradeniya and Its Antecedents.* Peradeniya: University of Peradeniya, 1992.

Indraratne, A. D. V. de S. (Ed.). *Increasing Efficiency of Management of Higher Education Resources.* Colombo: University Grants Commission, 1986.

-----. *Economics of Higher Education in Sri Lanka.* New Delhi: Navrang, 1992.

Jayasekera, U. D. *Early History of Education in Ceylon.* Colombo: Department of Cultural Affairs, 1969.

Jayasuriya, John Ernest. *Educational Policies and Progress During the British Rule in Ceylon (Sri Lanka) 1796-1948.* Colombo: Associated Educational Publishers, 1976.

-----. *Education in Ceylon Before and After Independence 1939-1968.* Colombo: Associated Educational Publishers, 1969.

Jayaweera, Swarna. "Education" in Fernando, T. and R. Kearney (Eds.). *Modern Sri Lanka: A Society in Transition.* New York: Syracuse University Press, 1979.

-----. "Recent Trends in Educational Expansion in Ceylon." *International Review of Education.* Hamburg: UNESCO Institute for Education, 15 (3), 1969.

-----. "Women and Education" in *UN Decade for Women: Progress and Achievements of Women in Sri Lanka*. Colombo: CENWOR, 1985.

Jennings, Sir Ivor. "The Foundation of the University of Ceylon." *University of Ceylon Review*, IX (3-4), n.d.

Kularatne, P. de S. *Foundation for a National System of Education*. Colombo: USIS, 1976.

Mathew, C. Cyril. *Diabolical Conspiracy*. Dematagoda, Sri Lanka: Rev. Karandeniye Wimalajothi, (undated).

National Association for Total Education-Sri Lanka (NATE). *Adult Literacy in Sri Lanka: Part I, Survey Report*. Colombo: NATE, 1990.

Roberts, Michael Webb. "Ragging at the Peradeniya Campus, Open Letter in Criticism," I & II. *TRIBUNE*, 20 (6), June 28, 1975.

Ruberu, T. Ranjit. *Educational Tradition Indigenous to Ceylon. Paedagogica Historica (International Journal of the History of Education)*, Ghent, Belgium: 1974.

Sanyal, Bikas C. et al. *University Education and Graduate Employment in Sri Lanka*. Paris: UNESCO, 1983.

Sarachchandra, E. R. "Some Popular Myths About Arts Students and Arts Faculties." *Nation*, 5 (32), May 30, 1971.

Strauss, Murray. "Family Characteristics and Occupational Choice of University Entrants as Clues to the Social Structure of Ceylon." *University of Ceylon Review*, 9, April 1951.

Sultan Bawa, M. U. S. *Some Observations on Science, Technology and Development in the Context of Sri Lanka*. Colombo: Proceedings of the Ceylon Association for the Advancement of Science, 28th Annual Sessions, December 1972, 1973.

Sumathipala, K. H. M. *History of Education in Ceylon: 1796-1965*. Dehiwala, Sri Lanka: Tisara Publishers Ltd., 1968.

Uswattearachi, G. "University Admission in Ceylon: Their Economic and Social Background and Employment Expectations." *Modern Asian Studies*, VIII (3), 1974.

POLITICS

Governance

Alles, A. C. *Insurgency 1971.* Colombo: Apothecaries, 1976.

-----. *The JVP 1969-1989.* Colombo: Lake House, 1990.

Austin, Dennis. *Democracy and Violence in India and Sri Lanka.* New York: Council on Foreign Relations Press, 1995.

Bastian, Sunil. "Political Economy of Ethnic Violence in Sri Lanka: The July 1983 Riots" in Veena Das (Ed.). *Communities, Riots and Survivors in South Asia.* Delhi: Oxford University Press, 1990 , 286-304.

-----.(Ed.). *Devolution and Development in Sri Lanka.* Colombo: ICES, & Delhi: Konark Publishers, 1994.

Bond, George. *The Buddhist Revival in Sri Lanka: The Religious Tradition, Reinterpretation and Response.* Columbia, S.C.: University of South Carolina, 1988.

Canagaretna, S. M. "Nation Building in a Multi-Ethnic Setting: The Sri Lankan Case." *Asian Affairs*, 1987, 14, 1-19.

Chandraprema, C. A. *Ruhuna: A Study of the History, Society & Ideology of Southern Sri Lanka.* Nugegoda, Sri Lanka: Bharat Publishers, 1989.

-----. *Sri Lanka: The Years of Terror - The JVP Insurrection 1987-1989.* Colombo: Lake House, 1991.

Committee for Rational Development. *Sri Lanka: The Ethnic Conflict, Myths, Realities and Perspectives.* New Delhi: Navrang, 1983.

Coomaraswamy, Radhika. *Sri Lanka: The Crisis of the Anglo-American Constitutional Traditions in a Developing Society.* New Delhi: Vikas, 1984.

Cooray, J. A. L. *Constitutional and Administrative Law of Sri Lanka (Ceylon).* Colombo: Hansa Publishers, 1973.

Crossette, Barbara. "Hatreds, Human Rights and the News: What We Ignore." *SAIS Review,* Winter-Spring 1993, 1-11.

De Silva, C. R. "The Constitution of the Second Republic of Sri Lanka (1978) and its Significance." *The Journal of Commonwealth and Comparative Politics,* XVII(2), 192-209.

-----. "Sinhala-Tamil Ethnic Rivalry: The Background" in Goldmann, Robert B. and A. J. Wilson (Eds.). *From Independence to Statehood - Managing Ethnic Conflict in Five African and Asian States.* London: Frances Pinter (Publishers), 1984, 111 -124.

De Silva, H. L. "The Indo-Sri Lanka Agreement (1987) in the Perspective of Inter-State Relations." *Ethnic Studies Report,* Vol. X, No.2, July 1992, 10-17.

De Silva, K. M. (Ed.). *Universal Franchise, 1931-1981: The Sri Lankan Experience.* Colombo: Department of Information, 1981.

-----. *Managing Ethnic Tensions in Multi Ethnic Societies: Sri Lanka, 1880-1985.* Lanham, Md.: University Press of America, 1986.

-----. "Buddhist Revivalism, Nationalism and Politics in Modern Sri Lanka" in James W. Bjorkman (Ed.). *Fundamentalism, Revivalists and Violence in South Asia.* New Delhi: Manohar, 1988, 107-158.

-----. "Separatism in Sri Lanka: The "Traditional Homelands" of the Tamils" in Premdas, Ralph R., S. W. R. de A. Samarasinghe, and Alan B. Anderson (Eds.). *Secessionist Movements in Comparative Perspective.* London: Pinter Publishers, 1990, 32-47.

-----. (Ed.). *Sri Lanka: The Problems of Governance.* New Delhi: Konark, 1993.

-----. "The Making of the Indo-Sri Lanka Accord: The Final Phase - June-July 1987" in de Silva, K. M. and S. W. R. de A. Samarasinghe (Eds.). *Peace Accords and Ethnic Conflict.* London: Pinter Publishers, 1993, 112-155.

-----. *The "Traditional Homelands" of the Tamils - Separatist Ideology in Sri Lanka: A Historical Appraisal.* Kandy: International Centre for Ethnic Studies, 1994.

-----, and Howard Wriggins. *J. R. Jayewardene of Sri Lanka. A Political Biography. Volume 1: 1906-1956.* London: Anthony Blond, 1988.

-----. *J. R. Jayewardene of Sri Lanka. A Political Biography. Volume II: 1956-1989.* London: Leo Cooper, 1994.

Dharmadasa, K. N. O. *Language, Religion and Ethnic Assertiveness: The Growth of Sinhalese Nationalism in Sri Lanka.* Ann Arbor: Michigan University Press, 1992.

Dissanayake, T. D. S. A. *The Agony of Sri Lanka: An In-depth Account of the Racial Riots of July 1983.* Colombo: Swastika (Pvt.) Ltd., 1983.

-----. *The Dilemma of Sri Lanka.* Colombo: Swastika (Pvt.) Ltd., 1993.

-----. *The Politics of Sri Lanka.* Colombo: Swastika (Pvt.) Ltd., 1994.

Fernando, Tissa and Robert N. Kearney (Eds.). *Modern Sri Lanka: A Society in Transition.* Syracuse: Maxwell School of Citizenship and Public Affairs, 1979.

Government of Sri Lanka. *Report of the Presidential Commission on Youth.* Sessional Paper No. 1. Colombo: Presidential Commission on Youth, 1990.

Gunaratna, Rohan. *War and Peace in Sri Lanka (with a post-accord report from Jaffna).* Kandy: Institute of Fundamental Studies, 1987.

-----. *Sri Lanka: A Lost Revolution? The Inside Story of the JVP.* Colombo: Institute of Fundamental Studies, 1990.

-----. *Indian Intervention in Sri Lanka: The Role of India's Intelligence Agencies.* Colombo: South Asian Network on Conflict Research, 1993.

Hensman, Rohini. *Journey Without a Destination. Is There a Solution for Sri Lankan Refugees?* Colombo: the author, 1993.

Hoole, Rajan et al. *The Broken Palmyra: The Tamil Crisis in Sri Lanka - An Inside Account.* Claremont, California: The Sri Lanka Studies Institute, 1990.

Hulugalle, H. A. J. *The Life and Times of Don Stephen Senanayake.* Colombo: Gunasena, 1975.

Jayantha, Dilesh. *Electoral Allegiance in Sri Lanka.* Cambridge: Cambridge University Press, 1992.

Jayatilleka, Dayan. *Sri Lanka: The Travails of a Democracy, Unfinished War, Protracted Crisis.* New Delhi: Vikas Publishing House, 1995.

Jayawardena, Visakha Kumari. *The Rise of the Labour Movement in Ceylon.* Durham, N.C.: Duke University Press, 1972.

-----. *Ethnic and Class Conflicts in Sri Lanka.* Colombo: Navamaga Printers, 1986.

Jayewardene, J. R. *Men and Memories: Autobiographical Recollections and Reflections.* New Delhi: Vikas, 1992.

Jeffries, Sir Charles. *Ceylon, The Path to Independence.* London: Pall Mall Press, 1962.

Jennings, Sir Ivor. *The Constitution of Ceylon,* 3rd ed. London: Oxford University Press, 1953.

-----, and H. W. Tambiah. *The Dominion of Ceylon.* London: Stevens, 1952.

Jiggins, Janice. *Caste and Family in the Politics of the Sinhalese 1947-1976.* Cambridge: Cambridge University Press, 1979.

Jupp, James. *Sri Lanka, Third World Democracy.* London: Frank Cass, 1978.

Kanapathipillai, Valli. "July 1983: The Survivor's Experience" in Veena Das (Ed.).*Communities, Riots and Survivors in South Asia.* Delhi: Oxford University Press, 1990, 321-344.

Kapferer, Bruce. *Legends of People, Myths of State: Violence, Intolerance and Political Culture in Sri Lanka and Australia.* Washington, D.C.: Smithsonian Institution Press, 1967.

Kearney, Robert N. *Communalism and Language in the Politics of Ceylon.* Durham, N.C.: Duke University Press, 1967.

-----. *Trade Unions and Politics in Ceylon.* Berkeley: University of California Press, 1971.

-----. *The Politics of Ceylon (Sri Lanka).* Ithaca, N.Y.: Cornell University Press, 1973.

-----, and J. Jiggins. "The Ceylon Insurrection of 1971." *The Journal of Commonwealth and Comparative Politics,* XIII(1), 40-64.

Keerawella, G. B. "The Janatha Vimukthi Peramuna and the 1971 Uprising." *Social Science Review,* Vol. 2, 1989.

Kemper, Steven. *The Presence of the Past: Chronicles, Politics and Culture in Sinhala Nationalism.* Ithaca, N.Y.: Cornell University Press, 1991.

Kodikara, Shelton U. *Indo-Sri Lanka Agreement of July 1987.* Colombo: University of Colombo, 1989.

-----. *External Compulsions of South Asian Politics.* New Delhi: Sage, 1993.

Leitan, G. R. Tressie. *Local Government and Decentralized Administration in Sri Lanka.* Colombo: Lake House, 1979.

-----. *Political Integration Through Decentralization and Devolution of Power: The Sri Lankan Experience.* Colombo: Department of Political Science, University of Colombo, 1990.

Little, David. *Sri Lanka: The Invention of Enmity*. Washington, D.C.: United States Institute of Peace, 1994.

Manikkalingam, Ram. *Prudently Negotiating a Moral Peace*. Colombo: Social Scientists Association, 1994.

Manogaran, Chelvadurai. *Ethnic Conflict and Reconciliation in Sri Lanka*. Honolulu: University of Hawaii Press, 1987.

-----, and Bryan Pfaffenberger (Eds.). *The Sri Lankan Tamils: Ethnicity and Identity*. Boulder: Westview, 1994.

Manor, James (Ed.). *Sri Lanka in Change and Crisis*. London: Croom Helm, 1984.

-----. *The Expedient Utopian: Bandaranaike and Ceylon*. Cambridge: Cambridge University Press, 1989.

Marga Institute. *Inter-racial Equity and National Unity in Sri Lanka*. Colombo: The Marga Institute, 1984.

McGowan, William. *Only Man is Vile: The Tragedy of Sri Lanka*. London: Picador, 1992.

Moore, Mick. *The State and Peasant Politics in Sri Lanka*. Cambridge: Cambridge University Press, 1985.

Movement for Inter-Racial Justice and Equality. *Someone Else's War*. Colombo: MIRJE, 1994.

Muni, S. D. *Pangs of Proximity: India and Sri Lanka's Ethnic Crisis*. Oslo: Peace Research Institute Oslo (PRIO), 1993.

Namasivayam, S. *The Legislatures of Ceylon 1928-1948*. London: Faber, 1951.

Nyrop, R. F. et al. (Eds.). *An Area Handbook for Ceylon*. Washington, D.C.: Government Printing Office, 1974.

O'Ballance, Edgar. *The Cyanide War: Tamil Insurrection in Sri Lanka 1973-88*. London: Brassey's, 1989.

Oberst, R. C. *Democracy and Persistence of Westernized Elite Dominance in Sri Lanka*. Boulder: Westview, 1985.

Peace Research Institute Oslo (PRIO). *Political Violence in Sri Lanka.* Oslo, 1989.

Perera, N. M. *Critical Analysis of the New Constitution of the Sri Lanka Government Promulgated on 31-08-1978.* Colombo: Dr. N. M. Perera Memorial Trust, 1979.

Perera, Sasanka. *Living With Torturers and Other Essays.* Colombo: International Centre for Ethnic Studies, 1995.

Phadnis, Urmila. *Religion and Politics in Sri Lanka.* New Delhi: Manohar, 1976.

----. "Sri Lanka: Crisis of Legitimacy and Integration" in Larry Diamond et al. (Eds.). *Democracy in Developing Countries, Vol. 3: Asia.* Boulder, Colo.: Riemer-Adamantine Press, 1989, ch 4.

Ponnambalam, Satchi. *Sri Lanka, The National Question and the Tamil Liberation Struggle.* London: Zed Press, 1983.

Raby, Namika. *Kachcheri Bureaucracy in Sri Lanka: The Culture and Politics of Accessibility.* Syracuse, N.Y.: Syracuse University Press, 1985.

Ratnatunga, Sinha. *The Politics of Terrorism: The Sri Lanka Experience.* Canberra: International Fellowship for Social and Economic Development, 1988.

Richardson Jr., John M., and S. W. R. de A. Samarasinghe. "Measuring the Economic Dimensions of Sri Lanka's Ethnic Conflict" in Samarasinghe, S. W. R. de A. and Reed Coughlan (Eds.). *Economic Dimensions of Ethnic Conflict: International Perspectives.* London: Pinter Publishers, 1991, 194-223.

Roberts, Michael W. *Caste Conflict and Elite Formation. The Rise of a Karava Elite in Sri Lanka, 1500-1931.* Cambridge: Cambridge University Press, 1982.

-----.(Ed.). *Documents of the Ceylon National Congress and Nationalist Politics in Ceylon, 1929-1950,* 4 Vols. Colombo: Department of National Archives, 1978.

-----.(Ed.). *Collective Identities, Nationalisms and Protest in Modern Sri Lanka.* Colombo: Marga Institute, 1979.

-----. "Noise as Cultural Struggle: Tom-Tom Beating, the British and Communal Disturbances in Sri Lanka, 1880s-1930s" in Veena Das (Ed.).*Communities, Riots and Survivors in South Asia.* Delhi: Oxford University Press, 1990, 240-285.

-----. *Exploring Confrontation. Sri Lanka: Politics, Culture and History.* Chur: Harwood Academic Publishers, 1994.

Ross, Russell R., and Andrea Matles Savada (Eds.). *Sri Lanka: A Country Study.* Washington, D.C.: United States Govt. Printing Office, 1991.

Russell, Jane. "Sri Lanka's Election Turning Point." (The General Election of 1977). *The Journal of Commonwealth and Comparative Politics,* XVI(1), 79-97.

-----. *Communal Politics under the Donoughmore Constitution, 1931-1947.* Dehiwala: Tisara Press, 1983.

Samarasinghe, S. W. R. de A. "Ethnic Representation in Central Government Employment and Sinhala-Tamil Relations in Sri Lanka, 1948-81" in Goldmann, R. B., and A. Jeyaratnam Wilson (Eds.). *From Independence to Statehood.* London: Frances Pinter, 1984, 173-184.

-----. "The Dynamics of Separatism in Sri Lanka" in Premdas, Ralph R., S. W. R. de A. Samarasinghe and Alan B. Anderson (Eds.). *Secessionist Movements in Comparative Perspective.* London: Pinter Publishers, 1990, 48-70.

-----. "The 1994 Parliamentary Elections in Sri Lanka: A Vote for Good Governance." *Asia Survey,* XXXIV(12) December 1994, 1019-1034.

Samarasinghe, S.W.R.de A., and Kamala Liyanage. "Friends and Foes of the Indo-Sri Lanka Accord" in de Silva, K. M. and S. W. R. de A. Samarasinghe (Eds.). *Peace Accords and Ethnic Conflict.* London: Pinter Publishers, 1993, 156-172.

Singer, Marshall R. *The Emerging Elite: A Study of Political Leadership in Ceylon.* Cambridge, Mass.: MIT Press, 1964.

Smith, D. E. (Ed.). *South Asian Politics and Religion.* Princeton: Princeton University Press, 1966.

Spencer, Jonathan (Ed.). *Sri Lanka: History and the Roots of Conflict.* London: Routledge, 1990.

Tambiah, Stanley J. *Sri Lanka: Ethnic Fratricide and the Dismantling of Democracy.* Chicago: University of Chicago Press, 1986.

-----. *Buddhism Betrayed? Religion, Politics and Violence in Sri Lanka.* Chicago: University of Chicago Press, 1992.

Tiranagama, Rajni. et al. *The Broken Palmyra: The Tamil Crisis in Sri Lanka, An Inside Account.* Claremont: The Sri Lanka Studies Institute, 1990.

Tiruchelvam, Neelan. "The Politics of Decentralization and Devolution: Competing Conceptions of District Development Councils in Sri Lanka" in Goldmann, Robert B. and A. J. Wilson (Eds.). *From Independence to Statehood - Managing Ethnic Conflict in Five African and Asian* States. London: Frances Pinter (Publishers), 1984, 196-209.

University Teachers for Human Rights (Jaffna). *Someone Else's War.* Colombo: Movement for Inter Racial Justice and Equality, 1994.

Vijayavardhana, D. C. *The Revolt in the Temple.* Colombo: Sinha Publications, 1953.

Warnapala, W. A. Wiswa. *Ethnic Strife and Politics in Sri Lanka: An Investigation into Demands and Responses.* New Delhi: Navrang, 1994.

-----. *Local Politics in Sri Lanka: An Analysis of the Local Government Election of May 1991.* New Delhi: South Asian Publishers, 1993.

-----. *The Sri Lankan Political Scene.* New Delhi: Navrang, 1993.

-----, and L. Dias Hewagama. *Recent Politics in Sri Lanka.* New Delhi: Navrang, 1983.

Weerakoon, Bradman. *Premadasa of Sri Lanka: A Political Biography*. New Delhi: Vikas, 1992.

-----, and Shelton Wanasinghe. *Reflections on Governance*. Colombo: Marga Publication, 1994.

Weerawardene, I. D. S. *Government and Politics in Ceylon, 1931-1946*: Colombo: Ceylon Economic Research Association, 1951.

Wickremeratne, Ananda. *The Roots of Nationalism: Sri Lanka*. Colombo: Karunaratne & Sons, 1995.

Wijesinha, Rajiva. *Sri Lanka in Crisis 1977-88*. Colombo: Council for Liberal Democracy, 1991.

Wilson, A. Jeyaratnam. *Oppositional Politics in Ceylon 1948-1968*, Government and Opposition, IV(1), 54-69; reprinted in Rodney Barker (Ed.). *The Opposition and New States*. London: Macmillan, 1972.

-----. *Electoral Politics in an Emergent State: The Ceylon General Elections of May 1970*. Cambridge: Cambridge University Press, 1975.

-----. *Politics in Sri Lanka, 1947-1979*. London: Macmillan, 1979.

-----. *The Gaullist System in Asia, The Constitution of Sri Lanka (1978)*. London: Macmillan, 1980.

-----. *The Break-up of Sri Lanka: The Sinhalese-Tamil Conflict*. Honolulu: University of Hawaii Press, 1988.

-----. *S. J. V. Chelvanayakam and the Crises of Sri Lankan Tamil Nationalism, 1947-1977*. London: C. Hurst, 1994.

Woodward, Calvin. *The Growth of a Party System in Ceylon*. Providence, R.I.: Brown University Press, 1969.

Wriggins, W. Howard. *Ceylon: Dilemmas of a New Nation*. Princeton, N.J.: Princeton University Press, 1960.

-----. "Impediments to Unity in New Nations: The Case of Ceylon." *The American Political Science Review*, LV(2), 313-21.

Human Rights

Amnesty International. *Report on Sri Lanka*. London: Amnesty International, Annual.

-----. *Sri Lanka: `Disappearances.'* New York: 1986.

Centre for the Study of Human Rights (CSHR), University of Colombo & the Nadesan Centre, *Review of Emergency Regulations*. Colombo: 1993.

Civil Rights Movement of Sri Lanka (CRM). *Human Rights and Our International Obligations - Sri Lanka's Record on Ratification of International Agreements*. Colombo: CRM, 1992.

Commission for the Elimination of Discrimination and Monitoring Fundamental Rights - Sri Lanka, *Annual Report*.

Goonesekere, R. K. W. *Fundamental Rights and the Constitution - A Case Book*. Colombo: Law and Society Trust, 1988.

Human Rights Task Force. *Annual Report*. Colombo: 1995

Law and Society Trust. *Sri Lanka - State of Human Rights 1994*. Colombo: Law & Society Trust, 1995.

International Relations

De Silva, K. M. *Regional Powers & Small State Security: India & Sri Lanka, 1977-90*. Washington, D.C.: The Woodrow Wilson Center Press and Baltimore: The Johns Hopkins University Press, 1995.

Kodikara, Shelton U. *Indo-Ceylon Relations since Independence*. Colombo: Ceylon Institute of World Affairs, 1965.

-----. (Ed.). *Dilemmas of Indo-Sri Lanka Relations*. Colombo: Bangladesh Centre for Ethnic Studies, 1991.

-----. *Foreign Policy of Sri Lanka*. 2nd ed. New Delhi: Chanakya Publications. 1992.

Liyanagamage. A. *The Indian Factor in the Security Perspectives of Sri Lanka.* Colombo: University of Kelaniya. 1993.

Mendis. Vernon L.B. *Foreign Relations of Sri Lanka: From Earliest Times to 1965.* (The Ceylon Historical Journal Monograph Series Volume II). Dehiwala: Tisara Publications, 1983.

Nissanka, H.S.S. *Sri Lanka's Foreign Policy: A Study in Non-Alignment.* New Delhi: Vikas, 1984.

Phadnis, Urmila. "Foreign Policy in Sri Lanka in the Seventies." *The Institute for Defense Studies and Analyses Journal,* VIII(I), July-September 1975, 93-124.

Press

Association for Education in Journalism. *The Taming of the Press in Sri Lanka.* Lexington, Ky.: Association for Education in Journalism with the support of the American Association of Schools and Departments of Journalism, 1974.

Coomaraswamy, Radhika. "Regulatory Framework for the Press in Sri Lanka." *Marga,* 6(2), Colombo: Marga Institute, 1981, 66-77.

Fernando, W. L. *The Press in Ceylon.* Colombo: Trade Exchange (Ceylon) Ltd., 1973. [6], 63p.

Gunaratne, Shelton A. "Government-Press Conflict in Ceylon: Freedom versus Responsibility." *Journalism Quarterly,* (Minnesota): 47(3) Autumn 1970: 530-543 + 552

Gunewardena, Victor. *Press as Promoter.* Colombo: Friedrich Ebert Stiftung, 1993.

-----. "The Press in Sri Lanka." *South Asia Journal,* 2(1) July-September 1988, 39-52.

Hulugalle, H. A. J. *The Life and Times of D.R. Wijewardene.* Colombo: The Associated Newspapers of Ceylon, Ltd., 1992.

Jayaweera, Neville. "Mass Media and State in Sri Lanka- The Uncomfortable Juxtaposition." *Media Asia.* 5(2), 1978, 68-77.

Keuneman, Pieter. "Ending of Press Monopoly." *Sri Lanka Today*, XXII(3&4), November-December 1973, 13-15.

Peiris, G. L. "Journalism and the Law: Emerging Trends" in *Selected Speeches*. Colombo: Government Press, 1988, 83-85.

Perera, Jehan. "Press System in Sri Lanka." *Media Asia*. 18(3), 1991, 137-151.

Senadhira, Sugeeswara P. *Under Siege: Mass Media in Sri Lanka.* New Delhi: Segment Books, 1996.

Warnapala, W. A. Wiswa. "Press and Politics in Sri Lanka." *Journal of Constitutional and Parliamentary Studies.* New Delhi: 9(2) April-June 1975, 125-155.

Why Lake House Seeks to Destroy the Coalition. Colombo: Sri Palihena (Suriya Printers), 1970.

Wijesinghe, Rajiva. "Towards a Productive Media." *Economic Review*, 17(2&3). May/June 1991.

Wijeyesinghe, Edward C. B. "Growth of Ceylon Journals in the Nineteenth Century." *The United States Education Foundation in Sri Lanka. Historical Essays.* Colombo: Hansa Publishers, 1976. 76-6a.

ECONOMICS

General

Athukorala, Premachandra, and Sisira Jayasuriya. *Macroeconomic Policies, Prices and Growth in Sri Lanka - Comparative Macroeconomic Studies 1969-1994*, Washington, D.C.: World Bank, 1994.

Das Gupta, B. B. *A Short Economic Survey of Ceylon.* Colombo: Associated Newspapers of Ceylon Ltd., 1949.

Bibliography / 197

/ 197

Bibliography / 197

Bibliography / 197

Bibliography / 197

Bibliography / 197

Bibliography / 197

/ 197

Bibliography / 197

/ 197

Bibliography / 197

Bibliography / 197

Bibliography / 197

Dharmasena, K. et al. (Eds.). *Essays in Honour of A. D. V. de S. Indraratna.* Colombo: A. D. V. de S. Indraratne Felicitation Committee, 1994.

Dunham, David and Charles Abeysekera. (Eds). *Essays on The Sri Lankan Economy, 1977-83.* Colombo: Social Scientists Association, 1987.

Friedrich Ebert Stiftung. *Aspects of Privatization in Sri Lanka.* Colombo: Friedrich Ebert Stiftung, 1988.

Hewavitharana, Buddhadasa (Ed.). *The Search for an Accurate Consumer Price Index for Sri Lanka.* Colombo: Friedrich Ebert Stiftung, 1992.

Indraratna Felicitation Committee. *Essays in Honour of A. D. V. de S. Indraratna.* Colombo: A. D. V. de S. Indraratna Felicitation Committee, 1994.

Institute of Policy Studies. *Sri Lanka - Economic Performance Review.* Colombo: (Annual).

------. *Sri Lanka: State of the Economy 1991/92.* Colombo: Institute of Policy Studies, 1992.

Kappagoda, Nihal, and Suzanne Paine. *The Balance of Payments Adjustment Process: The Experience of Sri Lanka.* Colombo: Marga Institute, 1981.

Marga Institute. *The Informal Sector of Colombo City (Sri Lanka).* Colombo: Marga Institute, 1979.

Rahman, Masihar. *Political Economy of Income Distribution in Sri Lanka.* New Delhi: Sterling Publishers, 1988.

Ronnie de Mel Felicitation Committee. *Facets of Development in Independent Sri Lanka.* Colombo: Ministry of Finance and Planning, 1986.

Samarasinghe, S. W. R de A. "Economic Adjustment: Effects on Health and Nutrition - Sri Lanka: A Case Study for the Third World" in David E. Bell and Michael R. Reich (Eds). *Health,*

198 / Bibliography

Nutrition, and Economic Crises: Approaches to Policy in the Third World. Dover, Mass.: Auburn Publishing Company, 1988, 39-80.

-----. "Economic and Ethical Implications of the Brain Drain of MDs from the Developing World: A Case Study from Sri Lanka" in Kiyoshi Aoki (Ed.). *Ethical Dilemmas in Health and Development.* Tokyo: Japan Scientific Societies Press, 1994, 119-139.

Sirisena, N. L. *A Multisectoral Model of Production for Sri Lanka.* Colombo: Central Bank of Ceylon, 1976.

Snodgrass, D. R. *Ceylon: An Export Economy in Transition.* Illinois: Richard Irwin, 1966.

Sri Lanka Association of Economists. *Structural Adjustment, and Growth.* Colombo: Sri Lanka Association of Economists, 1986.

Agriculture

Abeysekera, C. *Capital and Peasant Production: Studies in the Continuity and Discontinuity of Agrarian Structures in Sri Lanka.* Colombo: Social Scientists Association, 1985.

Bandaranayake, R. Dias. *Tea Production in Sri Lanka: Future Outlook and Mechanisms for Enhancing Sectoral Performance.* Colombo: Central Bank of Ceylon, Occasional Paper No. 7, 1984.

Bansil, P. C. *Ceylon Agriculture: A Perspective.* New Delhi: Dhanpat Rai, 1971.

Betz, Joachim. "Tea Policy in Sri Lanka." *Marga Quarterly Journal,* 10(4), 1989, 48.71.

Brow, James and Joe Weeramunda. (Eds). *Agrarian Change in Sri Lanka.* New Delhi: Sage, 1992.

Farmer, B. H. *Pioneer Peasant Colonisation in Ceylon.* Oxford: Oxford University Press, 1968.

Forrest, D. M. *A Hundred Years of Ceylon Tea: 1867-1967.* London: Chatto and Windus, 1967.

Gunaratne, W. and P. J. Gunawardena. "Poverty and Inequality in Rural Sri Lanka" in Khan, A. R. and E. Lee (Eds). *Poverty in Rural Asia*. Bangkok: I.L.O. Asian Employment Programme (ARTEP), 1983.

IBRD. *Report of the Agricultural Sector Survey for Sri Lanka*. Washington, D.C.: 1973.

Mendis, M. W. J. G. *The Planning Implications of the Mahaweli Development Project in Sri Lanka*. Colombo: Lake House, 1973.

Moore, M. P. and G. Wickramasinghe. *Agriculture and Society in the Low Country (Sri Lanka)*. Colombo: ARTI, 1980.

Richards, Peter and E. Stoutjesdijk. *Agriculture in Ceylon Until 1975*. Paris: O.E.C.D. Development Centre, 1970.

Samarasinghe, L. K. V. and S. W. R. de A. "Income Disparities in a Land Settlement in the Sri Lanka Dry Zone" in Bayliss-Smith, Tim and Sudhir, Wanmali (Eds.). *Results of the Green Revolution*. Cambridge: Cambridge University Press.

Samarasinghe, S. W. R. de A. (Ed.). *Agriculture in the Peasant Sector of Sri Lanka*. Peradeniya: Ceylon Studies Seminar, 1977.

Scudder, T. and K. P. Wimaladharma. *The Accelerated Mahaweli Programme and Dry Zone Development, Report No. 6*. New York: Binghamton Institute for Development Anthropology, 1985.

Industry

Athukorala, P. "Industrialization: Its Policies and Achievements" in Dunham, D. and C. Abeysekera (Eds). *Sri Lanka Economy - 1977-83*. Colombo: Social Scientists' Association, 1987, 252-292.

-----. "The Impact of 1977 Policy Reforms on Domestic Industry," *Upanathi* (The Journal of the Sri Lanka Association of Economists), 1(1), 1986, 69-106.

Catane, B. M. *An Assessment of Small Industries Development in Sri Lanka*. Paris: UNIDO, 1983.

Colombage, S. S. *Microeconomic Model for Sri Lanka.* Kuala Lumpur: Asian Pacific Development Centre, 1992.

De Silva, W. P. N. *Industrial Law and Relations in Ceylon.* Colombo: K. V. G. de Silva & Sons, 1964.

De Wilde, T. *Use of Technology: Rural Industrialization in Sri Lanka.* Moratuwa: Sarvodaya, 1980.

Edwards, C. *Industrial Policy in Sri Lanka: Lessons from South Korea.* Colombo: Institute of Policy Studies and University of Colombo, 1989.

Fernando, W. A. J. A. and I. Hewapathirana. *Some Aspects of Sri Lanka: Experience in Entrepreneur Development.* Colombo: Business Development Centre, 1986.

Hatch, Nigel. *Commentary on the Industrial Disputes Act of Sri Lanka.* Colombo: Friedrich Ebert Stiftung, 1989.

Herath, J. W. *Mineral Based Industries of Sri Lanka.* Colombo: Science Education Series No.15, Natural Resources Energy and Science Authority, 1986.

Hesselberg, Jan. *Artisan Production: The Case of Puwakdandawa.* Oslo: University of Oslo, 1980.

Hewavitharana, B. *Industrial Development and Location: Spatial Patterns and Policies in Sri Lanka.* Nagoya: United Nations Centre for Regional Development, 1992.

-----. *Industrialization, Employment and Basic Needs: The Case of Sri Lanka.* Geneva: I.L.O., 1986.

I.L.O. *Rural Industries and Employment in Sri Lanka.* New Delhi: I.L.O.- Asian Regional Team for Employment Promotion, 1987.

Osmani, S. R. *The Impact of Economic Liberalization on the Small Scale and Rural Industries in Sri Lanka.* New Delhi: I.L.O.- ARTEP, 1986.

Wickramanayake, B. W. E. *Rural Industries in Transition: A Case Study of Southern Sri Lanka.* The Hague: Institute of Social Studies, 1988.

Wickremasinghe, V. K. *The Development of Small Scale Industries in Sri Lanka - Experience and Prospects.* Colombo: Sri Lanka Economic Association, 1993.

Economic Overheads

Agrarian Research and Training Institute. *The Integrated Management of Major Irrigation Schemes.* Colombo: ARTI, 1991.

Karunatilake, H. N. S. *Demand and Priority of Commercial Energy in Sri Lanka.* Colombo: Sri Lanka Economic Association, 1993.

Perera, K. K. Y. W. *An Evaluation of the Trends in the Energy Sector and Potential for Developing Renewable Energy.* Colombo: Sri Lanka Economic Association, 1993.

UNDP/FAO. *Mahaweli Irrigation and Hydropower Survey- Ceylon,* Final Report, Vol. I, II & III, Rome: FAO/SF: 55/CEY-7, 1969.

Vitebsky, Piers. *Policy Dilemmas for Unirrigated Agriculture in Southeastern Sri Lanka.* Cambridge: Centre of South Asian Studies, University of Cambridge, 1984.

Trade and Commerce

Abeyratne, Sirimal. *Anti-Export Bias in the `Export-Oriented' Economy of Sri Lanka.* Amsterdam: VU University Press, 1993.

Athukorala, P. and Bandara. "Growth in Manufactured Exports, Primary Commodity, Dependence and Net Export Earnings, Sri Lanka," *World Development,* 17(6), 1989.

-----. "Export-Oriented Foreign Investment in New Exporting Countries: Patterns and Determinants with Evidence from Sri Lanka." *World Competition,* 13(1), 1989.

-----. "The Monetary Approach to Balance of Payments and Other Related Issues; Empirical Evidence of Sri Lanka." *Staff Studies*, 21(1&2), 1991, 1-26.

Corea, Gamani. *The Instability of an Export Economy*. Colombo: Marga Institute, 1975.

Cuthbertson, A. G. and P. C. Athukorala. *The Timing and Sequencing of a Trade Liberalization Policy: The Case of Sri Lanka* - World Bank Study. London: Basil Blackwell, 1989.

Deepak, Lal and Sarath Rajapathirana. *Impediments to Trade Liberalisation in Sri Lanka*. Aldershot: Gower Publishing Co. Ltd., 1989

Gunewardena, Elaine. *External Trade and the Economic Structure of Ceylon 1900-1955*. Colombo: Central Bank of Ceylon, 1965.

Jayasundera, P. B. and Y. Indraratne. Sri Lanka's Financial Sector Development with Special Reference to Taxation of Financial Instruments. *Staff Studies*, 21(1&2), Central Bank of Sri Lanka, 1991, 27-62.

Jayatissa, R. A. *Foreign Trade Experience in the Post Liberalisation Period*. Colombo: Sri Lanka Economic Association, 1993.

Rajapathirana, S. "Foreign Trade and Economic Development: Sri Lanka's Experience." *World Development*, 16, 1988, 1143-1157.

Siriwardhana, K. R. M. "A Comparative Analysis of Sri Lankan Tea Prices at the Colombo and London Landed Auctions." *Staff Studies*, 21(1&2), Central Bank of Sri Lanka, 1991, 75-97.

Sri Lanka Export Development Board. *National Export Development Plan: 1990-1994*. Vol. I & II. Colombo: Sri Lanka Export Development Board, 1992.

Finance, Banking, and Fiscal

Balaratnam, S. *Income Tax, Wealth Tax and Gift Tax in Sri Lanka*. Colombo: the author, 1979.

Bank of Ceylon. *Expanding Horizons: Bank of Ceylon's First 50 Years.* Colombo: Bank of Ceylon, 1989.

Colombage, S. S. *Monetary Policy in an Open Economy: The Experience of Sri Lanka.* Colombo: Sri Lanka Economic Association, 1993.

Dahanayake, P. A. S. *Economic Policies and Their Implications for the Foreign Exchange Availability in Sri Lanka.* Colombo: Central Bank of Ceylon, 1977.

De Valk, P. *The State and Income Distribution: With a Case Study of Sri Lanka.* The Hague: Institute of Social Studies, 1981.

Fernando, Nimal U. F. "Money Growth, Inflation, Output and Causality: The Sri Lankan Experience, 1978-1988." *Staff Studies,* 21(1&2), Central Bank of Sri Lanka, 1991, 63-74.

Jayamaha, Ranee. *The Monetary Transmission, Mechanism in Sri Lanka, 1977-1985.* Colombo: Central Bank of Sri Lanka, 1986.

Jayasundera, P. B. *Fiscal Policy and Operations in the Past 1977 Period.* Colombo: Sri Lanka Economic Association, 1993.

Karunatilake, H. N. S. *Banking and Financial Systems in Sri Lanka.* Colombo: Centre for Demographic and Socio-Economic Studies, 1986.

-----. *The Impact of Financial Sector Reforms of the Budget and the Balance of Payments.* Colombo: Sri Lanka Economic Association, 1993.

Kelegama, S. *Privatisation in Sri Lanka - Problems and Prospects.* Colombo: Sri Lanka Economic Association, 1992.

Lee, Jung Soo. *Improving Domestic Resource Mobilization through Financial Development in Sri Lanka.* Manila: Asian Development Bank, 1987.

Malhotra, V. P. *Report on Rural Credit in Sri Lanka.* Vol. I and II. Colombo: Central Bank of Sri Lanka, n.d.

Rodrigo, Chandra. A *National Wage Policy for Sri Lanka: An Investigation into Post-Independence Wage Performance and Policy Perspectives.* Colombo: Sri Lanka Institute of Development Administration, 1983.

Sirisena, N. L. *An Evaluation of the Role of Non-Bank Financial Institutions in Sri Lanka.* Colombo: Sri Lanka Economic Association, 1993.

Sirisena, P. T. *The Contribution of the Regional Rural Development Bank on the Upliftment of the Rural Economy.* Colombo: Sri Lanka Economic Association, 1993.

The Sri Lanka Association of Economists. *Structural Adjustment and Growth.* Colombo: 1986.

Weerasooria, W. S. *The Nattukotti Chettiar Merchant Bankers in Ceylon.* Dehiwala: Tisara Prakasakayo Ltd., 1973.

Wijewardena, W. A. "Monetary Policy and Instruments" in *40th Anniversary Commemorative Volume.* Colombo: Central Bank of Sri Lanka, 1990.

-----. *Capital Market in Sri Lanka - Current Problems and Future Prospect.* Colombo: Sri Lanka Economic Association, 1992.

Labor

Abeykoon, A. T. P. L. "A Labour Force Projection for Sri Lanka, 1981-2011." *Progress*, 3(2), 1983.

Crooks, C. R. and H. A. Ranbanda. *The Economics of Seasonal Labour Migration in Sri Lanka.* Colombo: Agrarian Research & Training Institute, 1981.

Dias, Malsiri. "Migrants to the Middle East: Sri Lanka Case Study." *Economic Review* (People's Bank, Colombo), 7(1), April 1981.

Eeleus, Frank and J. D. Speekmann. "Recruitment of Laborer Migrants for the Middle East: The Sri Lankan Case," *International Migration Review*, xxiv(2), Summer 1990, 297-322.

Goonesekere, S. W. E. *Child Labour in Sri Lanka: Learning from the Past.* Geneva: International Labour Office, 1993

Gunaratne, L. L. and P. W. R. B. A. U. Herat. *The Nature and Problems of Unemployment in Sri Lanka.* Colombo: Sri Lanka Economic Association, 1993.

Hewavitharana, Buddhadasa. *Rural Non-Farm Employment: Problems, Issues and Strategies.* Employment Series No. 4. Colombo: Institute of Policy Studies, 1992.

International Labour Office (I.L.O). *Matching Employment Opportunities and Expectations: A Program of Action for Ceylon.* Geneva: International Labour Office, 1971.

I.L.O.- ARTEP. *Employment and Development in the Domestic Food Crop Sector, Sri Lanka.* Report of the I.L.O.-ARTEP Rural Employment Mission to Sri Lanka, September 1984.

-----. *Impact of Out and Return Migration on Domestic Employment in Sri Lanka.* New Delhi: I.L.O. Office, 1986.

-----. *Rural Industries and Employment in Sri Lanka.* New Delhi: I.L.O. Office, 1987.

Institute of Policy Studies. *Employment and Unemployment Issues.* Colombo: Institute for Policy Studies, 1988 (mimeo).

Korale, R. B. M. *Employment and the Labour Market in Sri Lanka, A Review.* Colombo: Dept of Census and Statistics, Ministry of Plan Implementation, 1988.

Marga Institute. *Migrant Workers to the Arab World.* Colombo: Marga Institute, 1986.

Navaratne, P. *Wages, Terms and Conditions of Employment in Sri Lanka.* Colombo: Friedrich Ebert Stiftung, 1983.

Perera, U. L. J. *Hired Labour in Peasant Agriculture in Sri Lanka.* Colombo: Research Study Review, ARTI, 1980.

Samarasinghe, S. W. R. de A. "Problems, Policies and Strategies for Occupational Health and Safety in Sri Lanka" in Reich, Michael R.

and Toshiteru Okuba (Eds.). *Protecting Workers' Health in the Third World.* New York: Auburn House, 1992, 169-188.

Sanderatne, N. "The Effects of Policies on Real Income and Employment" in *Sri Lanka: The Social Impact of Economic Policies During the Last Decade.* Colombo: UNICEF, 1985.

Sirisena, W. M. "Invisible Labour: A Study of Women's Contribution to Agriculture in Two Traditional Villages in the Dry Zone of Sri Lanka." *Modern Sri Lanka Studies,* 1(2), 1986.

Wickramasekera, P. "Some Aspects of the Hired Labour Situation in Rural Sri Lanka: Some Preliminary Findings" in Hirashmia. S. (Ed.). *Hired Labour in Rural Asia.* Tokyo: Institute of Development Economies, 1977.

Wilson, P. *Economic Implications of Population Growth - Sri Lanka Labour World: 1946-81.* Canberra: Australian National University, 1975.

-----. *Changing Patterns of Employment in Sri Lanka, 1971-1996.* Colombo: Sri Jayawardenepura University, 1989.

Development

Agrarian Research and Training Institute. *Approaches to Development: The NGO Experience in Sri Lanka.* Colombo: ARTI, March 1991.

Centre for Regional Development Studies. *Sri Lanka Year 2000: Towards the 21st Century.* Colombo: 1995.

Dale, Reidar. *Organization of Regional Development Works.* Ratmalana: Sarvodaya, 1992.

De Silva, S. B. D. *The Political Economy of Underdevelopment.* London: Routledge & Kegan Paul, 1982.

Fernando, Neil and K. P. G. M. Perera (Eds.) *Regional Development in Sri Lanka.* Colombo: Sri Lanka Institute of Development Administration, 1980.

Hesselberg, Jan. *Welfare and Development in Sri Lanka.* Oslo: University of Oslo, 1984.

Marga Institute. *Housing Development in Sri Lanka 1971-1981.* Colombo: Marga Institute, 1986.

I.L.O. *Employment and Development in the Domestic Food Sector, Sri Lanka.* Bangkok: Regional Team for Employment Promotion, 1986.

Indraratne, A. D. V. de S. *The Ceylon Economy from the Great Depression to the Great Boom: 1930-1952.* Colombo: M. D. Gunasena & Co., 1966.

James, Estelle. "The Non-Profit Sector in International Perspective. The Case of Sri Lanka." *Journal of Comparative Economics,* 1989

Jennings, Sir Ivor. *The Economy of Ceylon.* Oxford: Oxford University Press, 1953.

Karunasena, A.G. *A Macroeconometric Model for Sri Lanka.* Colombo: Central Bank of Sri Lanka, 1988.

Karunatilake, H.N.S. *The Economic Development in Ceylon,* New York: Praeger, 1971.

-----. *The Economy of Sri Lanka.* Colombo: Centre for Demographic and Socio-Economic Studies, 1987.

Oliver, Henry M. *Economic Opinion and Policy in Ceylon.* Durham, N.C.: Duke University Press, 1957.

Perera, K. P. G. M. (Ed.). *District Integrated Rural Development Projects and the Rural Development Process of Sri Lanka* - A Symposium. Colombo: Ministry of Plan Implementation, 1982.

Ponnambalam, Satchi. *Dependent Capitalism in Crisis: The Sri Lankan Economy, 1948-1980.* London: Zed Press, 1981.

Rao, V. M., G. H. Peiris and S. Tilakaratne. *Planning for Rural Development - A Study of the District Integrated Rural Development Programme of Sri Lanka.* Bangkok: Asian Employment Programme, I.L.O., 1983.

Ratnapala, Nandasena. *Rural Poverty in Sri Lanka.* Colombo: The author, 1989.

Ratnayake, Piyadasa. *Towards Self-Reliant Rural Development: A Policy Experiment in Sri Lanka.* Colombo: Karunaratne and Sons Ltd., 1992.

Sahn, David E. "Changes in the Living Standards of the Poor in Sri Lanka during a Period of Macro-economic Restructuring," *World Development,* 1987, 15, 809-830.

Samarasinghe, L. K. Vidyamali. "An Evaluation of the Differential Impact of Public Policy on Spatial Inequalities in Sri Lanka" in Swindel, Ke Baba, J. M. and M. J. Mortimore. *Inequality and Development: Case Studies from the Third World.* London: Macmillan, 1989.

-----. "Polarization of Colombo: A Study in Regional Inequality." *Journal of Social Sciences,* Vol. V, No. 1, National Science Council of Sri Lanka, 1982.

Samarasinghe, S. W. R. de A. "Japanese and U.S. Health Assistance to Sri Lanka" in Reich, Michael R. and Eiji Marui (Eds.). *International Cooperation for Health: Problems, Prospects and Priorities.* Dover, Mass.: Auburn House Publishing Company, 1989, 91-118.

Snodgrass, D.R. *Ceylon: An Export Economy in Transition.* Homewood, Ill.: Richard D. Irwin, 1966.

Sri Lanka: Reform and Development 1992/93. Colombo: Institute of Policy Studies, 1993.

Sri Lanka Institute of Social and Economic Studies. *Essays in Asian Economics.* Colombo: Sri Lanka Institute of Social & Economic Studies, 1992.

Wijesinghe, D. S. *Some Experiments with a Multisectoral Intertemporal Optimization Model for Sri Lanka.* Colombo: Central Bank of Sri Lanka, 1986.

Environment

Ashton, P. S. and C. V. S. Gunatilleke. "New Light on the Plant Geography of Ceylon." *Journal of Biogeography*, 14, 1987, 249-285.

Central Environmental Authority. *Sri Lanka: National Conservation Strategy.* Colombo: Department of Government Printing, 1988.

-----. *Institutional and Legislative Framework in the Field of Environment.* Colombo: 1983.

-----. *Survey of Stationary Pollution Sources.* Vols. 1 & 2, Colombo: 1989.

-----. *Industrial Pollution in the Kelani River.* Colombo: 1985.

De Silva, A. L. M. and Ranjen Fernando. *Public Comments on the Proposed Coal-Fired Thermal Power Plant.* Colombo: Environment Foundation Ltd., 1987.

De Zoysa, Neela and Ryhana Raheem. *Sinharaja: A Rain Forest in Sri Lanka.* Colombo: March for Conservation, 1990.

Dissanayake, C. B. "Use of Geochemical Data Banks in Monitoring Natural Environmental- A Case Study from Sri Lanka." *Environment International*, 1990.

-----. et al. "Heavy Metal Pollution of the Mid Canal of Kandy; An Environmental Case Study from Sri Lanka." *Environmental Research*, 1986, 41.

Easton, R. O. *Coast Protection and Coastal Resource Development in Ceylon.* Washington, D.C.: U.S. Operation Mission Report, 1961.

Fernando, A. D. N. *The Ground Water Resources of Sri Lanka.* Colombo: Planning Division, Ministry of Irrigation, Power and Highways, 1973.

Fernando, Ranjen and S. W. R. de A. Samarasinghe (Eds.). *Forest Conservation and the Forestry Master Plan for Sri Lanka: A Review.* Colombo: Wildlife and Nature Protection Society of Sri Lanka, 1988.

Government of Ceylon. *Report of the Committee on Soil Erosion.* Colombo: Ceylon Government Press, 1931.

Gunatilleke, C. V. S. "Sinharaja Today." *Sri Lanka Forester.* 13 (3&4), January-December 1978, 57-64.

Jayewardene, Jayantha. *The Elephant in Sri Lanka.* Colombo: The Wildlife Heritage Trust of Sri Lanka, 1994.

Jeyaraj, E. E. "Some Examples of Environmental Assessment in Sri Lanka." *Proceedings of Seminar on Environmental Analysis and Assessment*, WHO/University of Moratuwa, X-1 to X-20.

Karunaratne, Nihal. *Udavattekale: The Forbidden Forest of the Kings of Kandy.* Colombo: National Archives, 1986.

Kuchelmeister, Guido. *Trees and the People in Sri Lanka.* Aachem: Aland Verlags GmbH, 1987.

Mel, Renuka. *Sri Lanka Energy Balance and Energy Data 1988.* Colombo: Ceylon Electricity Board, 1988.

Middleton, John T. *Air and Water Pollution in Sri Lanka: Report of UNDP Task Force on Human Environment.* Colombo: United Nations Development Program, 1977.

Munasinghe, Mohan. *The Sri Lanka Energy Sector: Trends and Future Policy Options.* Kandy: International Centre for Ethnic Studies, 1989.

National Science Council of Sri Lanka. *Environmental Management in Sri Lanka, Sub Committee Report.* Colombo: 1976.

-----. *Man and His Environment - Report of a Seminar.* Colombo: National Science Council, 1976.

-----. *A Preliminary Study on the Feasibility of Ocean Thermal Energy Conservation (OTEC) Power for Sri Lanka.* Colombo: National Science Council, 1980.

Natural Resources, Energy and Science Authority of Sri Lanka (NARESA). *Natural Resources of Sri Lanka: Conditions and Trends.* Colombo: NARESA, 1991.

NORAD. *Environmental Study of Sri Lanka.* Colombo: NORAD, 1989.

Porry, Jaako. *Forestry Master Plan for Sri Lanka.* Helsinki: Jaako Porry International Oy., 1986.

Tennakoon, M. U. A. *Drought Hazard and Rural Development: A Study in Perception of and Adjustment to Drought.* Colombo: Central Bank of Sri Lanka, 1986.

UNEP. *Environmental Problems of the Marine and Coastal Area of Sri Lanka*, National Report. Nairobi: United Nations Environmental Program, 1986.

Wickramasinghe, R. H. "Legal and Institutions Aspects of Environmental Management. Some Aspects of the Chemistry of the Environment of Sri Lanka." *Journal of the Sri Lanka Association for the Advancement of Science*, 1987, 179-186.

Wijayadasa, K. H. J. *Towards Sustainable Growth: The Sri Lanka Experience.* Colombo: Central Environmental Authority, Ministry of Environment and Parliamentary Affairs, 1994.

-----, and W. D. Ailapperuma. *Survey of Environmental Legislation and Institutions in the SACEP Countries - Sri Lanka.* Colombo: Central Environmental Authority, 1986.

Wijemanne, E. N. (Ed.). *Energy Pricing Options in Sri Lanka.* Geneva: Development Programme of the I.L.O., 1989.

Statistics

Central Bank of Sri Lanka, Colombo.

Annual Report. 1950-

Economic and Social Statistics of Sri Lanka. Periodic.

Prices and Wage Statistics: Retail, Producer and Input Prices and Wages. Annual.

Department of Census and Statistics, Colombo.

Annual Survey of Industries.

Census of Agriculture General Report. Decennial.

Census of Population and Housing - General Report. Decennial.

Labour Force and Socio-economic Survey. Periodic.

Report of the Registrar General on Vital Statistics.

State Sector and Corporation Sector Employment, 1985 and 1990.

Statistical Abstract. Annual.

Statistical Pocket Book. Annual.

Survey of Household Economic Activities. Periodic.

Vital Statistics [Vol.I] Marriages, Births and Deaths. Decennial.

Newspapers

Associated Newspapers of Ceylon Ltd., Lake House, P.O. Box 248, Colombo 10.

Dailies

Daily News (English)

Dinamina (Sinhala)

Janatha (Sinhala)

Thinakaran (Tamil)

Sunday Newspapers

Silumina (Sinhala)

Sunday Observer (English)

Thinakaran Vaara Manjari (Tamil)

Express Newspapers of Ceylon Ltd., P.O. Box 160, Colombo 14.

Dailies

Mithran (Tamil)

Virakesari(Tamil)

Sunday Newspapers

Mithran Varamalar (Tamil)

Virakesari Vaaraveliyeedu (Tamil)

Upali Newspapers Ltd., P.O. Box 133, Colombo 13.

Dailies

Divaina (Sinhala)

The Island (English)

Sunday Newspapers

Irida Divaina (Sinhala)

The Sunday Island (English)

Wijeya Newspapers Ltd., 8 Hunupitiya Cross Road, Colombo 2.

Dailies

Lankadeepa (Sinhala)

Sunday Newspapers

Irida Lankadeepa (Sinhala)

Sunday Times (English)

Colombo City

Midweek Mirror (English)

Leader Publications (Pvt.) Ltd., 24 Katukurunduwatte Road, Ratmalana

Sunday Newspapers

The Sunday Leader (English)

Popular Periodicals

Counterpoint (English monthly); *Lanka Guardian* (English fortnightly); *Pravada* (English monthly); *The Kandy News* (English monthly)

Scholarly Periodicals

Ethnic Studies Report, Journal of the International Centre for Ethnic Studies; *Kalyani - Journal of Humanities and Social Sciences,* Kelaniya University; *Marga,* Quarterly Journal of the Marga Institute; *Staff Studies,* Central Bank of Sri Lanka; *The Sri Lanka Journal of the Humanities,* University of Peradeniya; *Sri Lanka Journal of Social Sciences,* Biannual Journal of the Natural Resources, Energy & Science Authority of Sri Lanka; *Upanathi,* Journal of the Sri Lanka Association of Economists.

.